POLITICAL/CULTURAL IDENTITY

POLITICAL/CULTURAL IDENTITY

Citizens and Nations in a Global Era

P.W. Preston

SAGE Publications
London • Thousand Oaks • New Delhi

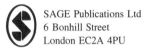
SAGE Publications Ltd
6 Bonhill Street
London EC2A 4PU

SAGE Publications Inc.
2455 Teller Road
Thousand Oaks, California 91320

SAGE Publications India Pvt Ltd
32, M-Block Market
Greater Kailash – I
New Delhi 110 048

British Library Cataloguing in Publication data

A catalogue record for this book is available from the British
Library

ISBN 0 7619 5025 7
ISBN 0 7619 5026 5 (pbk)

Library of Congresss catalog card number 97–067630

Typeset by Photoprint, Torquay, Devon
Printed in Great Britain by Biddles Ltd, Guildford, Surrey

Contents

Preface

In November 1989 I happened to be in Germany when the Berlin Wall was opened. At that time it was clear that events which were unfolding day by day would have a profound effect upon the future of European politics and upon the ways in which Europeans thought of themselves. However, when I returned to the UK later in the autumn of that year, expecting to find these matters hotly debated, I discovered a rather ill-tempered feigned disregard of these events. They could have been taking place on a different planet rather than a couple of hundred miles away. As I pursued the ways in which this extraordinary response was articulated, in an essay entitled *Europe, Democracy and the Dissolution of Britain*, it became clear that many of the UK ruling class wished that they were indeed taking place on another planet.

The sweeping patterns of structural change in Europe had a broad spread of implications for the polity of the UK. As I pursued these matters I became increasingly concerned with the general issue of the ways in which individuals construed their relationships to the ordered collectivities or polities of which they were members. I have tried to grasp these matters in terms of the idea of political-cultural identity.

The formal argument presented in this text sets to one side the resources of the extant disciplines of social science in order to recall the classical European tradition of social theorizing with its characteristic mixture of political-economic, social-institutional and culture-critical argument oriented to the elucidation of the dynamics of complex change, and on this basis affirming the utility of an ethnographic/biographical approach to the issue of political-cultural identity. The substantive arguments presented are informed by the formally derived summary claim that structural change entails agent response, so as the world changes around us, then so too does our sense of ourselves as political actors, and they point to the importance of the development of a tripolar global system where the main regions increasingly show discrete forms of industrial-capitalism and distinctive political communities with their own patterns of institutions, action and political-cultural identity.

The issues addressed here are both difficult and important and I am aware of the limited nature of the contribution of this text. I hope that readers will find it useful in their own work. It is certainly true, so far as I can see, that these issues are likely to become more important over the next few years as the different regions within the global system become more structurally integrated, and as these new forms of regional organization become more routinely evident in the lives of ordinary people.

Acknowledgements

The major themes of this book have been occasioned by patterns of reflection undertaken while travelling.

In 1988–9, as Europe began to be reconfigured, I had the good fortune to be in Germany at the University of Bielefeld, where I was the academic guest of Professor Hans-Dieter Evers. On my return I was moved to write on the impoverished character of the UK public debate in respect of the dynamics of complex change in Europe. Some years later, in 1993–4, I was the guest of Professor John Clammer at Sophia University, Tokyo, Japan. At the time the long dominant Liberal Democratic Party had lost power and the matter of Japan's future and its place in Pacific Asia were being vigorously debated. Again, the business of political-cultural identity was raised. In early 1994 I was in Australia where I was the guest of Dr Gary Rodan of the Asia Research Centre of Murdoch University, and here it was evident that the matter of identity exercised Australians with reference to their deepening relationships with Pacific Asia. And later in 1994, at the National University of Malaysia, where I was the guest of Professor Shamsul, the matter of identity was raised in the context of the post-colonial construction of an industrialized and 'eastern-looking' society. Finally, a little later, at the Institute of Southeast Asian Studies in Singapore I found a deep concern with constituting 'Singaporean identity' in the context of that country's role within the global system, matters which had found expression in the work of the institute's then head, Professor Chan Heng Chee.

The present book flows from these sources and offers a preliminary theoretical discussion of political-cultural identity in the context of an emergent tripolar global system. I should like to thank my colleagues and friends in Europe and Asia in whose company I first began to think about these issues, and I am indebted to Jack Brand, John Clammer, David Dolowitz, David Marsh, Earl Smith and my two readers from Sage, all of whom read some or all of the text and made many useful suggestions. The responsibility for the final product is, of course, mine.

Abbreviations

AFTA	ASEAN Free Trade Area
APEC	Asia Pacific Economic Cooperation
ASEAN	Association of Southeast Asian Nations
CCP	Communist Party of China
COCOM	Coordinating Committee for Multilateral Export Controls
DC	Developed Country
EAEC	East Asian Economic Caucus
EOI	Export Oriented Industrialization
FDI	Foreign Direct Investment
ISI	Import Substituting Industrialization
KMT	Koumintang
MITI	Ministry of Trade and Industry
MNC	Multinational Corporation
MOFA	Ministry of Foreign Affairs
NAFTA	North American Free Trade Agreement
NATO	North Atlantic Treaty Organization
NGO	Non Governmental Organization
NIC	Newly Industrialized Country
NIDL	New International Division of Labour
NIE	Newly Industrialized Economy
ODA	Official Development Aid
OECD	Organization for Economic Cooperation and Development
SCAP	Supreme Commander Allied Powers
TNC	Transnational Corporation

1

An Introduction to the Problem

The fundamental argument of the text is that political-cultural identity is a matter of the creative response of groups to the structural circumstances enfolding the collectivity which they inhabit. It can be suggested that, as the structural circumstances which have shaped the post-Second World War understandings of various groups within the global system are now in process of change, then the ways in which these groups have understood themselves will also be undergoing change.

The concerns of the text in respect of the issue of political-cultural identity could be pursued in a number of ways. This text is intellectually grounded in the classical European tradition of social theory with its characteristic concern to elucidate the dynamics of complex change within the developing industrial-capitalist system in order to advance the modernist project. In this tradition the key strategies of enquiry are political-economic, social-institutional and cultural-critical analysis. In general, social scientific reflection and enquiry is taken to be essentially hermeneutic-critical, a matter of the deployment within the public sphere of the intellectual machineries of the creative understanding of patterns of change. As a consequence of the particular intellectual grounding of this text, the material which comes to the fore is social philosophical in character and the empirical material is understood to be secondary.

In the text the opening discussions of identity and political-cultural identity point to the exchange of structures and agents. In principle both sides of this dialectic are of equal importance; however, in order to stress the rich detail of ordinary experience the arguments advanced tend towards the agent-centred (Cohen, 1994; Jenks, 1993). This is somewhat unusual in the context of the recent language-inspired preference for structural/cultural explanations which push the individual agent into the background, but in the opening chapters I am concerned to recall the rich detail of experience. In contrast, in the latter substantive discussions of patterns of change within the tripolar global system, which endeavour to summarily grasp a vast spread of detail, the arguments advanced tend towards the political-economic structural (Strange, 1988). The arguments advanced here are primarily drawn from international political economy and they allow us to characterize the global system and its regions. Only thereafter do we concern ourselves with the familiar exchange of structures and agents, where again a concern for agency comes to the fore.

In this chapter I will introduce the core theoretical concerns of the book with discussing identity and political-cultural identity (Chapters 2, 3 and 4 deal with theoretical matters), and will also introduce the substantive referents of the theoretical material, which take the form of a spread of illustrative material in respect of the regions of the emergent tripolar global system (Chapters 5, 6, 7 and 8 deal with substantive matters). I will begin with the occasion of the study.

The occasion of the study

Mills (1970) remarks that social scientific enquiry begins when private concerns coincide with public issues to spark the imagination of the individual researcher. In regard to the issue of political-cultural identity, in respect of my own case I can point to a series of private and public concerns.

I could begin with private concerns and the accidents of my own biography and record two sets of journeys: class travel, in the form of movement away from my background in the UK respectable working class to the equally respectable professional middle classes (and in the UK it should be noted this sort of class movement is always significant for the individual concerned); and geographical travel to various countries in Europe and Asia, although of course it is not the simple movement in space that matters; rather it is the intellectual/ethical relocation that counts, and here it is the movement away from the embrace of the political-cultural package called Britain/Britishness towards a richer and vaguer idea of self which is centred on an acquired rather than ascribed status (and this could be European-ness, or rootless cosmopolitan-ness, or even Englishness where this implies the reinvention of self in the absence of Britishness).

All this leads on to the public issues which have resonated with my concern for political-cultural identity, and three might be noted: first, the post-1989 drive for political unification in Europe based on the existing institutional programme of the European Union (Wallace, 1990); second, the related political-cultural ramifications of the collapse of the cold war settlement – a change that runs through the EU, the rest of the West and the wider global system (Hobsbawm, 1994); and finally the parallel recognition of an increasingly integrated tripolar global industrial-capitalist system (Thurow, 1994).

The coincidence of these private concerns and public issues opens up the issue of political-cultural identity and generates a core set of questions. If we come to think of ourselves as members of a political community, then how does this happen, what is involved in such an identity and how does it come to change, by what means and at what costs? In pursuit of answers to these questions we can begin with theorizing about identity and move on to political-cultural identity, and having noted the available theories dealing with the shift to the modern world, nation-statehood and modernity's discontents, we can go on to look at examples drawn from current patterns of change within the global system. Thereafter, if we put these elements together, we can move towards some preliminary conclusions in respect of the core set of questions.

The theory: the notion of identity introduced

As has been noted, this text is intellectually grounded in the classical tradition of European social theory. The classical social-scientific tradition affirms the modernist project of the rational apprehension of the social world and the resolution of questions of ordering society via discourse in the public sphere. The occasion of the modernist project lies in the shift from agrarian feudalism to industrial capitalism accomplished first in Europe in the seventeenth and eighteenth centuries. The reconstruction of intellectual ideas was bound up with the reordering of practical political-economic and social-institutional arrangements and within the ambit of these processes a particular role came to be central to the efforts of contemporary social theorists, which I have characterized as the attempt to elucidate the dynamics of complex change. The classical tradition of social theorizing is thus routinely multidisciplinary, ethically engaged and prospective in orientation (Gellner, 1964; Habermas, 1989).

The notion of complex change points to changes in political-economic structures, social-institutional arrangements and patterns of cultural understanding. These patterns of change are understood to be systemic, pervasive and inclusive. The business of social theorists and other actors is with the elucidation of patterns of change which are both ongoing and embrace the theorist. In other words, the task of the social theorists is to grasp a process which enfolds them. In this situation the end-points of the process can only be indicated on the basis of tendential analyses. It is a characteristic of this line of enquiry that notions of human identity in general, and political-cultural identity more particularly, are taken to be both intellectually elusive and routinely bound up in social-theoretical analysis. It is at least in part on the basis of provisional claims about the nature of humankind that lines of analysis of complex change within the system are made. The notion of identity is central to the classical social scientific tradition, with its concerns to analyse complex change within the system in order to advance the modernist project (in turn, taken as tendentially underpinned by the demands of reason). And as the notion of identity has figured quite centrally within the European tradition of social theorizing, we need to begin to sketch out some of the elements of these discussions so as to situate the particular approach which will be taken in this text.

The idea of the self: a biographical sketch of identity

It seems clear that personal identity is experienced as a rich arena of meanings. The matter of identity is not an attenuated formal realm. On the contrary, the self-image of all social actors is thoroughly elaborated. Identity is also structured. It is clear that identity has many aspects which derive from certain sources and find expression in particular social contexts. Identity is not a single homogeneous stock of traits, images and habits.

If we begin with a simple idea of identity as the way in which we more or less self-consciously locate ourselves in our social world, then we can make a simple schematic review of aspects of identity in the fashion of a substantive ethnographic/biographical report. This procedure is a way of grasping both the rich detail and the subtle structure of personal identity. The substantive business of identity can be unpacked in terms of the ideas of locale, network and memory. This trio points to the ways in which we inhabit a particular place which is the sphere of routine activity and interaction and is richly suffused with meanings, which in turn is the base for a dispersed series of networks of exchanges with others centred on particular interests/concerns, all of which are brought together in the sphere of continually reworked memory.

Acquisition and change, costs and contestedness

When the notion of identity is pursued in line with these headings it is clear that identity is an experientially rich matter. It is also quite clear that for the particular self the business of identity is largely unproblematical and secure. The richness, unproblematical nature and security of particular identities can be taken, both by people themselves and by commentators of various stripes, as the basis of claims to some sort of fundamental givenness of identity. A base in race, or ethnic group, or age-set, or gender, or historically generated cultural type or language can be presented as the occasion for a reductive naturalism in explanation (Smith, 1986), a non-social base or essence of identity. However, against such temptations it is quite clear that identity is the outcome of a complex series of social processes, and does not arise spontaneously but is learned and relearned over time. It is clear that identity does not express an essence but rather an acquired set of characteristics. It is also clear that aspects of identity admit of multiple readings/presentations (Gellner, 1964, 1983; Giddens, 1991).

As it is clear that identity is socially constructed, it is possible to speak of the business of making changes in an identity. It is usually said that making changes has costs. One set of costs could be in the social changes involved in reordering locale and network. A related cost could be in the psychological disturbances involved and the consequent reordering of memory. An important issue in this regard is difference between necessary and contingent change in identities: those which flow from our recognition of a new set of circumstances (Winch, 1958) and those changes which are effected only after a period of reflection upon new sets of circumstances. In the former case issues of identity are tied into fundamental structural patterns of social organization, whereas in the latter they are matters of personal choice and disposition.

In this vein, and against the familiar modernist view that identity, even if extensively acquired, is the vehicle of fundamental human traits of sociability and reason, it has been argued by postmodernists that identity is radically fluid, shifting and malleable. In this view, identity admits of making and remaking as the agent desires. And, moreover, the global industrial-capitalist system is taken to have reconstituted itself in such a manner as to positively invite the voluntaristic affirmation of chosen lifestyles and thus identities (Lyotard, 1979; Baudrillard, 1993). It seems to me that these claims are overstated (Harvey, 1989; Callinicos, 1989). The familiar talk of the rapidity of contemporary change takes us towards the realm of magazine social science and the territory of problem pages. None the less, against the more classically minded modernists we can suggest that the fixity of identity has been overstated. A sceptical modernist position can be affirmed which grants the pervasive nature of change but goes on to suggest both that we can acknowledge a fundamental humanity (sociability, reason) and record that change is slow.

The idea that complex identity (carried in language) is the outcome of complex social processes entails that any particular expression, any discrete identity, will be contested. The notion of identity can be unpacked in terms of the ideas of locale, network and memory and in each of these spheres the establishment of a particular identity flows from the routine dynamic exchanges of persons. Identities are socially made, they are not a private consumer construct from available elements. The particular person will confront a dense sphere of relationships with others, and in the background will stand the collectivity. One could think of identity as a shifting balance between what is privately remembered and what is currently publicly demanded. Identity is thus always shifting. It is never fixed.

Identity and language

In recent years social theorists have paid considerable attention to the nature of human language, and discussions have tried to work within the philosophy of language, in formal linguistics and in the social philosophical tradition of hermeneutics.

In the work of philosophy of language which derives from Wittgenstein, it has been made clear that in order to explicate the nature of humankind it is necessary to explicate the nature of language. After a first philosophy which attempted to reduce language to precise modelling of external reality, the second philosophy reverses the position and the idea of language is made central to the nature of humankind. Kenny (1973: 14) remarks that 'Words, Wittgenstein now insisted, cannot be understood outside the context of the non-linguistic human activities into which the use of language is interwoven: the words plus their behavioural surroundings make up the language game.' In place of the logico-mechanical truth functional schemes of the *Tractatus* we have the fluidity, flexibility and diversity of patterns of use sanctioned by social custom. This diversity-in-custom is expressed by Wittgenstein by using ideas of families of concepts clustering together, each cluster being a language game. And each language game constitutes a form of life. The implications are drawn out by Winch (1958: 15) who says:

> Our idea of what belongs to the realm of reality is given for us in the language that we use. The concepts we have settle for us the form of the experience we have of the world . . . there is no way of getting outside the concepts in terms of which we think of the world . . . The world is for us what is presented through those concepts. This is not to say our concepts may not change; but when they do our concept of the world has changed too.

And in the related work of linguistics human language has been presented as a formal system which is the vehicle for the constitution of the sphere of lived experience. Much of this work can be traced back to the linguist Saussure. The key idea is that language can be analysed as a system of signs, where each sign has a form (signifier) and a substance (signified). The linguistic sign is arbitrary and form and content are conventionally established by the community of language users. Culler remarks (1976: 22) that 'Each language articulates or organizes the world differently. Languages do not simply name existing categories, they articulate their own.'

In the social philosophical traditions of hermeneutics, language explicitly becomes the ontology of humankind. Gadamer comes to the position of noting that:

> The experience of the world in language is 'absolute'. It transcends all the relativities of the positing of being, because it embraces all being-in-itself, in whatever relationships (relativities) it appears. The linguistic quality of our experience of the world is prior, as contrasted with everything that is recognised and addressed as being. The fundamental relation of language and world does not, then, mean that world becomes the object of language. Rather the object of knowledge and of statements is already enclosed within the world horizon of language. (1960: 408)

And a little later he remarks that 'Being that can be understood is language' (1960: 432).

Overall, a key set of claims are made about language: first, that language is the ontology of humankind, which is to say that we are in essence inhabitants of structured sets of language-carried meaning; second, that priority has to be given to the structured sets of meanings, that is, persons are in a sense derivative of structures (and the familiar idea of individualism has to be taken not as a simple report on how things are but as a complex cultural construct characteristic of advanced industrial-capitalist societies generally and Anglo-Saxon societies more specifically); and third, that relationships between persons are fundamentally linguistic/semantic and are not amenable to reductive causal explanation.

The arguments presented imply that language-carried structures of meaning are both very complex and extensively structured. Thus language use is subtle, allusive, indirect, reflexive, self-conscious and intimately bound up with the routines of specific social practices (the idea that language is essentially referential is an outmoded view). Language use is extensively structured and, setting aside the technical matters of formal linguistic analysis, we can point to structuring in the 'horizontal' (ranges of the relevance of ideas with the *Zeitgeist*, fashions, themes, little traditions/big traditions and institutions), the 'vertical' (where the linkage of self, group, society and epoch all reflect each other) and the 'longitudinal' (where history is the source, stock and repository of meanings).

The implications of these claims are that human linguistic/social practices constitute the world of lived experience, that is, we inhabit forms of life. It is further claimed that it is from within the framework of a particular form of life that we constitute our experience of the physical world. It is further implied that notions of reason and ethics are internal to forms of life. However, at the present time, it is enough to note that the social construction of complex identities is accomplished in language, and identity is thus fluid, subtle and widely implicated in patterns of thought and action. Identity is not fixed, it has no essence and it does not reside in any given texts or symbols or sacred sites. It is carried in language and made and remade in routine social practice.

Self, society and the sphere of the collectivity

The relationship of individual and collectivity, and the manner in which the relationship might be grasped are difficult issues. Within the European tradition there has often been a divergence in overall explanatory orientation between those disposed to stress matters of structural determination and those who look to the outcome of a myriad of rational agent choices. In respect of the general nature of the modern world, we can argue that structural explanations are favoured by Marx and Durkheim, say, and agent explanations are favoured by Weber. In the more restricted area of the notion of culture, we can see that there is a similar distinction between arguments which stress the role of received structures and those which stress the practice of individuals (Jenks, 1993). Thereafter matters are more problematical within the Anglo-Saxon sphere as the popular ideologies of liberal individualism have wide formal and informal extension (MacIntyre, 1981). Yet the claims of liberalism to the pre-social existence of autonomous individuals are false, and the popular ideological expressions of possessive individualism are similarly untenable (Cohen, 1994).

It seems to me that we can cut through these debates for the time being by asserting two general points: first, that as a matter of social philosophy the collectivity is prior to the individual, and this conclusion we can reach via reflection upon the nature of language which is both central to the nature of humankind and inevitably social (Wittgenstein, 1953; Gadamer, 1960); and second, that as a matter of general substantive theorizing about the social world, the historical materialist analysis of the ways in which people make their own lives, and explain them to themselves in given circumstances, offers a way of grasping these issues in a reflexive fashion that draws directly on the concerns of the classical European tradition. Thereafter we can summarize matters by saying: first, the notion of the self points to a reflexive narrative construct which involves locale, network and memory; second, the formal notion of society points to the language-ordered relationships of persons; and finally, the notion of the collectivity points to the substantive body of persons with whom particular individuals necessarily live.

The focus: the idea of political-cultural identity

The idea of political-cultural identity is a particular answer to the wider question of the relationship of individual and collectivity. This relationship has been dealt with in different ways in different times and places. In Europe this relationship is construed at present in terms of private persons and a collectivity rationally ordered and appropriately legitimated. In the USA, in contrast, attention is devoted to the individual autonomous self and its myriad contracts, and the collectivity is read as a large-scale contracted sphere. And in Pacific Asia we can posit a central concern for family and community, with individual selves subordinate to that sphere. At this point, I will set aside all these broad differences and offer a general treatment constructed in terms derived from the classical European tradition.

Locale, network and memory

The idea of political-cultural identity expresses the relationship of individual selves to the community considered as an ordered body of persons. In schematic terms, we are looking at the way in which private identity is expressed within the public world, with thereafter a broad concern for how we acquire such an identity, how it changes and at what costs.

In terms of the notion of locale we are looking at person-centred understandings. The focus is on how an individual construes their relationship to the community they inhabit and how thereafter the person considers that their community relates to the wider world. This involves the political understandings of individuals and the political understandings of local collectivities expressed in folk knowledge/folk ideologies. In the first case, the political-cultural understandings of an individual will record accidents of biography. Thus in respect of given patterns of power/authority understandings will be informal and practical, dense, unremarked. And in respect of the formal sphere of politics understandings will be episodic (what has been noticed or has impinged upon the individual). Thereafter, secondly, it is clear that the political-cultural understandings of the local collectivity expressed in folk knowledge/folk ideologies will be particular, episodic and informal. Individuals will participate in folk knowledge/folk ideologies.

In terms of the notion of network, we are looking at how persons lodge themselves in dispersed groups, and thereafter how these group-ings construe their relationship to other groups within the wider collectivity. This seems to be a matter of membership of groups or organizations or subcultures. And this also seems to be a sphere of operation of ideologies, both delimited-formal as the group propounds its position and informal-extensive as the general cultural sphere is suffused with the articulated positions of many groups.

In terms of the notion of memory, we are looking at the ways in which individuals, groups and collectivities secure their understand-ings (and legitimations) of the power aspects of patterns of social relationships. In the European tradition this has routinely involved the invocation of an 'other' against which the group is thereby defined, for example, nation. In respect of this broad problem complex we could point to a series of familiar issues: the material of common sense and folk traditions; the material of little traditions; the material of institu-tional truths; the material of official histories (of organizations); the material of official histories of states; the material of great traditions; the material of the realm of popular culture spread through the media and the related material of the public sphere. In all these areas of enquiry the crucial concern is with the way in which the routines of everyday life link up to the realms of more or less self-conscious political thought and action.

Structural arguments to political-cultural identity

In place of the ethnographic/biographical approach, which is derived from the classical European tradition, these matters can also be approached from a rather more structural direction. In other words, we can look at how the collectivity embraces the individual self. This is the familiar realm of talk about nations, classes and groups, and it can be extended to allow us to talk about the ways in which sets of ideas present in formally articulated ideologies find expression in the mundane routines of everyday life with delimited-formal and pervasive-informal ideologies, great and little traditions, official ideologies and the extent of the development of the public sphere (an institutionally ordered sphere within which rational debate might be undertaken). It is here that we can begin to speak of power, dissimulation and coercion. In all this discussion, in contrast to the materials of the ethnographic/biographical approach, ideas working at the institutional level of the collectivity drive debate. It is clear that we have a rich and developed theoretical literature.

Ideas of nation, nationalism, statehood and nation-statehood

The classical European tradition of social theory concerned itself with analysing the shift to the modern world which was seen as a mix of system change and agent response. Smith, Marx, Durkheim, and Weber all had something to say about political identity: how it changed, how processes of change could be fraught, and about what end-points of change were desirable (models of humankind (Hollis, 1977)). Gellner (1964) argues that the task of social science is tentatively to interpret the process of ongoing pervasive change which both enfolds the theorist/citizen and typifies modernity. The central modernist project of the West can be understood as a broad commitment to the power of reason in respect of the understanding and ordering of the social world (Pollard, 1971). It is clear that there is a strong concern for political life lodged within this tradition.

In the historical shift to the modern world, political identity, institutionally secured order and legitimacy came to revolve around nationhood, statehood and citizenship. The first of these, the nation, can be understood to be an 'imagined community' (Anderson, 1983) where the basis of the community is a vernacular print language. In Europe, as overarching religious communities with trans-vernacular languages declined, new reading publics constituted themselves by using newly available vernacular print languages. In turn, as overarching religious authority declined and the power of secular institutions increased, the modern state emerged, a sovereign juridical institution laying claim to a specific territory within a network of states (Tivey, 1981). And finally, citizenship stresses membership of a community of political equals (Meehan, 1993). In sum, paradigmatically, a modern polity came to be a state within whose boundaries a nation of citizens lived, hence nation-statehood.

The group in control of the state can be characterized as a state regime, and in response to the constraint and opportunity afforded by changing structural circumstances the regime formulates a political project, a way of reading and reacting to structural opportunities which involves both locating their territory within shifting global structures and organizing their own population. State regimes promote political projects which they disseminate through their populations via formal and informal ideologies backed up by all the usual agencies of social control (and in this sense the notion of democracy lets us talk about the extent to which this is achieved via rational debate in the public sphere) (Jessop, 1988; Overbeek, 1990; Preston, 1994b). The key concern in all this is with the shift to the modern world, and with how groups read and react to the available problems and opportunities.

It could be noted that it is easy to read the histories of the developed countries in these terms. Moore (1966) speaks of routes to the modern world, and this gives us, for example, the eighteenth-century invention of the political-cultural project of Britain in the wake of the defeat in America and the ongoing wars with France, the nineteenth-century invention of America in the wake of the civil war, and the late nineteenth-century invention of modern Japan in the period of the Meiji Restoration.

In the perspective of the shift to the modern world, nationalism is a historically contingent response to changing circumstances (Nairn, 1988; Gellner, 1983; Hobsbawm, 1994). And in a similar vein there are theorists who point to the increasing integration of the global system and talk about the supersession of nation-statehood. None the less, we should note that there are other ways of grasping these issues, most obviously the way in which nationalists think of them. In which case nationalism expresses the unique truths and values of a group consti-tuted by some given natural features (via a race, or a language, or a religion, or an ethnicity, or culture or whatever) which must necessarily be asserted and defended against the claims of other different and inferior groups. It is clear that the tension between these two readings of nation runs down to the present.

Reprise: theory, focus and agenda

The present text will address the issue of political-cultural identity in terms of an ethnographic/biographical idea of identity, derived from the classical European tradition of social theory, which revolves around the concepts of locale, network and memory. In these terms the notion of political-cultural identity is taken to express a quite particular agent response to enfolding structural circumstances, a mix of necessary and contingent responses. If the structural patterns enfolding agents should experience change then the ways in which agents read themselves will also change (again, a mix of necessary and contingent responses). It seems clear that in the wake of the upheavals of 1989–91 which signal the end of the short twentieth century (Hobsbawm, 1994), the issue of political-cultural identity is emphatically represented both to extant power-holders within the global system and to social theorists, commentators and citizens.

Structural change and agent response: global changes and new political-cultural identities

In the post-Second World War period in the West the general issue of political-cultural identity had one overarching framework in the idea of the 'free West' (Walker, 1993). Against this model other images were ranged. In the countries of the Second World political-cultural identity was cast in terms of 'socialism'. In the Third World matters revolved around the pursuit of 'development'.

In the West the ideology affirmed the distinction between the realm of market-carried individual freedom and the realm of state-carried totalitarian unfreedom. The delimited-formal ideology offered a political-cultural identity for the political élite who were offered a role and a set of slogans to legitimate that role (and, of course, they had many institutions through which they could pursue their own career paths). It also offered a political-cultural identity for the masses who were enjoined to support the defence of freedom. The delimited-formal ideology found a political-cultural extension within the related areas of policy analysis and scholarship as the model of the West was stressed and the global system was read in bipolar terms (East/West).

The comfortable certainties of the cold war were undermined in the period 1985–91. Gorbachev unilaterally withdrew from cold war competition by initiating moves toward disarmament and *détente* (1985–9) and thereafter the Eastern bloc dissolved (1989–91). The object of ideological hostility and the central element of the official ideology of bloc-time simply disappears. At the same time, the end of the cold war has underscored the importance of existing debates about the direction of various parts of the global system. In the wake of the end of the short twentieth century and the related collapse of the received certainties of the cold war which had shaped the understandings of European and American thinkers, it has become clear that a new integrated tripolar global industrial-capitalist system is taking shape.

At the present time the global industrial-capitalist system shows a number of cross-cutting tendencies: first, to integration on a global scale, with a financial system that is integrated across the globe and extensive increasingly de-nationalized MNC operations; second, to division on a global scale, with areas of the world apparently falling behind the mainstream; and third to regionalization within the global system, with three key areas emerging where intra-regional linkages are deepening and distinctive variants of industrial-capitalism are discernible.

The reconstruction of global industrial capitalism: the European Union

In the post-Second World War period the countries of Western Europe were ordered at the macro-structural level in terms of the ideas, institutions and power relationships established by the Bretton Woods agreement, which placed the USA at the core of an open trading region. However, in the last third of the short twentieth century this system came under pressure with the oil price shocks of the early 1970s, the financial burdens of the war in Vietnam for the USA and the sub-sequent shift to debtor status in the Reagan years, and the partial and uneven globalization of the industrial-capitalist system.

In response to the early phases of structural change the countries of Western Europe slowly moved towards a closer union, and a spread of ideas and institutional mechanisms were in place when the extent of global change finally became unequivocally clear with the collapse of the USSR. The countries of Western Europe found an available reply in the guise of the European Union, itself a development of the European Economic Community which had been founded back in the early 1950s. The idea of the European Union was pushed to the fore in discussions about the future of the continent.

In a speculative way we could pick out the key elements of 'European-ness': a political economy in which state and market inter-act, with the state having a directive role; a social-institutional structure which affirms an idea of the importance of community, and sees economy and polity acknowledging the important role of the com-munity; and a cultural tradition which acknowledges established insti-tutions, a broad humanist social philosophy and a tradition of social-democratic or Christian-democratic welfare politics.

The reconstruction of global industrial capitalism: Pacific Asia

The countries of Pacific Asia attained the outline of their present configuration over the period of the expansion of the Japanese empire, the chaos of the Pacific War and the collapse of the Western empires. The Pacific region over the post-Second World War period has been divided by cold war institutions and rhetoric into a Western-focused group and a socialist bloc. The Western-focused group has been subject to the hegemony of the USA; however, considerable change is in progress and this can be summarized as the beginnings of a political-economic, social-institutional and cultural emancipation. At the same time the countries of the socialist bloc, which had spent decades following autarchic state-socialist development trajectories, are now opening up to the Western-focused group.

In respect of the sets of relationships within the region, it can be argued that the economic core is Japan and that around this core are a series of concentric spheres. In North-east Asia the countries of South Korea and Taiwan have close links with Japan. In South-east Asia the countries of ASEAN have become increasingly integrated within the Japanese sphere. In the sometime socialist bloc, China and Indo-China, there is extensive Japanese activity. And finally, in Australia and New Zealand there is extensive concern to reorganize economies and societies so as to attain a measure of integration with the Pacific Asian countries.

One key contemporary public issue concerns the arguments to the effect that the pattern of change in Pacific Asia is such that we can talk about a Pacific Asian model of development, where this is taken to be a particular variety of industrial capitalism distinct from the American or European models. A speculative illustration of the character of the Pacific Asian model would include these factors: the economy is state directed; state direction is top-down style and pervasive in its reach; society is familial and thereafter communitarian (thus society is non-individualistic); social order is secured by pervasive control machineries (sets of social rules and an extensive bureaucratization of everyday life) and a related hegemonic common culture (which enjoins submission to the demands of community and authority); and political debate and power is typically reserved to an élite sphere (and political life centres on the pragmatic pursuit of overarching economic goals).

The reconstruction of global industrial capitalism: the USA

The episode of the Second World War saw the emergence of the USA as the premier economic, political, diplomatic and military power in the world. The power of the USA was used to establish and underpin the Bretton Woods system within the sphere of the West and the military/diplomatic confrontation with the Second World. The position of the USA was unchallenged until the middle 1970s, when the financial burdens of the war in Vietnam occasioned the first changes within the Bretton Woods system. The period of the late 1970s saw inflation and economic dislocation within the Western sphere and in the Third World. In the 1980s the military build-up inaugurated by Reagan led to the USA becoming a debtor nation. In addition, the USA was the major sponsor of the doctrines of economic liberalization which have further undermined the order of the global system.

The end of the 'short twentieth century' (Hobsbawn, 1994) has seen the USA continuing to press for an open global trading system, but these arguments are now made within the context of a tripolar system and without the convenience of the existence of the Second World which provided an excuse for US hegemony within the sphere of the West. It is on the basis of this commitment to an open business environment that the US engages with its trading partners. The influence of the Washington-based IMF and World Bank is extensive in promoting liberalization and free trade, and recent expressions of these concerns have been the establishment of NAFTA and APEC.

In brief, the American political-cultural identity includes a series of key elements: a public commitment to an open market economy; a public commitment to republican democracy; and a strong preference for individualism, a tradition which celebrates the achievements of ordinary people and a cultural tradition of liberal individualism.

The reconstruction of global industrial capitalism: the Third World

The experience of the countries of the Third World in the post-colonial period has shown a diverse mix of advance, drift and stagnation. If we consider the very broad sweep of the countries of Pacific Asia, Latin America and the oil-rich Middle East, it is clear that there has been a sharp process of differentiation within what has in the post-war period been called the Third World.

In the case of Pacific Asia, it is clear that large areas of what might a few years ago have been called countries in the Third World have experienced relatively rapid development. The basis for economic success is elusive. In the 1980s the New Right claimed that the success of the area proved the correctness of market-oriented development policies; however, the countries of the area have all pursued state-directed development. The pace of development in the region as a whole over the 1980s has been so rapid that Pacific Asia is now spoken of as one of the three major economic blocs within the global economy.

It is similarly the case for other areas of what would have been called the Third World a few years ago that they have experienced a further round of dependent capitalist development. In the Middle East it is clear that the basis for economic success is primary-product exporting, in particular oil, but these countries have also invested heavily in industrial development. It is also clear that the countries of the Middle East have experienced considerable political dislocation in the shape of war and revolution. At the same time the progress of what has been called westernization, the introduction of modern social patterns, has been deeply problematical. Finally, in the case of Latin America the pace of advance is rather more problematical as social inequalities,

environmental problems and political instability work against economic successes. However, Latin America and the Caribbean fall within
the ambit of the USA-centred sphere of the global capitalist system. In
1993 the NAFTA agreement, which looks to a free trade zone within
the Americas, was inaugurated.

In contrast to the countries of Pacific Asia, the Middle East and Latin
America, the countries of Africa have experienced little progress in the
period of the 1980s. In Africa the initial legacies of the colonial period
included state and administrative machineries, legal systems, and
educated and mobilized populations. All these slowly ran down. In
Africa there were problems of political corruption, incompetence and
instability. The role of the military increased. A series of internal
conflicts occurred. At the same time, Africa experienced interference
from the two great powers as they pursued a series of overt and covert
proxy wars. At the present time the African countries' share of world
production and world trade is shrinking and is now very slight. Africa
seems to have experienced a slow detachment from the mainstream of
the global industrial-capitalist system.

If we try to summarize the post-Second World War period as a
whole, then we can say that by the mid-1970s the orthodox optimism
of the immediate post-war period had dissipated and was beginning to
be replaced by those fears about debt, instability and failure which
were to come to the fore in the 1980s. At the same time the counter-
optimism of the radical critics of the orthodoxy was similarly beginning to decline as unease grew about the further unequal development
of the global system. It is also true to say that the unease about the
post-Second World War settlement which underpinned the discussion
about development became acute as First World economies suffered
economic slow-downs and the societies saw rising problems. In the
First World the intellectual and political confusion of the period saw
the emergence of the New Right. In the Third World the New Right
sponsored a counter-revolution which aimed to sweep away the developmental role of the state in favour of the marketplace (Toye, 1987).
The overall impact upon the Third World has been to reinforce the
diversity of the area's patterns of integration within the global system,
a mixture of dependent development and semi-detachment.

Conclusion: towards an agenda of questions

In respect of the problem of political-cultural identity a series of
questions must be addressed; most centrally: how does it happen that
we come to think of ourselves as members of a political community,
what is involved in such an identity, what does it imply for action and
how does it come to change, by what means and at what costs? It is
clear that identity is socially constructed, carried in language, ex-

pressed in mundane routine, liable to revision and routinely contested as we move through life. Political-cultural identity expresses the way in which private self-understandings are expressed within the public sphere. A political identity will express a balance between private concerns and public demands.

2

Received Notions of Identity

The theorists of the nineteenth century pursued the modernist project of the rational apprehension of the social world and deployed political-economic, social-institutional and culture-critical analysis in order to elucidate the dynamics of complex change. However, towards the end of the century this style of theorizing fell into disrepute and the social science disciplines with which we are now familiar slowly emerged. In the contemporary social sciences there are a series of discrete areas of enquiry and each lays claim to a particular object sphere, a relevant method, a body of accumulated wisdom and the status of a professional discipline. Thereafter the professional expertise of discrete disciplines can be deployed within the knowledge marketplace.

In the post-Second World War period the US-inspired interdisciplinary package of the structural-functionalist analysis of industrial society established the contemporary social-scientific received wisdom in respect of analyses of identity and political-cultural identity. The issues were understood in terms of a general social consensus around a core value system with peripheral subcultures and deviants. However, the end of the short twentieth century has presented the general task of analysing patterns of complex change within the interdependent tri-polar global industrial-capitalist system. It is this general concern which frames the interest of this text. Overall, we can point to a renewed relevance for the classical tradition of social theorizing, with its prospective and engaged attempts to grasp the logic of complex change, and its associated distinctive concern for political-cultural identity.

The chapter will critically review the ways in which orthodox social scientists such as political scientists, sociologists, cultural analysts, and neoclassical economists typically approach the notion of identity. In general terms, each of these four approaches offers a particular route into the issue of identity and thereafter the matter of political-cultural identity which would be cast in terms of the following: first, states and ideologies (looking at power, citizenship and legitimation); second, society and social reproduction (looking at relationships, structures and learning); third, culture and tradition (looking at practices, ideas and involvement); or finally, market and consumption (looking at choice, competition and lifestyle). Thereafter, the discussion will review the approach to the issues of identity and political-cultural identity generated by the classical European tradition, which has typically taken the form of discussions of nationalism.

The classical tradition and the work of the short twentieth century

The theorists of the Enlightenment took the view that the social world could be understood and brought under human control. In turn, the classical nineteenth-century social theorists pursued the modernist project of the rational apprehension of the social world. The key strategy was that of political economy which encompassed the political-economic analysis of structures, the social-institutional ana-lysis of patterns of social life and the culture-critical elucidation of forms of understanding; in brief, a holistic, engaged and practical orientation to enquiry and action. However, towards the end of the nineteenth century this typical concern and strategy fell into disrepute, and in time the familiar specialist social science disciplines emerged. As these disciplines developed each laid claim to a particular object sphere, a relevant method, a body of accumulated wisdom, and on the basis of these three to the status of a professional discipline. Overall, the subsequent development of the legacy of the classical nineteenth-century social science in the First World over the period of the short twentieth century is one of expansion (as the formal institutionalized pursuit of social science burgeons), fragmentation (as separate dis-ciplines form and define themselves one against the other), consolida-tion (as disciplines develop their technical expertise and build up their stocks of knowledge), and eventual stagnation (as originally engaged scholarship slowly subsides into mere professional technical expertise).

The rational apprehension of the nature of the social world

The modernist project comprises a deep-seated set of assumptions about how the world might be understood and rationally ordered. It can be viewed as a cultural project centred upon the celebration of the cognitive mode of science and the demystification and rationalization of the world. It can also be viewed as a social-scientific project which centres on the rational apprehension of complex change, or it may be viewed as a political project which entails the affirmation of the formal and substantive democratic project. The classical nineteenth-century modernist project centred on the affirmation of the cognitive power of human reason and the proposal that reason be deployed in regard to both the natural and the human worlds.

The modernist project is bound up with the rise of European capitalism as alliances of intellectuals and commercial groups first brought together the agents, ideas and interests necessary to set the project in motion (Pollard, 1971). However, after the initial dramatic advances of the new form of life the metropolitan bourgeoisie drew back from the more radical implications. The modernist project appears in various guises as agent groups read structural circumstances and promulgate their views. It is a contested tradition. The best advocate for the modernist project has been the success of natural science. Gellner (1964) argues that science is the mode of cognition of industrial societies and that industrial society is the ecology of natural science. The nature of natural science is theoretically elusive, and as a practical activity in the world manifests all the usual social features of diversity of methods, styles and intentions, but it has been routinely invoked in all the delimited-formal variants of the modernist project, and in the specialist social science disciplines.

The emergence of professionalized specialist social sciences

In general there are two aspects of the shift from classical nineteenth-century social theory to the familiar intellectual patterns of the short twentieth century: first, the movement towards discrete social science disciplines; and second, the coloration given to this movement by the existence of distinct national intellectual traditions. The elaboration of the familiar spread of technical social-scientific disciplines was different in different countries as the shift from the early modern period to the developed modernity of the years of the short twentieth century proceeded. An additional matter was the relative eclipse of the British and European positions and the rise of the USA to a hegemonic status within the First World. The relative decline of the European theorists saw a rise in the influence of US social scientists. In the USA the divisions of intellectual labour were particularly clearly drawn within a cultural context well disposed to the practice of deploying expert knowledge in the marketplace (Preston, 1996).

In the shift from the broad prospective analysis of complex change oriented to dialogue in the public sphere, which was the typical concern of classical nineteenth-century social science, to the pursuit of discipline-bound technical expert knowledge oriented to a professionally delimited knowledge marketplace, much of the critical edge of nineteenth-century work was lost. As Bauman (1976) puts it, in place of negative-critical work we have positive-constructive work. It is characteristic of discrete disciplines of learning that they lay claim to privilege in respect of methodologies, areas of concern and accumulated bodies of knowledge. On the basis of these positions they claim privileged expert knowledge. In the marketplace of contemporary capitalism the claim to expert knowledge is the basis of a further claim to an exclusive possession of this expertise, that is, to the status of a profession. The result is clear and in terms of the schematic trio of practice – scholarship, policy and politics – the balance shifts away from scholarship conjoined to politics and towards a policy sphere that expands to embrace the political. In Habermasian (Habermas, 1989) terms, the fragmentation of the classical nineteenth-century modernist project allows the substitution of claims to technical expertise to displace the imperative of democracy. In the contemporary modern world an ever broadening spread of experts of one sort or another lay claim to the purportedly technical expert professional knowledge which is taken to be necessary in order to legislate for the broad mass of the population (MacIntyre, 1981).

The inter-war years and the dilemmas of the post-war period

As the legacy of classical nineteenth-century social theory slowly declined into the familiar spread of discipline-bound social sciences a series of new intellectual departures were made. The new work produced in the inter-war period can be taken to have contributed significantly not only to the elaboration of narrowly discipline-bound work but also to the subsequent possibility of restating in contemporary guise the concerns of the classical nineteenth-century tradition. Out of a wealth of material we can point to the following significant economic, political and social analysis: the elaboration of neoclassical economics and its partial eclipse by Keynesianism; the collapse of Marxist work into official Marxism-Leninism, and the related rise of the Frankfurt School; the first statements of structural-functionalist sociology; and the pursuit of anthropology. It was from the shifting patterns of debate within and between disciplines, as these were further shaped by the episodes of depression and war, that the post-Second World War pattern of social science concerns emerged.

In the post-Second World War period the efforts of the discipline-bound social sciences found expression in a complex package deal of theories of industrialism which for a time attained the status of a more or less unchallenged orthodoxy (Giddens, 1979). The critical traditions of the Enlightenment were consigned to the sidelines as structural functionalism offered its naturalistic and conservative analyses of industrial society.

The central image presented was of the social world as a self-regulating harmonious system which was held together by common values, and this social system could be analysed in terms of a series of functional sub-systems, each of which was the concern of a particular discipline (economy, polity, society, culture). The central image is unpacked in a series of related areas: first, the model of industrial society which is the goal to which the logic of industrialism is driving all societies; second, the process of modernization whereby the less developed countries shift from traditional to modern societies; third, the process of the convergence of East and West as both are driven by the logic of industrialism; and finally the realization of the end of ideology as scarcity is overcome and conflict disappears. It was an optimistic scheme. However, critics objected that it was little more than the generalized model of the post-Second World War USA.

In the early 1970s a series of overlapping doubts began to assail the theorists, policy analysts and political agents of the First World. Among intellectuals, the project of modernity in its short twentieth-century guise came into question from both the liberal right and the democratic left, and in the intellectual confusion of the end of the short twentieth century a denial of the project of modernity in the form of ideas of postmodernity was offered. Among policy analysts, confidence in respect of the post-Second World War settlement, which involved state-sponsored welfare to stabilize monopoly capitalism, faltered as confidence in strategies of intervention dipped in the face of accumulating failures. And among political agents, confidence in the progressive nature of the polity splintered as the post-Second World War settlement dissolved into a disputatious market-obsessed interregnum that was overtaken by the end of the short twentieth century and the establishment of a phase of general confusion.

The general debate among scholars, policy analysts and political agents has been confused, and much has been made of the distinction between modernity and postmodernity; however, a series of more or less coherent themes has been advanced for debate: first, that the industrial-capitalist economic system is now both global and tripolar; second, that the industrial-capitalist political system is now adjusting to the global and tripolar economic system and this manifests itself in the supersession of the nation-state in favour of global, regional, national and local institutional structures; third, that social theorists and others must grant that the extent to which these processes can be understood is very limited; and finally, that social theorists and other commentators can contribute to a collective grasp of these processes by contributing to the re-establishment of a series of public spheres. Overall, the end of the short twentieth century has represented in contemporary guise the key issue which was addressed by the classical theorist of the nineteenth. Once again, social theorists must grapple with the business of complex change.

The matter of identity within the specialist disciplines

The development of the specialist disciplines of the social sciences over the period of the short twentieth century has bequeathed to present-day theorists a body of work at once richly elaborated and highly restrictive. The prospective, engaged and future-oriented work of classical nineteenth-century social science has been eschewed in favour of putatively value-neutral and technical exercises in social-scientific enquiry. However, against the self-images of these technical practitioners it is relatively easy to show how the material presented by each discipline offers a clear statement in regard to the nature of humankind and its social organization. In other words, notwithstanding the internal diversity of the specialist social sciences, and contrary to the claims to technical value neutrality, it remains the case that each sphere affirms a conception of humankind and thereby a notion of the proper ordering of the collectivity. These buried claims in respect of human self-identity and political-cultural identity are the basis of exercises in social theorizing and they needs must be uncovered if we are to treat reflexively the notions of identity and political-cultural identity.

Politics: power, citizenship and legitimation

In the intellectual tradition of political theory persons are construed as denizens of polities. A series of commitments in respect of the nature of persons is immediately made: persons are rational; persons are able to judge their own interests and those of the collectivity within which they live; persons are able to reflect upon different lines of action and to select rationally from available courses of action; and persons are able to distinguish rights and duties. A related series of commitments in respect of the nature of polities is also made: polities are rationally ordered groups of persons; polities have established structures of securing order and coming to agreement about appropriate courses of collective action; and polities have established mechanisms for resolving conflicts (both extra-polity and intra-polity). And finally a series of commitments in respect of the relationship of person and polity is made: the relationship is rational, consensual, ordered and admits of change upon reflection and in accord with procedure.

In the history of political theory there have been various ways in which the nature of the polity, the nature of the people and their relations have been construed. In the modern period the debate has revolved one way or another around the idea of democracy (Macpherson, 1973; Plant, 1991). Held (1987) offers a broad synoptic overview built around the notion of democracy, which is traced back to a fundamental discussion in ancient philosophy of the ideas of equality, liberty, citizenship and law and presented in two broad modern forms: protective democracy and developmental democracy.

The liberal tradition, which Held calls protective democracy, is traced back to the work of Hobbes, who looks to the circumstances of the English Revolution or Civil War, and argues from the model of the new natural sciences to the fundamentally material nature of humankind, which in turn generates within each individual a concern for material advance which may be secured at the expense of others. On the basis of this fundamental asocial competition, Hobbes argues for the rule-setting role of the sovereign. The fundamental themes of

English liberalism are presented with the commitment to individualism, the stress on the autonomy of the self, the expectation of competition and the rational necessity of establishing contractually a minimum state to order social relationships. It is in this sense that the state is protective. The tradition is pursued by Locke, who puts family units rather than individuals at the core and makes it clear that the business of the state is with the protection of property, and in the nineteenth century the line is pursued in the utilitarianism of Jeremy Bentham and James Mill. It finds radical expression today in the work of the New Right.

The origins of the modern democratic tradition, Held's developmental democracy, are lodged within the critical alternative tradition of the English Revolution, the Levellers and Diggers with their radical egalitarian democracy; the work of Tom Paine and Jean-Jacques Rousseau continues the line of argument. The key claims revolve around the notions of equality, common citizenship and political freedom which came to have practical expression in the American and French Revolutions. And thereafter the arguments were pursued in the nineteenth century and found further expression in the work of Marx.

Within the very broad ambit of the tradition of political theory we can identify a series of issues which can be regarded as fundamental: first, the matter of power – how it is concentrated and deployed; second, the matter of citizenship – who belongs to the polity, how the members of the polity in general are regarded and how they exercise power; and third, the matter of legitimation – how power is legitimately deployed within the polity – what the basis of authority is and how the whole matter is self-consciously explained.

However, it should also be noted that it is possible to distinguish political theory from political science where the latter has a distinctively American origin and is concerned with the behavioural analysis of matters political. The underlying model affirmed is liberal – there are persons who come together according to common traits in order to pursue explicit interests within the framework of the state machineries. This approach has been influential in the post-Second World War period.

None the less, in the modern period within Europe we can detail the ways in which the two broad traditions, liberal and democratic, find expression within contemporary debates. In the post-Second World War period the countries of Europe operated within the dual framework of the Bretton Woods liberal world trading regime and the more particular ideological/security frame of the cold war bloc system. And in the post-Second World War period the countries of north-west Europe developed social-democratic polities which looked to strategies of social-institutional inclusion on the basis of planned Fordist political economies. The package was successful until the early 1970s. However, the package was always contested by more liberal theorists, and the theorists of the New Right attained great influence in the USA and the UK in the 1980s, and even some influence within Europe. Yet at the present time commentators suggest that a renewed interest in the politics of the democratic tradition can be identified, Habermasian or communitarian replies to the decline of social democracy and the related celebration of liberalism.

Overall, in the sphere of political theory, in brief, persons are understood as citizens within polities which collectively essay legitimating ideologies. The key concerns of enquiry revolve around states (which have been the key institutional form of modern polities) and ideologies.

Society: relationship, structure and learning

In the intellectual tradition of sociology, persons are construed as denizens of societies. A series of commitments in respect of the nature of persons is immediately made: persons are understood to be necessarily lodged within networks of relationships with others; persons are understood to be necessarily lodged within structured relationships with others; persons are understood to be necessarily lodged within power relationships with others; and persons are taken to have a sphere of possible action around them within which rational action can be initiated. A series of commitments in respect of the nature of society is also made: society comprises persons in relationship; and society has its own structure and dynamic (both synchronic and diachronic). Finally, a key commitment in respect of the relationship of person and society is made: the social is logically prior to the person.

In the history of sociological theory there have been various ways in which the nature of society, the nature of the people and their relationships have been construed. One characteristic of debate has been the ways in which the distinction between persons and the collectivity has been drawn, with schemes focusing on persons favouring voluntaristic contractual notions of society whereas schemes focusing on society have looked to structural holistic explanations of particular patterns of life. In respect of the history, Hawthorn (1976) offers a broad synoptic review of the development of contemporary sociology which is built around the models of humankind affirmed by particular theorists who are in turn taken to be lodged within national traditions, where the nature of the sociological work produced depends particularly on the relationship of practitioners and the state.

In the UK, the period from 1870 through to the outbreak of the First World War was a period of high bourgeois optimism and labour-based counter-optimism during which political economy was superseded by neoclassical marginalism as the science of economic life (Pollard, 1971). The residue social-scientific concerns for ethics, society and ideas became the sphere of sociology, and L.T. Hobhouse produced a social evolutionist gradualism and thereby set the subsequent dominant tone of all UK sociology with the ameliorist analysis of social problems (Abrams, 1968).

In the French and German intellectual traditions, theories of market economics figured much less strongly and the contributions of history and philosophy remained more prominent. In France during the latter years of the nineteenth and early twentieth centuries, the work of Durkheim became influential and the position of sociology was assured as a practical reforming discipline which found favour among those committed to the political project of the Third Republic. However, after the First World War the confidence of French intellectuals became dissipated and in the inter-war period a series of dispersed enquiries was pursued. Meanwhile in Germany the humanities and the arts were traditionally seen as the vehicles of personal cultivation and arguments in favour of more practical social science were regarded as positivistic. However, as Germany shifted decisively into the modern world in the later years of the nineteenth century the practical demands of the period became pressing. It was here that Max Weber made his ambiguous contribution to the illumination of the interests of the bourgeoisie and the German power-state. However, the débâcle of the First World War, a failed revolution and the emergence of the fragile Weimar Republic had the effect of reducing the influence of practical social science as the majority of intellectuals withdrew to the old traditions of the humanities.

In the USA the shift to the modern world had taken place within the material circumstances given by a rich and largely uninhabited continent and the intellectual framework of an ostensibly radical but in practice profoundly conservative individualistic social philosophy. The notion of progress familiar to Europeans was not available to American thinkers except in the guise of material advance. In the absence of any perceived need to reflect upon the possibility of structural reforms, the work of American social theorists turned to the pragmatic pursuit of a multiplicity of more particular reforms. However, it was in the inter-war period that the influential theoretical work of Talcott Parsons took shape. And in the period of unquestioned US hegemony in the wake of the Second World War, it was the theories of industrial society inspired in part by Parsons which came to dominate the social science of the First World.

On this subject, it can be noted that it is possible to distinguish between the classical European tradition of sociology and the restricted technical material of professionalized sociology (close to official naturalistic structural functionalism). The argument made by Gellner (1964) rejects the piecemeal, empirical and pragmatic work of US-inspired work in the post-war period in favour of an emphatic reaffirmation of the theoretically ordered engaged practicality of social theorizing which should be seen to be oriented to the display of the dynamics of the modern industrial system. In this Gellner recalls the concerns of the classical tradition with the prospective and engaged analysis of the dynamics of complex change.

Within the broad ambit of the sociological tradition we can identify a series of issues which can be regarded as fundamental: first, the matter of relationship – the ways in which persons are related one to another thereby to constitute society; second, the matter of structure – the ways in which these relationships are systematically patterned thereby constituting social structures which are reproduced over time; and third, the matter of learning – the ways in which persons become social and the related ways in which societies progress or become more civilized. In brief, in the sphere of the discipline of sociology persons are understood as discrete elements of wider systems of relationships which are reflexively apprehended as societies, which are thereafter ordered in a complex way; the key concerns of enquiry revolve around society and learning.

Culture: practice, ideas and involvement

In the intellectual traditions concerned with culture persons are construed as inhabitants of language-carried traditions. A series of commitments is immediately made in respect of the nature of persons: persons are understood to be inhabitants of structured webs of meaning; persons are understood to be bestowers of meaning; and persons are understood to be bestowers of value. Related commitments are also made in respect of the nature of language-carried traditions: traditions are the base of current understandings and actions; traditions are routinely reworked in ordinary practice; and language systems are conventional social constructs. And finally, a series of commitments is made in respect of the relationship of persons and traditions: the tradition is logically prior, as is the language vehicle, both of which are conventional (the one historical, the other formal) and admit of reconstruction. Overall, in the history of cultural analyses there has been a series of ways in which the nature of culture, people and their relationships have been construed.

There is no single contemporary disciplinary tradition which attends to the matter of culture. Instead the matter is approached in a series of ways: in cultural anthropology (where concern is shown for patterns of understanding, in particular among traditional societies); in political sociology (where concern is shown for the sphere of ideology); in literature and the humanities (where concern is shown for ideas, ethics and the arts); and in the recently presented strategy of cultural studies (which looks at the production of patterns of understanding in contemporary modern society) (Inglis, 1993).

The tradition of anthropology runs back to the late nineteenth century when what began as travellers' tales turned into the systematic elaboration of the dynamics of non-European peoples encountered in the process of the expansion and ordering of First World empires. Contemporary anthropology inherits this tradition (Jenks, 1993).

The tradition of political sociology runs back into the concerns of the classical nineteenth-century tradition of social theory which was concerned with the business of the analysis of complex change the better to order it, and in this context the routine inspection of the occasion of the claims of particular groups grew up. It has been associated with the Marxist tradition in particular, in recent years influentially in the Frankfurt School (Fay, 1975; Eagleton, 1991).

The tradition of literature and humanities would embrace a broad spread of works of art concerned with the values, patterns and dilemmas of human life (Williams, 1958; Wolff, 1981). The material enters the more familiar realm of the social sciences in the particular guise of cultural studies. The tradition of cultural studies has a dual base in the post-First World War assertion of the cultural/ethical value embedded in great literature (and the emancipatory value of studying the canon) and the post-Second World War assertion of the cultural/ ethical value embedded in the patterns of life of ordinary working people (Hoggart, 1958). The sphere of concern of contemporary cultural studies is both with the values and ideas lodged within ordinary practice and the emancipatory potential of self-conscious reflection upon received ideas and practices, most obviously pursued via the notion of hegemony but also present in the concern for art (Inglis, 1993).

Within the very broad ambit of the tradition of cultural analysis we can identify a series of issues which can be regarded as fundamental: first, the matter of practice, the nature of the routines of everyday life; second, the matter of ideas, the ways in which patterns of life are self-consciously explained to those who perform them; and third, the matter of involvement, the ways in which persons are lodged in and related to ongoing tradition. Overall, the sphere of cultural analysis, in brief, construes persons as the carriers/users of sets of ideas embedded within language and carried within developing traditions, and the key concerns of enquiry revolve around culture and tradition.

Economy: choice, competition and lifestyle

In the intellectual tradition of orthodox economics persons are construed as autonomous individuals with endogenously arising needs which are rationally satisfied via contractual exchanges in the free marketplace. In this tradition the matter of livelihood is taken to revolve around choice within a competitive marketplace in order to establish a chosen lifestyle. A series of commitments in respect of the nature of persons is immediately made: persons are ontologically autonomous with inherent needs; persons are rational maximizers of material goods; and persons are rational choosers among proffered schedules of goods. A related series of commitments in respect of the nature of the marketplace is also made: markets are spontaneously ordered, rational and efficient. And finally, a series of commitments in respect of the nature of the exchange of persons and marketplace is made: the contracted relationships of discrete individuals constitutes the marketplace which is the best vehicle for the achievement of individual needs and wants.

As a delimited-formal ideology the overarching claim is made that free markets maximize human welfare and in turn this emerges as a series of interlinked claims: economically, the claim is that as free markets act efficiently to distribute knowledge and resources around the economic system, then material welfare will be maximized; socially, the claim is that as action and responsibility for action reside with the person of the individual, then liberal individualistic social systems will ensure that moral worth is maximized; politically, the claim is that as liberalism offers a balanced solution to problems of deploying, distributing and controlling power, then liberal polities ensure that political freedom is maximized; and epistemologically, the claim is that as the whole package is grounded in genuine positive scientific knowledge, then in such systems the effective deployment of positive knowledge is maximized.

In the history of theorizing matters economic there have been various ways in which the nature of the pursuit of livelihoods within society has been construed and we can note the familiar trio of classical nineteenth-century political economy, institutional economics and neoclassical economics. These approaches are quite distinct (Dasgupta, 1985; Hodgson, 1988; Cole et al., 1991). The first is concerned with the prospective and engaged analysis of patterns of complex change which are construed as essentially economic and political. The second is concerned with realistically modelling economic systems which are taken to be lodged within social systems. And the third is concerned with the positive analysis of market behaviour. It is clear that within the very broad ambit of the orthodox tradition we can identify a series of issues which can be regarded as fundamental: first, the matter of choice, how autonomous individuals come to exercise choices among proffered alternatives; second, the matter of competition, how the sphere within which autonomous choices are exercised comes to be spontaneously ordered; and third, the matter of lifestyle, the ways in which choices made within a competitive environment are aggregated into lifestyles. Overall, in the work of orthodox economics, persons are understood as individuals exercising choices within a market in order to create lifestyles, and the key concerns revolve around markets and consumption.

Complex change, identity and political-cultural identity

The classical tradition had a quite particular set of concerns which cannot be reduced to an aggregate of the interests of the particular disciplines of the present-day social sciences. The fundamental pre-occupation of the classical tradition was with the analysis of complex change and its methods were prospective, engaged and practical. The work as a whole was firmly rooted within the sphere of social theory and oriented to the pursuit of the modernist project of a rational democratic society. In this brief concluding section we will recall the nature of the classical tradition; indicate the ways in which its concerns find expression within the narrower area of political-cultural identity; and in particular we can note discussions about nationalism.

The scope of the classical tradition recalled

The disciplines detailed above have developed in the period of the short twentieth century and are the product of a complex exchange between received tradition and the dynamics of the formation of institutionalized, professionalized spheres of enquiry. Against the spread of commitments in respect of objects and procedures of enquiry of these quite particular styles of social theorizing, it is clear that the classical European tradition of social theorizing was concerned with elucidating the dynamics of complex change within the political-economic, social-institutional and cultural spheres of the social world in the overall process of the shift to the modern world. The task of the classical theorists concerned the elucidation of the details of these complex and intermingled processes. It was a problem which had to be attempted in a multidisciplinary, prospective and engaged fashion. The orientation of the work was practical. However, the work was an attempt to elucidate patterns of change which were ongoing and which enfolded the theorist. It was therefore fundamentally interpretive-critical (Gellner, 1964), grounded in social-philosophical reflection and only thereafter substantive (as scholarship, policy advice or political action). The principal addressees of the work were the inhabitants of the public sphere, with scholarship as a parallel critical realm. The analyses which were produced were typically open-textured, and there was none of the concern for theoretical closure which typifies contemporary discipline-bound technical professional social-scientific work. The later style of work can only be pursued when the social world is taken to be essentially unproblematic and ordered, such that external-style descriptions can be made.

The focus on the analysis of complex change

The notion of complex change indicates inter-related, pervasive and extensive patterns of change within the social world. In respect of the industrial-capitalist form of life we can speak of the political-economic development of increasingly powerful market-centred productive systems, the parallel construction of state systems and the subsequent construction of nations (together forming the basis for familiar talk about nation-states). Overall, the process of historical industrial-capitalist development worked in two ways: first, intensive development, as capitalistic relations deepened to include more and more spheres of human social life within the rationalized sphere of the capitalist market; and second, extensive development, as the system expanded geographically to draw in more and more forms of life whose traditional patterns were reconstructed in line with the demands of capitalistic rationality. In turn, these developments are the basis for talk about the global industrial-capitalist system.

In the classical tradition the analysis of the historical development of the global industrial-capitalist system is essentially an interpretive-critical attempt to grasp patterns of change which are extensive, pervasive and enfold the theorist. Much of the work has tended towards the structural/institutional. A related complementary line of work has dealt with the historical/cultural aspects of the developing form of life. It should also be noted that intermingled with both of these areas of work is a routine concern with the detail of the lives of the ordinary inhabitants of the developing form of life, and this points to the business of ethnographic research.

There are two routes into this material: formally, the strategy of ethnographic research is logically entailed by the status of the work of the classical tradition as social philosophically grounded interpretive-critical enquiry, because if social theorists wish to elucidate the dynamics of complex change then they need to talk about structural change and agent response (which of course are mutually implicated in processes of structuration), and this entails grasping the patterns of understanding of agents – and that involves ethnographic work; and substantively, if we wish (in contrast to the more schematic efforts of the professionalized social sciences) to pursue engaged prospective work in respect of complex change then we need to grasp the rich detail of forms of life, and again this requires ethnographic types of work (Giddens, 1984: 284–5; Giddens, 1987: 6, 66, 113).

Identity in general

In the classical tradition the issue of identity has figured quite centrally in analyses of complex change. The discussion has involved two broad issues: the unstable nature of identity in the modern world, and the ambiguous nature of the system within which identity was constructed.

As the industrial-capitalist system developed, old forms of life and patterns of self-understanding experienced radical reconstruction. One aspect of the intellectual preoccupation with identity has been the way in which self-identity has been regarded as insecure. As the system changes so too does the agent, and in a rapidly changing environment all familiar claims to the security of the individual self fall. The theme of the insecurity of modern self-hood has been widely pursued within social theory (Bauman, 1991).

The extent to which the pursuit of the modernist project entails affirming a pattern of life that can be taken to be intrinsically ambiguous is made clear in Bauman's (1989) analysis of the holocaust. The modernist project is seen to be able to create the successes of natural science, and at the same time the technologies of war and control. The modernist project is also seen to be able to order society rationally, to enhance civilization and at the same time to create rational bureaucracies amenable to direction by the state (and thus suffused with violence). And further, the project routinely deploys an epistemic/ methodological means–ends rationality, and thus escapes from religion and magic to fashion the secular world that we know, but at the same time renders technical rationality a 'morality *sui generis*' and out of reach of familiar social ethics of community, democracy and so on. The modern world is a bureaucratic rational enterprise with the potential for both ordered progress and ordered irrationality. On the holocaust specifically, the bureaucratic rational state production of death was an expression of modernity rather than an aberration. The possibility for more holocausts is lodged in the form of life that we inhabit. The implications for defensive reform, so to say, would seem to be the democratization of the state in pursuit of pluralist systems of authority/power, the remoralizing of social science by overcoming the technical-rational model, and the abandonment of grand-scale social engineering in favour of piecemeal change. Overall, any discussion of identity in the modern world must embrace the implications of its social construction, instability and ambiguity.

The elucidation of political-cultural identity

It is within the framework of the broad modernist project and the structures given by states that modern political-cultural identities develop. In the context of the classical European tradition of social theorizing, the sphere of self-conscious reflection upon these processes, the notions of identity and political-cultural identity present themselves, as might be expected, as compounds of the materials of the separate disciplines. Against the moves to simplify and to pick out one element as the key to identity which are characteristic of the discipline-bound social sciences, within the classical tradition the matter is routinely taken to be complex: (a) persons are taken as ineluctably social (in Smith via moral sentiments, in Marx via social relations, in Durkheim via social rules – only Weber presents individualistic argument); (b) persons are taken to be embedded within productive systems (in Smith via self-interest, in Marx via the overweening demands of the dynamic system, in Durkheim via the shifting demands of the dynamic system, and in Weber via more self-conscious but nonetheless rather forced choices); (c) persons are taken to be embroiled in an increasingly rational cultural sphere (not visible in Smith's pre-Industrial Revolution work, but central to Marx and Durkheim and for Weber a source of overwhelming concern and distress); and (d) persons are taken to be lodged in changing and developing systems which are themselves lodged in history (a theme common to all classical theorists). And in a rather more substantive fashion, we can recall that the central preoccupation of the theorists of the classical tradition was with the elucidation of complex change in the process of the shift to the modern world. In this connection, it is possible to speak of the political-economic structures of power which order the global system. In a related fashion, it is possible thereafter to analyse the particular social-institutional arrangements which link particular territories to the overarching global structures. On the basis of these analyses, finally, it is possible to analyse the ways in which these patterns are expressed within the sphere of culture.

States, nations and nationalism considered

The rise of states and the related derivative construction of nations is widely discussed. The fundamental claim routinely presented is that the familiar pattern of nation-states is historically novel. The change from pre-national dynastic polities to contemporary secular nation-states has been fraught with multiple conflicts and has taken place over a comparatively brief historical period; any disposition to regard the nation-state as an unproblematic given must be resisted. Analytically there are three basic elements to treat: first, the idea of the state which is a politico-legal entity; second, the nation which is or is taken to be a community of people sharing in some important way a common culture; and third, the nation-state which is a nation organized as a state. It is clear that the familiar image of the long-established, historically deep-rooted, culturally homogeneous nation-state is both narrowly based upon the western European case and distinctly misleading. For a group to come together and formulate, lodge and secure acceptance of claims to nation-statehood is a complex task. However, out of this process, at this juncture we can pursue the cultural aspect, the idea of nation. In this material the notion of political-cultural identity comes to the fore and the general notion of identity moves into the background.

Modern ideas of nation-statehood originated in the work of the Scottish and French Enlightenment theorists, broad schools of social philosophy which produced many of the familiar ideas of contemporary social thought. The ideas of nation and of state, and of nation-statehood, were closely intertwined with political programmes of republican democracy which were fashioned in the shift to the modern world. It can be said, at the outset, that the business of achieving nation-state status was never straightforward and the contemporary pattern of nation-states is the product of a series of phases of formation. In the majority of cases, nation-states have been formed from elements of wider political systems. As each of the various routes to nation-statehood was sketched out, it became available as a model for subsequent aspirant nation-states (Anderson, 1983).

The first batches of new nation-states were constituted in North America and Latin America. The rebellions in both areas were occasioned by economic conflicts with their respective metropolitan centres, and problems of geographic and social distance exacerbated these conflicts. These nascent modern nation-states had the ideas of the Enlightenment to draw on and eventually claims to independent status were lodged, although the actual achievement of independent nation-statehood was not a simple process in either region. In regard to the present USA, the war of independence was as much a civil war as an inter-state war, with a large loyalist minority supporting the English. It is also true that among the English population there was much sympathy for the American rebels. The newly formed republic had a precarious early existence and the creation of an American identity took until well into the twentieth century. In Spanish America the route to nation-statehood proved to be even more difficult with multiple lines of conflict where, in addition to tensions between colonial and metropolitan powers, as in the North American case, there were ethnic, political and religious conflicts. The wars of independence were spread over nearly twenty-five years, and Anderson (1983) remarks that the nationalist impulse in Latin America was in fact rather weak and uncertain.

The second phase of nation-state formation involves Europe, and the rise of both states and nations is a complex matter. Anderson, who treats the idea of nation as a cultural artefact, intimately linked to formalized print languages, makes the period of the fifteenth to nineteenth centuries one of the slow crystallization of national language communities organized increasingly into states. The business of the creation of modern-type states, as feudalism gave way to capitalism, and nations, as print language slowly created communities of language users, was slow and their fusion into modern-day European nation-states was in the main a nineteenth-century phenomenon. Anderson argues that European nation-states emerged out of various dynastic empires, that is, pre-national orders, and it was not until the aftermath of the First World War that the dynastic empires of Austro-Hungary and czarist Russia disappeared.

The third phase of nation-state formation occurred as the colonial empires of the Europeans disintegrated. The emergence of the post-colonial new nations has been attended by a pervasive expectation that replacement élites would pursue the goal of effective nation-statehood (Preston, 1994b). Thereafter, finally, in the wake of the 1989–91 dissolution of the USSR and the post-Second World War bloc system, there has been a surge of nation-state formation in Eastern Europe. It could be seen as another *sui generis* wave of nation-state formation, or as a delayed realization of nineteenth- and early twentieth-century European dynamics. Beyond this, of course, is the thought from Gellner that if all language-based ethnicities secured nation-statehood then there would be approximately 4000 nation-states where there are now roughly 200.

The ideas of nation, state and nation-statehood can be regarded as resources available for people to use to make sense of their circumstances. The ideas were the result of particular historical episodes and, once made, were available for remodelling for use in new situations. This is true of the key political-cultural notions of nation, nationality and nationalism. Anderson argues that familiar ideas of 'nationality . . . as well as nationalism, are cultural artefacts of a particular kind' (1983: 13), and he suggests that to 'understand them properly we need to consider carefully how they came into historical being, in what ways their meanings have changed over time, and why, today, they command such profound emotional legitimacy' (1983: 13). Anderson accepts that nations are inventions and suggests that there are three basic elements to the imagined community of nationhood:

> The nation is imagined as limited because even the largest . . . has finite . . . boundaries, beyond which lie other nations . . . It is imagined as sovereign because the concept was born in an age in which Enlightenment and Revolution were destroying the legitimacy of the divinely-ordained, hierarchical dynastic realm . . . Finally, it is imagined as a community, because, regardless of the actual inequality . . . the nation is always conceived as a deep, horizontal comradeship. (1983: 16)

In regard to this business of the invention of nations it can be seen that at this point a considerable cultural shift has taken place. In a schematic fashion we can report that the experience of the ordinary person had entailed first, membership of a broad religious community held together by sacred language and pilgrimage, and hierarchical in form; then second, submission to a loose dynastic secular authority, a lord and a local noble; and third, the routine experience of inhabiting an essentially timeless life-world. But this has changed for the first people to take the step, the Americans, and the experience of the ordinary person now entails first, membership of a national community held together by a shared vernacular language constituted and expressed in the manifold forms created by print capitalism; second, submission to a sovereign republican state authority; and third, a

routine experience of inhabiting an essentially historical and progressive life-world.

The idea of nation/nation-statehood is a historical and cultural
artefact, maintained by a battery of mechanisms (flags, parades,
anthems, etc.). It is also the central political-cultural experience of most
people in the developed industrial-capitalist countries, including social
scientists. Benjamin (1987) has drawn attention to the way in which the
received idea of the nation-state can be reflected back into the procedures of social-scientific analysis. In brief, social-scientific enquiry
can become overly unit-minded because social scientists typically live
the experience of group membership. Giddens (1987) has argued that
sociology has typically taken society to be coterminous with the nation-
state, and has done this entirely unconsciously. Strange (1988) has
made the same point for political science. Giddens suggests that social
scientists must think in terms of transnational networks of power.

Conclusion: the limits of the received orthodoxy

The social scientific traditions of the short twentieth century offer a
series of ways of coming at the ideas of identity and thereafter political-
cultural identity which are at once quite precise and very restricted.
The images of humankind are bound by the demands of particular
delimited professionalized spheres of argument and activity. It seems
to me that if we reach back to the work of the classical European
tradition of social theorizing, with its central preoccupation with the
elucidation of the dynamics of complex change, then we can begin to
sketch out much richer notions of identity and thereafter political-
cultural identity. However, one available area of work must be acknowledged and set carefully to one side, that is, the pervasive rhetoric
of nation/nationalism. In place of these received debates we must
acknowledge the idea of the richness, specificity and changing nature
of both identity and political-cultural identity.

3
An Ethnographic/Biographical Approach to Identity

An alternative approach to the issue of identity informed by the concerns of the classical European tradition will be offered in this chapter. The notion of political-cultural identity will be the subject of the following chapter. The approach advocated in this text centres on the exchange of received structures and creative agents, and this can be understood in ethnographic/biographical terms which focus on locale (the place where people live), networks (the ways in which people interact) and memory (the understandings which are sustained and re-created over time). In this way the richness and detail of identity structures can be grasped.

Available strategies for grasping ethnographic detail

It is clear that there are many sources for this type of interpretive ethnographic material, and they derive from varieties of critical social commentary. In a formal fashion they can be sketched in terms of the materials of nineteenth-century critical social commentary, humanist Marxism and cultural studies (and this last noted is the key area). I will approach the matter via the idea of culture; once the spread of the term is noted then the role of interpretive, ethnographic and biographical work can be seen clearly.

The idea of culture

The notion of culture presents itself within the social sciences and humanities in diverse guises. Jenks (1993) reviews the multiplicity of meanings of the term by pursuing the notion of culture in a series of intellectual locations: in the humanities, where culture is taken to need defence against encroaching industrial modernity; in the exchanges of structure and action, where the issue of the precise status of collective representations of social life is raised; and in the context of matters of stratification and status, where it is clear that cultural capital can be used to constitute exclusive social groups.

In the humanities, in particular, the material of philosophy and literature in the nineteenth century, a series of uses of the notion of culture can be identified, all of which express the doubts of the cultured in regard to the dynamics of mass industrial society: first, the nineteenth-century reaction to industrialism which stressed culture in opposition to the rise of industrial society (S.T. Coleridge, Thomas Carlyle and Matthew Arnold, all of whom reacted against industrialism and stressed the role of the intellectual in defending culture, which they understood as acquired skills and sensibilities); second, a related idea, the classical notion of culture as civilization in opposition to barbarism; and third, within the traditions of German cultural sciences, the philosophical notion of culture as acquired learning/sensibility is presented. The theme present in these versions of the idea of culture is the threat to civilized acquired ideas and sensibilities posed by the rise of a brutalizing industrial capitalism. In this context, culture is unique to humankind and must be affirmed against the ahuman logic of the economic system.

The relationship of structure and action, and the matter of the collective representation of social forms, introduces a broad body of work. In respect of culture and social structure we can cite Durkheim, early evolutionist anthropology and more recent structural-functionalist social anthropology. In all these spheres of enquiry culture is understood as a symbolic realm which arises within the frame of social structures. And with the relationship of culture and social action the available material flows from those whom Jenks styles the 'Heidelberg cultural philosophers', the work of Ranke, Dilthey, Rickert and Weber, which derives from Kant. As might be expected, the work stresses the role of sets of ideas in constituting the social world, as cultural traditions or as the sets of ideas which individuals affirmed in action, and a little later the cultural anthropology of Clifford Geertz moves in similar areas of concern. Jenks goes on to note the work of Marx, where the idea of historical materialism made culture an emergent property of economic structures, and the concern for the sphere of ideas is pursued thereafter in the humanist Marxist tradition exemplified by Lukács, Gramsci, Goldman and the Frankfurt School, and the concern to indicate how social structures and practices carried complex sets of cultural resources can be taken to be of continuing interest, most recently pursued in the work of 'cultural studies' (Inglis, 1993).

In contrast, Jenks also pursues the ways in which the notion of culture can carry claims to the appropriateness of given patterns of social stratification. We can see this with, for example, the ideas of the superiority of the colonizers in respect of the colonized, and related ideas in respect of the relationships of various races. In the UK these sorts of relationships/judgements are repeated in the context of ideas of social class (Parkin, 1972). The idea of cultural reproduction has been pursued in the work of Bourdieu (1984) who points to the ways social groups both inhabit a particular cultural space, or habitus, and possess in the schedules of taste which they affirm stocks of cultural capital. In these contexts culture becomes something which is possessed by the

individual, as cultured or uncultured (Bauman, 1976), and this possession can be deployed to secure advantage in the social world.

In summary, Jenks distils the varieties of ways of deploying the
notion of culture into four clusters of meanings: first, culture as a
cognitive category, a state of mind (with an ideal goal implied), which
is the proper concern of the arts and ethics; second, culture as the level
of collective social development, with this sphere of concern designated as 'culture and society'; third, culture as the arts, where a
restricted sphere of self-conscious expression is designated (and may
be reserved for particular groups, with their own self-images); and
fourth, culture as the way of life of a people, the sphere of complex
practical activity, or praxis.

Culture as praxis

In the context of this book the notion of culture as praxis is of particular
relevance. I am interested in the sets of ideas embedded within routine
practice and familiar institutions, and wish to read them as implicated
in the reports of self which we make, in other words, in self-identity.
The sphere of practical activity constitutive of self-identity will comprise locale, network and memory. The linkages between self and its
locale are dense. A particular concern of cultural studies has been with
unpicking these links and displaying their dynamics.

The idea of cultural studies

Turner (1990) notes the recent rise in interest in cultural studies, and
presents the overall concern of cultural studies as being with the
decoding of cultural meanings as they are widely dispersed in historically located and familiar social practices, artefacts and institutions. In
Turner's work a key metaphor suggests that culture is like a literary
text which can be read and reread.

These themes are also addressed by Inglis (1993) in a text which
announces the author's version of cultural studies as an ethically
engaged concern for the values inscribed in ordinary life. The role of
cultural studies is to unpack and display these patterns of value, a task
involving a mixture of high theory, local knowledge and engaged
commitment. The background to cultural studies is noted as comprising three main areas. In the first place the rise of the study of English as
a source of values/culture which might guide life in the wake of the
First World War is recorded. The Royal Commission chaired by Henry
Newbolt reported in 1919 on English in schools, and in 1917 work on a
new degree at Cambridge had been started. All this was the background for the work of F.R. Leavis and his colleagues who offered an
independent-minded radicalism which celebrated the moral worth of
ordinary everyday life – a middle route between Bloomsbury high-
minded individualism and mechanical Marxism. And so in the second

place, European Marxism has also contributed to cultural studies. In Germany a similar concern for patterns of power and the ways in which these were read into culture was pursued in a rather different way by the Frankfurt School. In Italy the work of Gramsci on hegemony was similar. Then, thirdly, there was the scattered contribution to cultural studies derived from the nineteenth-century preoccupation with language – Saussure, J.L. Austin and Wittgenstein. And in total, all this work was the seed-bed for the post-Second World War emergence of cultural studies. Turner (1990) reads the work as a distinctively British tradition. In all this, Richard Hoggart turned the concerns of Leavis away from high literature to ordinary life and popular culture. Raymond Williams spoke of the structures of feeling of everyday life and related these to economic structures and patterns of power, and these were also the concerns of E.P. Thompson and Stuart Hall.

Thereafter, Inglis (1993) reviews a series of debates on method and slowly moves away from a critical concern for ordinary patterns of life within capitalism (with its concerns for the interactions of structures, institutions and ideas) towards a general cultural anthropology (which plots patterns of belief). The author goes on to specify art as a repository of value, and points to biography as the locus of value and experience. Inglis follows Clifford Geertz in seeing culture as the ensemble of stories which we tell about ourselves, and so biography – which can be read as the story we tell about ourselves – becomes a way of accessing the whole social sphere within which we are lodged.

Interpretation, ethnography and biography

The formal and substantive role of interpretive ethnographic-type material is integral to the classical tradition because ethnographic research is logically entailed by interpretive-critical enquiry, and this entails grasping the patterns of understanding of agents which in turn involves ethnographic work (Giddens, 1976, 1984), and if we wish to pursue engaged prospective work in respect of complex change then we need ethnographic work in order to grasp the rich detail of forms of life. It is clear that there is a series of contemporary routes into the field of ethnography, in particular, the legacies of the work of nineteenth-century literature and criticism, the humanist Marxist school and more recent work of cultural studies. All these strategies bear on the patterns of action and thinking evidenced in ordinary forms of life. In this general field of concern, a recent sophisticated contribution has been made by the anthropologist Norman Long.

The actor-oriented approach presented by Long (1992) derives from an interactionist social anthropology. The work centres on the experience of ethnographic fieldwork. Such exercises are taken to be theory-drenched interventions in the ordinary patterns of life of those with whom anthropologists deal. The preparation of a formal scholarly statement in respect of fieldwork exercises represents a subsequent theoretically informed intervention in the discourses of traditions of scholarship. The strategy of enquiry has clear characteristics. It is interpretive, that is, it is concerned to spell out the detail of the processes whereby ordinary patterns of life are made and remade. It is dialogic, that is, the conduct of fieldwork exercises and their subsequent formal presentation takes place via conversations (with informants and colleagues). The fieldwork exercise is a social process itself and the formal report, the contribution to scholarship, is similarly a specific social process and the final text is thus a complex cultural construct. In orientation the approach may be said to be hermeneutic-critical. It is elucidatory in intention, aiming in a reflexive fashion to spell out the ways in which the agents involved make sense of their respective worlds and the various exchanges between these worlds. The hermeneutic-critical elucidation of the detail of the social processes of the construction of the detail of ordinary life is applied in a quite particular context, that of development studies. The patterns of life typically dealt with are those of peasant farmers, the various development agencies with whom they deal, and the social anthropologist or development theorist who offers particular reports on these matters to an equally specific audience.

A major concern of the actor orientation has been with the way in which those concerned in the matter of rural development construe and order their various interactions. The central and crucial claim made is that those involved be seen as agents, that is, as having their own understandings of their situations, their own expectations of change and their own strategies for securing such objectives. The world of rural farming and development is seen to comprise a complex series of exchanges between such agents: those who are labelled farmers, peasants, petty traders, agricultural-extension workers, aid groups and state-planners. The development theorist is seen by those propounding the actor-oriented approach to be one more agent in the complex exchanges under way. It quickly becomes apparent that the exchanges between intervenors and recipient groups are very complex indeed. As Long (1992: 37) puts it:

> Intervention is an ongoing transformational process that is constantly re-shaped by its own internal organizational and political dynamic and by the specific conditions it encounters or itself creates, including the responses and strategies of local and regional groups who may struggle to define and defend their own social spaces, cultural boundaries and positions within the wider power field.

In general, the strength of the actor-oriented approach derives from the detail of ethnographic fieldwork exercises and the rigour of reflexive criticism. Overall, three points are argued: first, that research must pay attention to the micro-scale detail of the social processes of the construction of patterns of life; second, that research must deconstruct untenable rational models of plan-making and grant that intervention is a complex social process involving many agents; and third, that the further theoretical elucidation of these matters requires the supersession of the distinction between structure and agency. Finally, it is clear that any programme of reflexive criticism entails clarity in respect of the expectations of the theorists. In Long's case this points to the supersession of familiar positivist interventionist development studies in a reaffirmation of the central preoccupations of classical social-scientific traditions with the business of elucidating complex change in pursuit of the modernist project.

It seems to me that within the classical European tradition, and these more recent areas of reflection, the role of interpretive, ethnographic and biographical work can be seen clearly.

Identity considered systematically

It seems safe to begin by asserting two general points in respect of the notion of identity: first, that for Europeans in the post-Second World War period the issue has not figured particularly centrally within either ordinary life or social-scientific reflection, as the matter has been regarded as largely unproblematical; and second, where the issue has been addressed, formal scientific enquiry has been cast either in psychological terms (dealing with personal breakdown and crisis or, more positively, the aesthetic sensibilities of artists or commentators) or social-structural terms (centring on notions of nationalism, regionalism or, latterly, ethnicity).

In the post-Second World War period Europeans (including, 'ordinary people', scholars and policy analysts) were enjoined by political élites to understand themselves in terms framed by the official ideologies of the cold war, which revolved around the putative freedoms of liberal democracy and consumer capitalism. All this changed in the period 1989–91 when the received ideas which together comprised the post-war settlement abruptly collapsed. Today a new tripolar global system, shifting and unstable, must now be grasped, and along with it the identities of those lodged within its structures.

If we recall the core tradition of European social theorizing with its concern to elucidate the dynamics of complex change, then it is clear that the issue of identity figures centrally. The present text draws on this tradition, but the arguments are cast in contemporary social-scientific idioms: (a) speaking generally of making arguments (rather than following the inclination to formal mechanical models typical of the nineteenth-century theorists with their own notion of science so influenced by nineteenth-century natural science); (b) taking it for granted that we can run arguments which plausibly detail the structures within which individuals and groups can be taken to move (although the detail of these arguments is not pursued and nor is there any commitment from myself one way or another as to their status); and (c) concentrating on the ways in which agents read the structures within which they move (and which thereby they constitute). In brief, I would argue that we can begin to understand identity only if we grasp its specificity, complexity and contingency. We can get a preliminary handle on the strategy proposed by thinking in substantive descriptive terms. If we simply describe the elements from which our own identity is constructed we can generate a broad intellectual agenda. Accordingly, to begin I would assert that identity is a matter of locale, network and memory.

The notion of locale points to the immediate sphere of practical activity within which we move. It will be ordered around a set of routine practices. It will involve a series of familiar and regularly used locations. It will involve a specific group of people, again routinely seen. It will involve a taken-for-granted yet richly known background, a place. And all this we can summarize as a locale. Then, secondly, the notion of network points to the wider spread of contacts which people have and use, a spread of contacts which grows out of the spread of practical activities which are pursued within the familiar locale but which move beyond familiar boundaries. The contacts could be distant family and kin networks, professional and business networks, or simply the tourist and leisure activities undertaken in pursuit of pleasure. The entire dispersed ensemble of people and places we can summarize as a network. And third, the notion of memory points to the ways in which practical activities deposit residues in memory and provide the basis for ideas of continuity. Memory comprises a store of experience and knowledge to inform future activity. It is a sphere of reflective self-understanding, a fluid sphere liable to alteration in the light of new events or merely via the passage of time. We can distinguish personal memory which is the stuff of autobiography and memoir, and collective memory which is a contested public sphere.

In brief, my concern for identity will set the matter of structures to one side. I will simply take them for granted. Instead I will read identity as a substantive individual way of locating oneself in the social world. This approach to identity foregrounds issues of ethnography and biography, and directs our attention to the routines of ordinary life.

Locale, network and memory

If we begin with a simple idea of identity as the way in which we more or less self-consciously locate ourselves in our social world, then we can make a simple schematic review of aspects of identity in the fashion of a substantive ethnographic/biographical report. The substantive business of identity can be unpacked in terms of the ideas of locale, network and memory. This trio points to the ways in which we inhabit a particular place, which is the sphere of routine activity and interaction and is richly suffused with meanings, which in turn is the base for a dispersed series of networks of exchanges with others centred on particular interests, all of which are brought together in the sphere of continually reworked memory. This trio of substantive areas of identity creation can be unpacked and reworked in what is at once a more formal yet schematic fashion to address the nature of experience as depth, spread and extension (think of the trio of ideas as an image of how an empty space can be given structure). It is also possible, recalling the role of language in carrying identity, to rework this schema in terms of hierarchical, spatial and temporal referents. However, in what follows, the substantive material will be foregrounded (think of the following derived headings as chapter titles for your autobiography).

A sense of locale, the depth of experience

It seems clear that there are patterns of activity and understanding which are close to us and intimate, and others which are more remote from our routines and from our intimates. In this sense identity has depth in that some matters are more important than others. These patterns of activity and understanding overlay one another. We do not change our identity like a suit of clothes, but in different social situations different aspects of self come to the fore and other aspects move into the background. I want to summarize this experience of the rich depth of identity in terms of the notion of locale. It is the sphere of routine activity and interaction and is richly suffused with meanings.

FAMILY   It is a commonplace that modern industrial-capitalist society is dominated by the nuclear family. It is a commonplace that young people are dependent until late adolescence. It is a (false) commonplace that the troubles of society are caused by the breakdown of the family. Yet it seems to me that identity has a family aspect at its heart. In brief, we can note that if we are asked our identity the first reaction is that we give our family name.

LOCAL AREA   If the notion of locale encompasses routine activity and understanding then we must point to the immediate sphere within which the family is located. We can speak of the 'local area' – the street, the neighbours, the local shop, maybe the local café or food centre. In this sphere family overlaps routinely with community. Identity has a local aspect close to its heart. In brief, we can note that if we are asked our identity one reaction is to tell the questioner where we live.

COMMUNITY   As we move outwards from the family we shift to the local area and thence to a slightly wider grouping. It is the sphere where we begin to operate as members of an ordered grouping – a community. A community will have symbolic locations – the pub, the church, the police station and the town hall. It seems to me that identity has a community aspect. It is the place where people live. In brief, we can note that if we are asked our identity one reaction is to tell the questioner where we are from.

INSTITUTIONS It seems to me that identity has an institutional aspect which centres on the organizations within which people routinely operate. These organizations are away from the immediate sphere of family and locality. And although they may be located within the geographical territory of community, they may well be separate from it. These formal organizations may be voluntary, a church or community group and so on, or commercial, a health club or discount schemes where one becomes a member and so on, or professional, with associations or unions. However, the key organization to which people belong will be the place of work. In brief, we can note that if we are asked our identity one reaction is to tell the questioner what we do for a living.

LITTLE TRADITIONS These spheres of activity and understanding are essentially local. It is a matter of individual lives within restricted spheres. It has been argued that such local spheres generate their own patterns of semi-formal understanding in the guise of moral tradition (Scott, 1976, 1985). It can be argued that association with these local spheres of activity and understanding identity has a cultural expression in 'little tradition'. Individuals participate in the local little tradition. In brief, we can note that if we are asked our identity one reaction is to tell the questioner how 'people like us' live, think and act.

FORMAL REALMS As persons move out of the informally structured sphere of family, locality and community they encounter formal organizations, as noted, and thereafter the immediate presences in their locale of the formal institutions of the state: the tax man, the social security officials, the health administrators, the officials of the local authority and so on (Hay, 1996). All these formal institutions affirm institutional truths to which persons in exchange with them have to submit one way or another. It seems to me that identity has a formal institutional aspect which acknowledges the realm of state institutions and their several impacts upon persons. In brief, if we are asked our identity one reaction is to tell the questioner our ID number.

GREAT TRADITIONS The formal institutions of the state affirm truths to which persons are required to submit but they also embody broader sets of ideas – the official truths which the state affirms. It seems to me that these spheres of identity have a cultural expression as 'great tradition' and/or 'official ideology'. In brief, if we are asked our identity one reaction is to tell the questioner our socio-political status (and this can be cast in material or cultural terms).

THE REALM OF MEDIA   Most generally, and resonating with all the foregoing levels, we have the realm of media-carried identity where this centres on the mass media of newspapers, magazines, advertising, radio and television. The sphere of the media comprises meanings. The exchange of the media with the social worlds upon which it comments is diverse and we can schematically note first, the routine social level, as in the output of light entertainment which ties identities back into patterns of commonsense reflection upon the social world (think of a soap opera); second, the routine economic level in the form of consumer-oriented material which ties identities back into given political-economic structures (think of advertisements or programmes devoted to consumer activities, food, cars, holidays and so on); and third, the routine political level in the form of news and current affairs which ties identity back into given political institutional structures and understandings (think of news programmes with their standard agendas). In brief, if we are asked our identity one reaction is to tell the questioner what we read or watch.

SOME ISSUES   In the context of this characterization of the depth of experience, the locale, we can note a series of areas of concern/debate: the shift from private to public sphere; the shift from private folk knowledges to public ideological knowledges; and the ways in which the entire sphere is a realm of contested understandings, hence the closer to the private/folk end of the hierarchy the more autonomy (over what might be a limited realm) the person has, and similarly the closer to the public/ideological end of the hierarchy the more the person is subject to pressures to conform to the views affirmed in the institutions of the system itself.

The distinction between private and public sphere is a familiar one within political theory. The distinction is quite sharp in the liberal tradition, with the private sphere prioritized and taken as needing defence against the expansion of the claims of the public. In the democratic tradition the distinction is marked differently as between a sphere of personal activity in respect of personal goals and the sphere of public debate in respect of the collectivity. However, in terms of an ethnographic/biographical exposition it seems clear that the distinction will be fundamentally unclear as it does not mark a shift in social status but rather a boundary between rather different but interlinked spheres of activity and understanding. For example, if I leave home and travel on the bus to the welfare office in order to collect my welfare cheque I do not make one shift from private to public person, rather I begin as a person, then become a passenger and finally become an applicant. It is a series of shifts, a series of social locations. None the less, all that said, if there is no abrupt change in status then it does seem to be the case that the particular roles played can be described in terms of movement along some sort of continuum: from the domestic sphere, through a community space and into an official realm. It is a shift from private to public.

A shift from private folk knowledges to public ideological knowledges accompanies this movement along the continuum, a shift from what we know to be true within our domestic sphere to what we are obliged to grant is the case within the official realm.

It is clear that this sphere of activities is a realm of contested understandings. In the domestic sphere we can exercise control (over what might be a structurally limited but cognitively dense area of activity) whereas in the community or official realms we exercise much less control (over what might be a structurally more significant realm which is simultaneously cognitively shallow for us). In sum, it seems clear that there are patterns of activity and understanding which are close to us and intimate, and other patterns which are more remote from our routines. These patterns of activity and understanding overlay one another. In this sense identity has depth. I want to summarize this experience in terms of the notion of locale, the sphere of routine activity and interaction, richly suffused with meanings.

A knowledge of networks, the spread of experience

It seems clear that we invest our attention in the domestic sphere, thereafter the world of work, then the formal institutional sphere, and as a loose array of ideas throughout the whole ensemble of the world of the media, which is simultaneously present in the detail of life and superficially distant from it. The spread of identity is an aspect of that depth which we noted above: where the elements lodged within identity issue in a depth or richness of experience, the same series of elements also points to the broad spread of acquaintance which makes up the identity. The spread of identity can be readily grasped in the notion of networks, those people and places with whom we interact at a distance from our familiar locale.

The family sphere is the most immediate location for those sets of relationships which constitute identity. The family may be geographically close or more dispersed. A young nuclear family will be concentrated but an older family with children away from home will be dispersed – and the dispersal may be relatively restricted (in the same town) or quite distant (another town or another country). The extended family of aunts and uncles and so on may be widely distributed. In a similar way the locality will have a particular extent, a territory within which routine patterns of activity and understanding are pursued, places which are visited, places which were visited, places rich in association. And the community will have a particular extent. It will have sites which embody the notion of community, and it will have boundaries.

As we shift from the domestic sphere into the world of formal organizations we find that certain journeys and destination points are taken into our identity, distant places which we visit: the journey to work, the workplace and the various other organizations to which we belong and with which we interact. The little tradition which will encompass these activities and understandings will include a reference to the territory, routes and boundaries which make up the particularity of the place. And finally, there are the media, rich in meanings. In the media realm we participate in imagined communities, and these are imagined as bounded.

In this way we can see that the patterns of relationships which constitute identity do have a spread; they are not concentrated in one place, they encompass a particular space. We have a spread of experience. One way of thinking about the spread of experience we have is to think in terms of networks: family networks, local and community networks, and professional networks. The spread of relationships which constitute identity is extensive. In the context of an appreciation of the spread of experience networks, we can see that there is a series of issues to note: the move from the local and familiar to the general and unfamiliar; the move from the local and safe to the general and unsafe; and the move from realms of control to realms of less control.

The role of memory, the extension of experience

It seems clear that the sets of relationships which constitute identity are lodged within time, they have extension over time, they persist and they decay, and they do both at varying rates. The residue of these shifting extended patterns of relationships is lodged in memory. Private memory is idiosyncratic, it is the material of biography. The sets of ideas that will be affirmed by a group, the memories acknowledged by a collectivity, will be history, either the informal folk history of the group in question, or more formally as official history, or more scholarly as the history produced by historians. In other words, we can remember in a variety of ways (Samuel, 1994).

It seems to me that we recall the mundane details of family change such as lines of relationship and patterns of descent (some formalized for property reasons). It seems to me that we recall the ways in which the locality/community in which we live change. It seems to me that we inhabit cultural little traditions (and these change). It seems to me that we inhabit cultural great traditions (and these change) (Hoggart, 1958, 1995).

A key use of the past, both informal and official, is when we invoke the past to explain and judge the present. Overall, it seems to me that we affirm ideas of progress (identity is thus lodged in developing time)

(Pollard, 1971). And in the context of this chronological aspect of identity we can note a tension between the detail of personal or community memory/tradition and the generalized demands of mass culture. Many have argued that history in this sense is a zone of conflict between the powerful and their subordinates, a battle for historical memory (Wright, 1985).

Identity: learning, language and contestedness

It is clear that identity has a complex structure (depth, spread and extension). It is also clear that identity is the outcome of a complex series of social processes. Identity does not arise spontaneously but is learned. The learning in the immediate sphere of the locale will be direct. One will learn how to fill in the blanks in the schedule of questions presented above as one moves through one's routines. In a similar way the network of the self will be learned in practical routine activity. The learning in the more public sphere will be less direct, a matter of the presentation of private self in the public sphere. Learning how to salute a flag is not the same as learning one's way around the local neighbourhood. It is a shift from the intimate detail of practical forms of life to abstract general formulations. It is an exchange with ordered understandings ranging from folk knowledges through in-stitutional knowledges to official ideologies.

In all this, it is clear that identity is carried in language, and that this opens up a sphere of reflexive enquiry of some complexity, the mechanics of the language-carried self-conscious construction of iden-tity. Yet for my purposes it is enough to note that the social construc-tion of complex identities is accomplished in language. The sets of social relationships which constitute identity are understood within language. All sets of social relationships are contingent. The con-tingency of social relationships and the fluidity of the language of identity means that identity is a fluid and subtle construct. It is widely implicated in patterns of thought and action. Identity is not fixed, it has no essence, it does not reside in any given body of texts or symbols or sacred sites. It is carried in language and made and remade in routine social practice.

In the light of the contemporary concern for language, and the work of the critical theorists, it is clear that we must treat identity as contested. The idea that complex identity carried in language is the outcome of complex social processes entails that any particular expres-sion, any discrete identity, will be contested. In the domestic private sphere the contested nature of identity will be a product of the power relationships between persons, in the family, locality and community. In the public sphere the contested nature of identity will be a product of the power relationships between groups. One could think of identity as a shifting balance between what is remembered and what is currently demanded. Identity is thus always shifting; it is never fixed.

Individual social selves are at issue, not individualism

It is necessary to add a disclaimer. The notion of individual self which is used in this text sees such individuals as lodged within networks of relationships, in other words, the notion of social relationship comes first and the idea of an individual comes second. It seems to me that this is a familiar position within the classical tradition of social science, in particular sociology. In this sense the claim I make is not particularly novel or interesting, but there is a clear occasion for its presentation, because in the UK over the 1980s there has been an emphatic public political restatement of the tradition of political liberalism.

The political ideology of liberalism does begin its theorizing with claims about the discrete autonomous asocial individual (who thereafter constitutes society via a series of contracts). In this text the material of the tradition of liberalism is not accepted and in its place is an affirmation of the notion of formal and substantive democracy (Preston, 1994b). The recently presented arguments of the New Right are a derivative of the tradition of liberalism. The model of an individual which the New Right presents is an element of that delimited formal ideology which has been the principal vehicle of the legitimation of their state-regime project. In other words, the New Right's notion of an individual is an ideological confection. This would not matter very much except for two things: first, their model of an individual has been widely disseminated in popular thinking (as it is, after all, merely a variant of a long-established official ideology); and second, it is the model of an individual which is lodged within a wide spread of the UK social sciences, in particular, orthodox economics, and it needs to be set to one side in order to make clearer arguments about the social world and the matter of identity.

Individual social selves and analysing self-consciousness

A further disclaimer must be added. The present text is concerned with political-cultural identity, read as structural. The psychology of individual selves is not directly relevant and is not pursued. However, in a recent discussion Cohen (1994) argues that anthropology has preferred structural arguments from which individuals are thereafter derived and that this has resulted in the routine misreporting of ethnographic material. In this discussion Cohen opens up the issue of the balance between structural and agent-centred routes into the matter of personhood, and thereafter identity. Against the preference for structural argument, which is affirmed in this text, Cohen insists both that an adequate account of any pattern of human life must take cognizance of the lived experience of particular human beings, and this revolves around a sense of self, and that any ethnographic report will be predicated upon the anthropologist's sense of self as the touchstone around which interpretations are made. The lines of substantive and formal reflection coincide, so far as Cohen is concerned, in the demand that anthropologists acknowledge the sphere of the self.

Cohen begins by arguing that anthropology has wrongly neglected the self and that its ethnographies are thereby wrongly made. Cohen notes that a concern for self arose in the late 1970s and 1980s when a reflexive concern for the writing of ethnographies was current (sometimes called postmodernist anthropology). Somewhere in these critical commentaries is an important truth about the relationship of the anthropological self to the anthropologized self, and related lessons about how we can construe self-consciousness generally. Cohen takes the view that attention to the business of self will act as a kind of bottom-up corrective to structural top-down treatments of individuals. The nature of self-hood and the relationship of self and society will thereby be better illuminated. Cohen wants to insist that selves are not essentially passive recipients of structural forces and that, on the contrary, they are active participants in the creation of the societies/cultures which they inhabit.

Cohen continues his discussion and insists that selves are creative. And again this is asserted against those disposed to offer structural explanations which rather drive out the authorial self. Cohen is insisting that, within the frameworks of received cultural structures, selves are creative actors and that the ways in which individuals will read and react to structures are idiosyncratic and personal. On this we might comment that to open up a sphere within ethnographic description for 'selves' seems unobjectionable. It opens up another area of descriptions, the subjective meanings which agents attach to events. To suggest that the responses of agents to enfolding structures are actively rather than mechanically affected also seems unobjectionable. We can talk about motives and intentions. However, Cohen insists that the readings of agents will be not merely idiosyncratic but personal, and this moves you into the territory of individualism. It is this ever-present asocial and pre-social self which undermines Cohen's argument, because it is not possible to affirm the ontological priority of persons.

It is clear that Cohen wants to reassert the centrality of self but without affirming ideologies of individualism. However, it is not clear that he succeeds: (a) Cohen nowhere establishes his key assumption in respect of the priority of self; instead he asserts it and then presents ethnographic material to illustrate the claim; (b) Cohen offers a notion of society as an aggregate of selves, but this argument will not work as you cannot move in an inductive fashion from particular individuals to the general of society, and if you do ask about the relationship of individual and society then it is clear that the latter is logically prior;

(c) Cohen is concerned to reread ethnography in the light of his assertions in respect of selves and this, as we saw with Long, is interesting but it is essentially about how to make descriptions and not about abstract issues in theory; (d) all of which raises a question about the precise intellectual role/place of ethnographic reportage.

At the end of his reflections Cohen considers the confusions of ethnographic work between official versions of how things are and the reality. The former tend to read out selves. Cohen insists that anthropology should attend to the creative authorial self, and as an injunction to govern research this is fine, but it is not coherent theory. As with Long, the plea for attention to individual selves as a corrective to overly structural analyses is interesting, for there is surely a realm of personal experience, the sphere of the self, to address in descriptive ethnography. However, as with Long, it seems to me that Cohen also opens the door for the return of a variety, perhaps a polite one, of individualism. It is also noticeable that the notion of memory is not dealt with and surely it is in memory that coherent selves are constructed. In this text, the notion of an individual is understood to be constituted as the intersection of a series of social relationships which are reflexively monitored and given coherence in memory.

Reprise: locale, network and memory

The available discipline-centred strategies of analysing the notion of identity point to particular characterizations of humankind and thereafter build analysis around these characterizations. In the classical European tradition the business is much more complex. I would argue that we can only begin to understand identity if we grasp its specificity, complexity and contingency. A preliminary grasp of these issues can be secured by the strategy of thinking in substantive and descriptive terms, and the key ideas which can order such ethnographic/ biographical material are locale, network and memory. First, the notion of locale points to the immediate sphere of practical activity within which we move. It will be ordered around a set of routine practices. It will involve a series of familiar and regularly used locations. It will involve a specific group of people, again routinely seen. It will involve a taken-for-granted yet richly known background – a place. Second, the notion of network points to the wider spread of contacts which people have and use, a spread of contacts which grow out of the spread of practical activities which are pursued within the familiar locale. The contacts could be through family, business or pleasure. And third, the notion of memory points to the ways in which practical activities deposit residues (individual and collective) in memory: a basis for ideas of continuity; a store of experience and knowledge to inform future activity; a sphere of reflective self-understanding; a fluid sphere liable to alteration in the light of new events or merely via the passage of time.

In the post-Second World War period Europeans have taken the matter of identity for granted, and within the broader ambit of settled patterns of global relationships the same was broadly true for the USA. In Pacific Asia matters were perhaps less clear, with a Western-focused group and a Communist bloc coexisting uneasily within the region during the years of the cold war. However, the situation whereby identity could be regarded as unproblematic changed in the period 1989–91 when the received geo-strategic, institutional and political-cultural ideas, which together comprised the interlinked post-war settlements, abruptly collapsed and destroyed familiar frameworks of identity in the process. As the global structural forces which run through societies are reconfigured, then inevitably the ways in which the members of those societies think of themselves will change.

Conclusion: attending to the practices of ordinary life

Overall, any research in matters of identity and political-cultural identity would have to address the following lines of reflection: first, identity can be taken to be the outcome of complex social processes which embed the person in a series of social contexts; second, one aspect of these processes locates persons in polities; third, systemic change implies reworking received political-cultural identities; and finally, an ethnographic/biographical approach looks to locale (the place where people live), networks (the ways in which people interact) and memory (the understandings which are sustained and re-created over time). It is from reflection upon these complexes of problems that an appreciation of the difficulties of the issues of identity and political-cultural identity might be constructively established.

4

The Idea of Political-Cultural Identity

The particular concern of this chapter is with the ways in which agents come to understand themselves as members of political collectivities, how such understandings are expressed in routine practice, and how such understandings are institutionally embodied and thereafter formally legitimated in the public sphere. The ways in which individuals or groups construe their relationship to extant political-cultural structures will effect the extent to which such agents take themselves to be able to react creatively to structural change. And the ways in which such agents understand their power will feed into their routine practical actions.

I have argued that the classical European tradition of social theory was concerned with analysing the shift to the modern world and addressed problems of political-economic structural change (the development of science and the power of the material base), social-institutional change (the extension of rational order within the social sphere) and related cultural movement (the tenets of modernity find wide routine expression in politics, the humanities and the sphere of the arts). Within the many-stranded analysis of the classical tradition there is a strong concern for political life. Marx (ideology), Weber (rational/traditional action) and Durkheim (collective belief systems) all had something to say about political-cultural identities and political life. In general, in the sphere of political-cultural identity the contestedness of identity is centrally important. It is here that we can begin to speak of delimited-formal and pervasive-informal ideologies; great and little traditions; official ideologies; and the extent of the development of the public sphere (an institutionally ordered sphere within which rational debate might be undertaken).

This chapter will look at the more specific idea of political-cultural identity in terms derived from the classical tradition of social theorizing. In broad terms, political-cultural identity expresses our relationship to the community considered as an ordered body of persons. Such a political-cultural identity could work at a series of levels: first, person-centred (how an individual construes their relationship to the community they inhabit); second, group-centred (how persons lodge themselves in groups and how a grouping of persons construes its relationship to other groups within the community); and third, collectivity-centred (how persons ordered as groups thereafter construe themselves in relation to other separate groups). The chapter will look first, in an ethnographic/biographical fashion, at the detail of political-cultural identity as it is present in routine practical activity. Then, second, the chapter will look at the business of the ways in which agents come to understand themselves as members of political collectivities, at how such patterns of political-cultural understandings are institutionally embodied and how thereafter such understandings are expressed in routine practice. The third concern will be with the ways in which individuals or groups construe their relationship to extant political-cultural structures, as this will affect the extent to which agents take themselves to be able to react creatively to structural change.

It is from this general discussion that we can draw an idea of political-cultural identity where such identity expresses our relationship to the collectivity considered as an ordered body of persons, a polity. In terms of the characteristics of identity listed above, we are looking at the way in which private identity is presented within the public world.

Construing the collectivity: locale, network and memory in political-cultural structures of identity

The theorists of the classical European tradition of social theory concerned themselves with analysing the shift to the modern world, with grasping the nature of political-economic structural change as the old feudal agrarian pattern declined. In the context of such analyses, patterns of social-institutional change were considered, often in terms of a contrast between polar types (tradition/modernity) and, as a reflexive extension to these analyses, the ways in which sets of ideas shifted and offered narratives in respect of the changes themselves were a key concern. Within this thoroughly complex area of debate there is a strong concern for the changing nature of political life and political-cultural identity, the ways in which agents read the patterns of change which enfold their lives. As the shift to the modern world was accomplished, new forms of life carried new patterns of identity and political-cultural identity.

The diverse ways in which agents had made the new system and were in turn bound by that system was a routine concern for the theorists of the classical tradition. Marx addressed these ideas in terms given by the strategy of historical materialist analysis and revolved around the notion of ideology, which concept has figured variously in subsequent social-scientific work (Eagleton, 1991). A little later Durkheim cut through this problem complex in terms of a distinction among collective belief systems and social organizational forms between mechanical and organic solidarity. Durkheim argued that the decline of solidary relations typical of the former pattern of life was in process of being replaced by a new integrative social ethic of individualism. And in the transitional work of Weber we find a neo-Kantian analysis of the cultural rationalization of the world accompanying the growth of bureaucratically ordered industrial-capitalism. It is clear that these major theorists all dealt with the issue of political-cultural identity in the context of rapid social change. In various ways the exchange of structures and agents reworked available affirmed ideas of identity. It was also clear to the theorists of the classical tradition that processes of change could be fraught. And the whole process of change and theorizing about change entailed adopting clear positions in respect of what end-points of change were desirable. In this sense, the theorists all affirmed particular models of humankind (Hollis, 1977).

The models of humankind which these theorists respectively affirmed were not simple generalizations from their personal experience, the way in which we might speak casually about these matters; rather, they were self-conscious constructs. The material can be regarded as philosophical anthropology. It comprises a mixture of critical observation and philosophical reflection. The results are necessarily abstract and they can easily become simply schematic, in the sense that there is little real intention to uncover the keys to grasping personhood; rather, the models are proffered in order to enable lines of substantive enquiry to proceed (for example, the models of humankind affirmed by the standard quartet of social sciences noted in Chapter 2 were schematic in this sense). Against any simple reliance on these abstract models, and as a prophylactic against schematism, I wish to recall the dense and complex detail of political-cultural identity. Of course, my own philosophical anthropological commitments cannot be set on one side, so at the back of the accumulation of detailed reflection is a view of personhood as social and creative. The reflections of this text are therefore finally grounded in this respect in the optimistic traditions of formal and substantive democracy (Preston, 1994b).

The notion of political-cultural identity can be approached in a preliminary fashion in terms of the ideas of locale, network and memory. As this trio provided an ethnographic/biographical route into the matter of identity so too can they provide preliminary access to the issue of political-cultural identity, that complex spread of practices and ideas whereby the person is related to the ordered collectivity.

The strength of locale

In terms of the notion of locale we are looking at person-centred understandings. The focus is on how an individual construes their relationship to the community they inhabit and how thereafter the person considers their community relates to the wider world. This involves the political understandings of individuals and the political understandings of local collectivities expressed in folk knowledges (claims to fact), common sense (claims to mundane practical knowledge) and folk ideologies (claims to ideals).

The political-cultural understandings of an individual will record accidents of biography and, in respect of given patterns of power and authority, understandings will be practical, dense and unremarked. In respect of the formal sphere of politics, understandings will be episodic, addressing merely what has been noticed or what has impinged upon the individual. And in a similar way, the political-cultural understandings of the local collectivity will be particular, episodic and informal. There will be an available stock of local knowledge, and individuals will participate in folk knowledges, common sense and folk ideologies.

The immediate context of locale will provide the person with a series of sources of knowledge (practices/ideas) in respect of the collectivity, and we can review these sources, running from the locale's core to its periphery: family; neighbourhood; community; organization; institution; and media realm. All these discrete yet interlinked spheres will provide knowledge which will inform the relationship of person and collectivity.

So, first, in the family sphere there will be the ways in which the members of the family severally construe their relationship to those centres and agents of power which they recognize. This could include the manner of approach and judgements adopted (practice/ideas) to those formal agents of authority encountered in routine practice (the agents of the state, or other analogous institutional spheres), and these could be deferential, accommodative, evasive or aggressive. Here the person operates as an individual and as a member of a family. Then second, in the neighbourhood sphere of the street, the local shop or meeting place the person will encounter the routines of practices/ideas in respect of the politics of local life, including, for example, how to deal with neighbours within the local sphere (gossip, opinion, complaint) and how to handle publicly voiced common sense in respect of formal politics (for example, commentary on topical issues in the media). Here the person operates as an individual and as a member of a small local group. Third, in the community sphere the person will encounter both the lowest tier of formal political institutions and organizations (local state, and analogous institutional spheres) and the lowest tier of community-based political groups and social movements. Here the person operates as an individual and as a member of a group. Fourth, in the organization sphere the person will encounter sets of ideas which express the relationship of groups to the collectivity, for example, as a member of an artisanal group, or a professional group or trade union. Here the person operates as a member of a social group. And similarly, in the institutional sphere of the state machinery – registration, taxes, welfare and so on – the person operates as an individual, a member of a group and a member of the collectivity. And then, finally, in the media realm the person both participates vicariously in the issues of the day and runs the media word back through routine in the light of media stories. This sphere is an element of the public sphere of rational debate, but more directly it is the sphere of popular culture and it is suffused with delimited-formal and pervasive-informal ideological material. It is in this sphere that the ordered collectivity turns back upon itself in systematic reflection.

All these spheres of practice/ideas have been presented as a simple schematic list. However, they are integrated and these spheres of political-cultural identity find coherent expression in little tradition. Moving beyond this notion, and anticipating latter comments, the formal institutional aspect of political-cultural identity (the realm of the state and analogous institutions, and their several impacts upon persons) associated with these spheres has a cultural expression as 'great tradition' and/or 'official ideology'. And most generally, and resonating with all these levels, we have the realm of media-carried political-cultural identity (mass media of newspapers, advertising, television and their routine overlap with consumerism – which ties them back into fundamental political-economic structures). In other words, political-cultural identity can be taken to be a coherent package, an integrated whole, which can be discovered in practice/ideas at micro and macro levels.

On the basis of this characterization of locale, a series of areas of debate can be identified: first, the shift from private to public sphere; then second, the shift from private folk knowledges to public ideological knowledges; and finally, the ways in which the hierarchy is a realm of contestedness, as the closer to the private/folk end of the hierarchy the more autonomy (over what might be a limited realm) the person has, and similarly the closer to the public/ideological end of the hierarchy the more the person is subject to pressures to conform to the views affirmed in the institutions of the system itself.

FROM PRIVATE TO PUBLIC SPHERE   It is possible to draw a distinction between the private sphere and the public sphere. The former can be characterized as essentially the mundane realm of ordinary life – of family, work, leisure. The realm is, of course, suffused with the demands of the broader system within which it is necessarily embedded. In some respects the demands of the system do not bear very directly upon this sphere (for example, modes of dress in leisure hours). In some respects the demands of the system do bear very directly upon this sphere (for example, in the regulation of time so that labour power is rationally ordered). In some respects the demands of the system are subverted, denied or turned aside (for example, in the ways in which local networks can constitute a black economy which escapes regulation by officialdom, the archetypal denizens of the rationally ordered public sphere). It is often argued that one of the characteristics of industrial capitalism is its tendency rationally to reconstruct areas within the private sphere in accordance with the demands of the logic of the system – hence the familiar example of clock-time – and these processes continue today.

The private sphere will have its own patterns of power and its own schedules of what is desirable. The public sphere will also have patterns of power and schedules of what is desirable. For our purposes, it is important to note that the shift from private to public sphere is significant. On the one hand, the sets of political-cultural ideas which govern the action of individuals towards the collectivity within the private sphere can be taken to grow organically out of the routine practice of that private sphere; it is a grass-roots upward route to political-cultural ideas, no matter how deeply overlain by the demands of the powerful. On the other hand, in the public sphere we encounter the realm of formal ideas which are self-consciously promulgated by a variety of political actors. In the modern world, the key actor has been the state (and associated mechanisms of parliaments and parties and pressure groups, etc.). In the public sphere we find the promulgation of top-down sets of political-cultural ideas.

The shift seems to imply a move from a realm of political-cultural ideas tested and legitimated in tradition to a realm of ideas tested and legitimated in (more or less) open public discourse. And related to this, the shift seems to imply a lessening of detail and a move to simplification (in the media-dominated realm of the public sphere we find all pretence at rational debate eschewed in favour of public-relations slogans and sound-bite politics). Also, the shift seems to imply a loss of power on the part of the ordinary person. On these issues, in sum, one would want to insist that the private sphere does have an element of relative autonomy. And one would want to insist that the key characteristic of the public sphere is the extent to which it manages to act as a rational sphere.

FROM PRIVATE KNOWLEDGES TO PUBLIC KNOWLEDGES The sets of ideas current within the sphere of ordinary life can be characterized as political folk knowledge, the accumulated knowledge current within a population in regard to the ways of the wider world and their place within that world. It is likely that such folk knowledge will comprise a variety of claims, including practical knowledge, prejudice and myth. Such folk knowledge will be current within the group in question and it could take a semi-formal guise as 'little tradition', an idea to which we can return in the later discussion of memory.

The sphere of public ideological knowledge can be contrasted with the sphere of folk knowledge. The sphere of public ideological knowledge will contain a variety of claims all of which will be in some fashion self-conscious: the formal sets of ideas of organizations, institutions and the state. The public ideological sphere is a routinely contested sphere.

There is a dilemma here in respect of the balance of explanation of the constitution of the self. As Cohen (1994) has argued, notwithstanding the ineluctably social nature of humankind and human life, we can establish spheres of reflection/action which are for a little while pulled out of the mainstream of social life. On Cohen's argument this opens the further issue of the use by individual selves of agreed social truths as frameworks, ways of structuring interaction. Cohen suggests that this is how these cultural resources do and ought to work. The agreed untruth works as a way of ordering social interaction. In this Cohen points not merely to the realm of convenient functional untruths, the ritual displays of public life, but also, more contentiously (it seems) to the public sphere generally as suffused by distancing ritual. Again, it seems to me, Cohen's a priori affirmation of the autonomous self is present and (again) drives reflection too far towards individualism. However, more familiarly, the sphere of folk knowledge, common sense and folk ideology is a routinely contested sphere, and any consensus will be provisional.

THE CONTESTED NATURE OF UNDERSTANDINGS   The closer to the private/ folk end of the hierarchy, the more autonomy (over what might be a limited realm) the person has and similarly, the closer to the public/ ideological end of the hierarchy, the more the person is subject to pressures to conform to the views affirmed in the institutions of the system itself. The spread of sanctions in ordinary life is large and subtle. In the formal sphere matters are reversed. As Weber pointed out, eventually the state relies on violence and individual selves can be obliged to conform.

The resources of the network

In terms of the notion of network we are looking at how persons lodge themselves in dispersed groups, and thereafter how these groupings of persons construe their relationship to other groups within the wider collectivity. There seem to be two elements to consider: first, the matter of membership of groups or organizations; and second, the sphere of operation of ideologies, both delimited-formal (as the group propounds its position) and pervasive-informal (as the general cultural sphere is suffused with the interacting and competing articulated positions of many groups).

In terms of political-cultural identity we invest our immediate attention in the practice/ideas of locale which in turn are the basis for networks which move beyond locale to reach more distant places. We interact with distant others as individuals (family and kin networks, and leisure), members of organizations (commercial and professional links), and members of collectivities (trade links, national units, international organizations). As we move along these networks, the stock of ideas which we have from our base is liable to become less relevant to other new situations. As we move along our networks, a mix of familiarity, novelty and incomprehension will be encountered. At one extreme we merely re-create our base at the point along our networks to which we have moved (as tourists we might re-create our home base in the holiday location; as professionals we are likely to meet with other professionals to discuss similar problems in new contexts; and as members of collectivities we deal with common concerns and problems). More optimistically, we do encounter novelty in the form of new persons and places and read these experiences back into our stock of knowledge. The distinction in respect of the response to novelty has in recent years been cast in terms of tourists/travellers. And then, at the opposite extreme, knowledge of new situations falls away into stereotypes and ignorance (as we move along trade links where partners become ever more remote from familiar locales, or we meet others only as instances of another collectivity – thus in the cold war period 'Westerners' met 'Easterners', as they do today in a different fashion in Germany).

In the context of networks we can see that there is a series of issues to note: first, the move from the local and familiar to the general and unfamiliar; second, the move from the local and safe to the general and unsafe; and third, the move from realms of control to realms of less control.

FROM LOCAL/FAMILIAR TO GENERAL/UNFAMILIAR The local sphere is familiar and carries its own available strategies of understanding in the form of folk knowledge, common sense and local ideology; the form of life will carry along with it forms of understanding. However, when the individual moves away from the local sphere the cognitive resources of the locale become less immediately relevant as the newly encountered place will have its own cognitive resources.

The members of a family and kin network living in a place remote from the familiar locale will have a different knowledge appropriate to their locale. Or in the context of organizations, the sets of expectations in respect of how members of formal organizations can interact with members of other organizations or the machinery of the state will also be dependent upon the local context – if the context changes then so too will the local sets of rules of prudent procedure. Or again as members of collectivities, if we interact at a distance from our familiar locale then we do so in more simplified/stereotyped ways.

Overall, in terms of the knowledge available to guide action we are moving from the local/familiar to the general/unfamiliar. In terms of the knowledge available to guide action we are moving from a sphere dense in detail to one which is relatively impoverished of detail. And in general, an individual would move from the status of 'local' to that of 'stranger' (or 'foreigner').

FROM LOCAL/SAFE TO GENERAL/UNSAFE   The local territory is known and thus safe (even if the form of life in question has areas which are politically fraught, these will be known and routinely negotiated via avoidance, self-censorship, disguised and indirect references, and so on). As we move along various networks we move into areas where the local political rules are not known and these areas are therefore potentially unsafe. In conversation in the local place we will know what it is to be frank, but in a new place we will not know the rules and we might restrict our comments.

FROM MORE TO LESS CONTROL   In the local sphere with familiar sets of political-cultural resources it is possible to remain in control. The political-cultural environment is known and might therefore be con-trolled (although this is not the same as being guaranteed safe). In an unfamiliar place with unfamiliar sets of rules/understandings we cannot exercise such control.

Overall, a shift outwards along a network can be seen to involve moving into more problematical territory; we are not sure how to go on. However, a contrary experience is available; as we move outwards along a network we move into problematical territory which is seen as a sphere not of danger but of freedom or release from routinely experienced patterns of action/understanding.

The reserves of memory

In terms of the notion of political-cultural memory we are looking at the ways in which individuals, groups and collectivities secure their understandings of the patterns of social relationships (and one key aspect which will be grasped and explained/legitimated in memory will be patterns of power). We could suggest that for individuals memory is a matter of personal coherence whereas for collectivities memory is a matter of order and legitimation.

Political-cultural memory can take a series of forms: the material of folk traditions; the material of little traditions; the material of official histories of organizations and institutions; the material of official histories of states; the material presented in the media; and the material underpinning the public sphere. In these various spheres we are looking at the production, dissemination and practical effect of sets of ideas about how the polity and its inhabitants are ordered and might develop. At the local level such reflections will be informal and the body of judgements will be passed on through little traditions, but thereafter the positions adopted will become more self-conscious, either in terms of the truths affirmed by organizations or embedded within institutional routines, or as delimited-formal ideologies with, of course, their pervasive-informal extension. In the First World in the modern period the central political-cultural memory has come to be the nation. Anderson (1983) presents this as an imagined community with an official history (how persons ordered as groups thereafter construe themselves in relation to other separate groups). The nature of nationalism has been a central preoccupation in the modern period.

The business of memory is linked to the matter of change. Thus we recall change in a series of spheres: the mundane details of family change such as lines of relationship and patterns of descent (some formalized for property reasons), and the ways in which the area/community in which we live changes. We note also that cultural traditions shift and change, and the past is invoked to explain and judge the present (and in the First World we affirm ideas of progress so that all identity is lodged in developing time) (Hoggart, 1958; Pollard, 1971; Wright 1992).

There is a series of simple points to be made about political-cultural identity in the context of memory: (a) we can distinguish private and public memory; (b) we can distinguish unselfconscious and self-conscious memory; (c) we can note the specific construct of the national past; and (d) the latent conflicts in respect of memory.

PRIVATE AND PUBLIC MEMORY   We can distinguish between private and public memory where the former is personal, idiosyncratic and untidy and the latter is ordered. As we move through life we accumulate memories which draw the disparate events of experience into a co-herent narrative, and random experiences become a personal set of memories (and are taken as coherent). The sphere of public memory is ordered and is present as organizational records/truths, as institutional records/truths, as official state records/truths. In these spheres what is remembered is considered, weeded and regulated.

The tension between private and public memory is thus quite sharp. In the sphere of public political culture the claims that are made by various groups or individuals on the basis of memory (as to how things were and are and might be, with continuity usually construed as a virtue in political-cultural debate) bear upon questions about patterns of power within that collectivity. The sphere of public memory is not merely a considered sphere but it is considered in the light of the interests of the powerful. A challenge by an individual affirming a counter-memory will be resisted. A challenge by a group affirming a counter-memory might well meet with a stronger reaction.

The realm of official public memory is claimed by the machineries of the state as these memories are part of the legitimating ideology of the polity. Yet to this sphere of the official public memory we can counter-pose an idea of a rational public memory, a critical counter-factual with which to evaluate official truths.

UNSELFCONSCIOUS AND SELF-CONSCIOUS MEMORY   In the case of private memory we can distinguish between the unselfconscious understandings of particularity, the celebration of familiar patterns of life as unproblematic, and the reflexively self-conscious understandings of individuality, the celebration of the historical uniqueness of received and changing sets of circumstances. The distinction comes from Heller (1984) and points to the extent to which individuals or groups are self-critical, that is, the extent to which they are able to reflect rationally and critically upon the pattern of life they follow.

THE NATIONAL PAST   In the public sphere in the First World we have a routine presentation of the national past (Wright, 1985). The national past is an official public memory of the past of a collectivity which serves the concerns of the élite. Wright argues that a 'national past' comprises the stories we routinely assume about ourselves, rather than explicitly tell. In this sense everyday life includes an element of historicity, the appreciation of being lodged in developing time: 'Everyday life is the historically conditioned framework in which the imperatives of natural sustenance (eating, sleeping . . .) come to be socially determined: it is in the intersubjectivity of everyday life that human self-reproduction is wedded to the wider processes of social reproduction' (Wright, 1985: 6). The banal routines of everyday practice are suffused with historical memory and these are one strand of the complex linkages, practices and ideas which lodge specific persons in specific social locales.

This aspect of living is grasped in Heller's notion of particularity, the unreflective self-understanding of those who accept and affirm the norms of the wider group to which they belong. Contrariwise, individuality is a distanced appreciation of the cultural norms binding us. Particularity was made into the core ethic of bourgeois society, the egocentric doctrine of individualism plus the mystificatory notion of the private pursuit of greed occasioning maximum social well-being. However, the rise of modernity not only ushered in bourgeois particularity but also a new realm of freedom, of individuality and hence also insecurity.

In everyday historical consciousness agents explain their world/selves via plausible tales, stories, narratives or histories. It is a part of the business of making sense. It is embedded in routine, the sphere of the taken-for-granted. It is also strongly implicated in the response of groups and individuals to change. Wright, considering the case of the UK, argues that the national past is a story told to inhabitants to render things meaningful and clear in the context of the flux and disenchantment of the modern world. Wright mentions two particular styles the national past adopts: the use of auratic sites where history is taken as most particularly present; and remembered war, which is taken as a sphere of non-routine when actions made a difference.

Wright points out that there is a clear political aspect to all this as the group to whom we are routinely enjoined to belong/submit is the nation. We are offered a national past, an official history. The nation replaces other more local communities and it re-enchants the world. A story is woven which tells us who we are, where we came from and where we are going. The political issue for Wright lies in the question of whether or not 'everyday historical consciousness might be detached from . . . the dominant symbolism of nation and drawn into different expressions of cultural and historical identity' (Wright, 1985: 26). The counterpart to the national past is an appreciation of the historical nature of the life of a community which is free of this overriding élite claim.

THE CONTESTED NATURE OF MEMORY   We can note a tension between the detail of personal or community memory/tradition and the generalized demands of official memory or mass culture. Many have argued that history in this sense is a zone of conflict between the powerful and their subordinates, a battle for possession and control of historical memory.

Learning the political-cultural collectivity

The material in the foregoing section offered a sketch of the rich detail of political-cultural identity. It is clear that such political-cultural identities are not given but must be learned and relearned within the general social world. The processes of learning and relearning can be schematically unpacked in terms of a quartet of ideas: first, the business of becoming a political agent within a collectivity; second, the nature of those understandings which are expressed in routine practice; third, the nature of those understandings which are lodged within institutions; and finally, the elaborate spread of understandings which are present as narratives available to given audiences and available to inform action. This is the realm of ideologies.

Becoming a political agent within a collectivity

The process whereby persons become initiated as political agents involves a set of ways of learning the appropriate locale, network and memory. The experiences begin in childhood with figures outside the domestic sphere to whom significant others defer or display fear, or towards whom they act as supplicants. That the social world is suffused with a myriad patterns of power relationships will be a process of learning for the new recruit. A series of issues present themselves: first, the processes of induction into communities, whereby a person learns the basic sets of rules, and the rituals of rites of passage which move the person from initial status positions through to later positions (Cohen, 1994); second, the use of auratic sites (Wright, 1985; Eco, 1987) which have symbolic power for the community (and which may be used by the collectivity or privately); and third, the strategy of taking pilgrimage-style journeys (Anderson, 1983) from the periphery of political-cultural collectivities to the sacred sites at the centre (public and private).

INDUCTION AND RITES OF PASSAGE   The business of becoming a member of a society is a familiar area of reflection for sociologists, anthropologists and psychologists. One might suggest that the notion that lies at the heart of the diverse tales on offer is that of learning. In Wittgensteinian terms the social world is a web of rules. It is sets of rules which constitute social practices. We learn the rules and we 'know how to go on'. The process of learning sets of rules is practical. A language game carries a form of life, and we learn the linked activities in practical activity.

We can argue that the same process occurs in respect of learning to be a member of a political collectivity. The distribution of power, status, rights and duties throughout society (and the ways in which these are discursively legitimated) will be learned along with the range of other social skills.

It is routinely held that this learning is accomplished early in life. It seems clear that there are patterns of power, status and legitimating explanations within families and these will be learned by the child. And as the child moves out of the domestic sphere new patterns of power will be encountered and learned.

A particular expression of this learning how to go on will be the formal episodes of status change – the movement from one status to another which is marked by the community in a ceremonial fashion. The shift from childhood to adulthood will usually mark the shift to full membership of the political community.

AURATIC SITES   Auratic sites have symbolic power for the community and may be used by the collectivity or privately. These auratic sites are taken to have a particular cognitive and affective relevance for the community in question. The sites are places where the sets of ideas affirmed by the community find particular expression – and as such are available for ceremonial purposes and may be engaged with collectively or privately. These sites are social constructs which serve the purpose of allowing the affirmation of political-cultural identities: the example which Eco (1987) offers is of historical reproduction museums in the USA which meticulously recreate places, scenes and events from the 'old West'. However, these are meticulous reconstructions of mythic places, scenes and events, and as such are hyper-real. In a similar fashion for the UK Wright (1985) points to the burgeoning production and consumption of 'heritage' which is a similar ritual sphere.

These auratic sites offer exemplifications of political-cultural identities; they are resources whereby individual selves can locate themselves with reference to the collectivity. Cohen (1994) insists that such ritual should not be read deterministically, as culture imposing itself on selves, but should be read as offering a framework with reference to which individual selves can locate themselves.

PILGRIMAGE JOURNEYS Anderson (1983) argues that there are three basic elements to the imagined community of nationhood:

> The nation is imagined as limited because even the largest . . . has finite . . . boundaries, beyond which lie other nations . . . It is imagined as sovereign because the concept was born in an age in which Enlightenment and Revolution were destroying the legitimacy of the divinely-ordained, hierarchical dynastic realm . . . Finally, it is imagined as a community, because, regardless of the actual inequality . . . the nation is always conceived as a deep, horizontal comradeship. (1983: 16)

In the historical process of the production of this cultural artefact two matters were crucial: print capitalism and pilgrimage journeys.

Anderson looks at the way in which both pre-existing religious communities and dynastic realms were displaced by the rise of the secular nation-state. Anderson begins by looking at the cultural system of religious communities. He wants to know how they were constituted in practice, and he points to a shared sacred language and common paths of pilgrimage within a hierarchically ordered meta-institution. People with different vernacular languages shared the same sacred language, took the same pilgrimages to express their faith and lodged themselves within the hierarchy according to trans-ethnic rules: thus was constituted a community of believers. But the world religions declined, in Europe first, from the Renaissance onwards. Over a similar period the dynastic realms were weakened. Simultaneously we see the rise of mercantile capitalism and the particular sphere of print capitalism.

The rise of modern language communities created the possibility of nation-communities. Print capitalism destroyed the primacy of Latin, the sacred language of Europe and the language of administration, by solidifying vernacular languages with editions of sacred texts, grammars and dictionaries. A new reading public emerged among the educated people generally rather than simply the clerics and bureaucrat servants of the dynasty in power. As religious community was displaced as a central social experience, so too were dynastic polities. The political pattern first broke in the Americas. Anderson now re-introduces the theme of pilgrimage and offers an argument by analogy to the creation of nations. The particular journey/pilgrimage which he has in mind is the bureaucratic journey. Colonial schools came, over time, to send recruits into colonial administrations. In the American empires of the Europeans the journeys of the colonial-born were restricted. As they moved through their careers looking to the pilgrimage centres of their bureaucratic spheres, London, Paris, Madrid or Lisbon, they found their progress blocked. Their journeys finished in the colonial territories. They were an out-group suffering discrimination, and this they came to recognize. The behaviour of the metropolitan administrations split the colonial élite groups away from the metropoles. It is this experience, plus again a community of readers, this time of colonial newspapers (print capitalism again), that Anderson posits as the germ of American nationalisms. This is how the potential nationalist group was constituted. Add to this the circumstances of vast geographical remoteness from the metropoles, economic disputes, the political and social ideology of the Enlightenment, a political occasion for rebellion and we have a sketch of how groups came together, formulated, lodged and had accepted, after wars of liberation, claims to nation-statehood. And thereafter the idea was re-exported to Europe and thence with industrial-capitalist expansion and colonialism to the rest of the world. In brief, so far as Anderson is concerned the germ of modern nationalism is to be found in those secular pilgrimages of the relatively disadvantaged who thereafter constituted themselves as a community. And the ritual role of pilgrimage continues.

Understandings expressed in routine practice

The ordinary social world is suffused with meanings. One aspect of this spread of meanings carried in routine will deal with the relationship of persons and collectivities: ideas of political-cultural identity and political practice will be carried within the realm of ordinary practical activity. A series of issues can be addressed: first, the idea of little traditions (Scott, 1971) whereby the nature of the political collectivity and the scope for local action are carried in a spread of common-sense ideas (for example, 'you cannot fight city hall'); second, the idea of the ideology in everyday life whereby the sets of ideas of the élite mesh with the concerns of the subordinate group and find a quite particular expression as non-ideological ideology and non-political politics (for example, the collapse of political activity/thinking into technocratic developmentalist nation-building in Singapore (Chua, 1995)); finally, the idea of everyday nationalism (Shamsul, 1996) whereby the ideas promulgated by the élite are picked up and self-consciously deployed by the subordinate groups.

LITTLE TRADITIONS   The idea of the little tradition points to the practical and ethical resources of the local community which flow from their everyday practice. These resources offer ways of ordering their ordinary lives and ways of resisting the claims of outside powers – such as the state machinery. The notion recalls the sociological work of Robert Redfield on small-town America, and E.P. Thompson with his cultural history of the dispossessed and ignored. The material of the little tradition will be rich in political-cultural resources as it will detail the ways in which authority might bear upon the local community and the ways in which authority might effectively and properly be resisted.

IDEOLOGY EXPRESSED IN EVERYDAY LIFE   A similar area of debate looks to the general societal expression of delimited-formal ideological materials disseminated by élite groups. Chua (1995) has looked at the non-ideological ideology of pragmatism which is disseminated by the government of Singapore and which finds routine expression in the ordinary lives of the population. In the scheme of ideas disseminated by the government all value-based political judgements and proposals are assimilated to the pursuit of material advance, which goal is presented as both utterly obvious, non-controversial and amenable to technical expert ordering. In this way political life flows away into the sphere of technical debate, and all value-based criticism is either irrational and irrelevant posturing or, where the criticisms have purchase, dangerously disruptive and therefore disallowed on technical grounds. Chua does note that political life does not thereby vanish from the polity, for not only are elections regularly held (no matter that these might be rather empty contests) but a vast area of informal substitute political life has grown up – the sphere of gossip and rumour. All this recalls the Gramscian notion of hegemony whereby the sets of political ideas of the élite are taken into ordinary common sense and thus attain a maximum effectiveness.

EVERYDAY NATIONALISM   A further related area of discussion has been addressed by Shamsul (1996) who looks not at the élite dissemination of non-ideological ideology but at the ways in which élite-disseminated ideology finds expression in everyday practice. In this instance the ordinary people are consciously using the elements of élite-disseminated ideology to inform their routine practice. It is a variety of social mobilization. The particular person acts consciously as a political commentary/actor and produces an 'everyday nationalism'. It is clear that in multi-ethnic communities such mobilization is socially and politically ambiguous, able to produce tension and violence as well as a sense of collective endeavour. Shamsul has the situation in Malaysia in mind, but the point could be made for contemporary Europe as well (Ignatieff, 1994).

Understandings embodied in institutions

The notions of structure and agency point to the activity of knowledgeable agents within the context of received structures. As Marx remarked, humankind makes its own history but not in conditions of its own choice. In respect of the matter of political-cultural identities there are cognitive resources available which can be taken to be lodged within the established practices of formal institutions. These resources can be located both within ordinary routines and in the more formal statements of the objectives of the institution. A series of issues can be addressed: first, the spread of cognitive resources lodged in the routines and official objectives of organizations which together imply/ reflect broader patterns of social organization and hence identity and political-cultural identity; second, the promulgation of institutional truths which self-consciously offer particular readings of the nature of the social world (and thus persons, having identities and political-cultural identities); and third, the more overtly engaged cognitive resources found in official ideologies (nationalisms).

RESOURCES LODGED IN ROUTINES   The notion of the little tradition can be extended to the workings of formal organizations and institutions. In the routine practice of such organizations and institutions are carried sets of ideas which resonate with the political culture of the society at large. As an example, in business organizations within the industrial-capitalist world one would expect to find uncritical acceptance of the predominant role of instrumental rationality, the unequivocal benefit of material goods, the appropriateness of personal ordered behaviour and so on. In these ways the cultural resources of the industrial-capitalist system find expression within key organizations and the patterns of professional behaviour of those engaged in these businesses. Similarly, in formal institutions there will be parallels between the ways in which action internal to the institution is ordered and the ways in which the wider society is ordered. As an example, in the state's civil service one would anticipate patterns of personal activity which reflected or exemplified the institutional commitments of that service – an ordered hierarchical working practice, a routine deference to authority, a commitment to long-term service – and in the particular organs of the state one would expect institutional objectives to be reflected in the actions of the employees – in the health service to caring, in the social-welfare service to controlling supplicants and in the security service to identifying and controlling wrong-doers.

INSTITUTIONAL TRUTHS   A related set of resources can be pointed to in the sets of explicitly presented ideas to which institutions give a collective assent: mission statements, official positions, formal responses and so on. In all these cases the parallels between institution and wider society which we noted above will find a particular considered expression. As an example, the organizations representing the concerns of senior businessmen routinely speak in a directorial version of management-speak. And in a similar way, trades unions adopt a particular rhetoric of aggression which exemplifies their claims to be the counter-voice to the economic élite in an unequal society. In a sceptical fashion, Galbraith (1989) suggests that institutional truths are best seen as a realm of convenient untruths. However, the continued repetition of the familiar stock of convenient untruths represents another way in which established power and its ideological legitimations are reaffirmed.

OFFICIAL IDEOLOGIES   The realm of official ideologies provides a further stock of political-cultural ideas. In the modern period such official ideologies have typically been cast as nationalisms, but there are other more self-consciously progressive sets of statements. The twentieth century has seen a series of emphatic programmatic exercises from European states and political movements, from the left and the right. In Western Europe the fascist regimes of Italy, Spain and Germany produced elaborate official ideological schemes. And in the European Second World the intellectual work of Marx was invoked by the state to offer a purportedly scientific official ideology, Marxism-Leninism. On the basis of these formulations the policy orientation of the state was vindicated and critics silenced (MacIntyre, 1962). And in a similar way in the Third World in the wake of decolonization a number of developmental official ideologies have been presented, and in socialist China another elaborate official ideology replete with personality cults grew up around Mao Zedong.

Understandings related in narratives

In the sphere of political-cultural identity the contestedness of identity is centrally important. As we understand ourselves and our group and our collectivity, then so do we order our activities. The sphere of self-conscious reflection is a cognitive one, and while much activity is taken for granted, in the realm of self-conscious activity there are sets of ideas that are promulgated and disputed.

It is here that we can begin to speak of an inter-related set of ideas (moving from ideas current within the mass towards ideas promulgated among élites): narratives of self/community, or folk traditions and little tradition; narratives of collectivity, or delimited-formal ideologies and great tradition; and the extent of the development of the public sphere, which is an institutionally ordered sphere within which rational debate might be undertaken.

NARRATIVES OF SELF/COMMUNITY   The material of folk traditions and little traditions will express the accumulated knowledge of the local community, the resources of tradition. It is here that we will find the informal stories dealing with the history of the community, the key popular figures and episodes in the history of the community. The figures may be popular in the sense of being taken to have stood for the ordinary people, but they can just as well belong to the élite or indeed to mythical realms (think of the ways in which figures from literature or media can be associated with an area, and may become tourist attractions). The function of such popular figures is symbolic; they exemplify the community. The record of the local hero is not required to be historically accurate. The same may be said about local events; it is enough that they happened and thus mark out the history of the community. These events give the history of the community some light and shade; the circumstance which is not looked for is a history empty of event. Of course, it may well be that, while these tales derive from particular historical persons or episodes, in collective informal recollection they are made and remade to address contemporary problems. Hobsbawm and Ranger (1983) have argued that tradition is invented, and we may be confident that the same is true of local-level tradition.

NARRATIVES OF COLLECTIVITY   The sphere of delimited-formal ideology is self-conscious and offers particular readings of structural circumstances which are intended to inform the practice of particular audiences/agents.

The tales which the members of self-conscious collectivities tell are of a different character to local-level folk history. In the case of the informal histories affirmed by ordinary people the material is essentially domestic, a record of what happened to our community cast in unproblematical terms of people and events. In contrast, the exercises in the manufacture of narratives undertaken by a collectivity are immediately self-conscious or artful. In these representations the intention is not merely to record but to distinguish and to separate. The narratives of collectivity tell the members of a group not merely where they have come from and what happened in their history, but, crucially, how they are different from other groups. It is in this sphere of material that we meet delimited-formal ideologies; one aspect of these devices will be to characterize particular groups and offer them routes to the future. It is likely that these delimited-formal ideological narratives will be produced by élites and broadly disseminated among the general population. And, of course, one key concern lodged within the classical tradition of social science is with the characterizing and comparative ranking of competing ideological schemes (Preston, 1985).

One familiar trait of such ideological tales, in particular as they refer to the constitution of the collectivity in question, is the attempt to naturalize the group, to suggest that it is something other than a collectivity constructed in narrative, in social life. The familiar strategies look to extra-social explanations in biology/history, claims to an ethnic or racial purity as the basis for the narratives of collectivity. The strategy of turning to an extra-social ground of collective identity has also been linked to the rationalizing drive of modernity, the extension of the sphere of life subject to rational scientific enquiry. In the history of Europe the consequences of the assimilation of these lines of argument have been profound, and Bauman points to the episode of the holocaust (Bauman, 1989).

THE PUBLIC SPHERE Habermas (1971) has argued that humankind shows three deep-seated interests in knowledge: the empirical-analytic, the historical-practical and the emancipatory. On the basis of the last-noted interest in human freedom Habermas contrives an intellectual space for a critical theory of society. A set of key claims in respect of the nature of human language is articulated as the basis of a theory of social-political development secured via the affirmation of the ideal goal of free debate in respect of the collective process of securing rational progressive social order. Habermas argues, in brief, that lodged within human language is a disposition to pursue not merely open debate but also the practical condition of such debate, namely an open democratic polity (Habermas, 1989).

A key issue in respect of the political culture of modern society is therefore the extent to which the public sphere is developed so as to enable rational open debate. Anderson (1983) calls this a pedagogic politics whose central character is a strong preference for open debate in pursuit of a rational consensus. On the basis of such a characterization, we can turn to deal with the patterns of debate in extant public spheres. It is here that the collectivity ordered self-consciously as a polity will offer its narratives of political identity: the free West, socialism, democracy and so on.

Acting in relation to the collectivity: political-cultural structures of identity and agent responses

The ways in which individuals or groups construe their relationship to extant political-cultural structures will affect the extent to which such agents take themselves to be able to react creatively to structural change. And the ways in which such agents understand their power will feed into their routine practical actions.

Routine practical action

A simple way of presenting these matters is to speak of the ways in which political culture is expressed in routine mundane action: from unselfconscious actions (where political-cultural ideas are merely expressed unnoticed in routine, for example, prejudices), through to self-consciously active patterns of action no matter how trivial they may seem (we could point to the activities of low-level moral entrepreneurs advising us on this and that).

In respect of these matters we could talk about arguing (within family, community and organization), complaining (to whoever will listen), lodging protests (about this and that, to whoever will acquiesce in our approach), and disregarding, ignoring and prejudging the claims of others (strategies applied across the range of our contacts).

In brief, it can be claimed that political action at the mundane level will rarely be an articulated politics; instead, it will be expressed in a diversity of seemingly non-political strategies or find modest articulation in the form of complaint.

Construing agent relationships to structures

The relationship between structures and agents can be construed more actively, and in this context it is clear that the relationship is mediated by the images of the agents in question. Agents can act politically only in the light of the understandings they have of their circumstances. It is clear that there is plenty of scope for confusion here – for misreading circumstances and acting unwisely as a result.

If we approach this business around the person/group we are confronted with the task of elucidating the detail of the ways in which the people involved construe their relationship to the collectivity of which they are a part. The business of forming a political-cultural identity has been discussed at length above. In this section we are interested in the ways in which agents position themselves – the way they place themselves within the stories they tell about the collectivity as a whole.

If we approach this business around the collectivity or polity we are confronted with the task of elucidating the sets of ideas which inform the actions of agents: the realm of political ideology. One element of the routinely and vigorously contested ideological realm is precisely the extent to which non-élite agents are taken to have the capacity to act. Recall Gramsci: if your ideas are routinized in common sense then they block action against your ideas. The notion of ideology is usually taken to be a matter of mobilizing people for action, but I rather think that the ideologies of the powerful – necessarily the most widely disseminated and influential – are concerned with demobilizing.

On these issues we can talk about mobilizing, demobilizing, and apathy, acquiescence and resignation. It is only on the basis of a view of the agents' relationship to structures that lines of possible action will be entertained. The first noted concern, mobilization, recalls the classical style of discussion of political leadership and political ideology as designed to encourage people to become active. However, as the second noted concern indicates, it can be argued that modern state machines and their professional politicians have a vested interest in keeping their populations uninvolved. An argument derived from the assimilation of politics to technical administration would point to this conclusion, and an example has been presented by Gellner (1964). A simpler argument would point to the vested interest of élites in maintaining their own power (Preston, 1994b). And here, to pick up the third noted area of concern, one reaction among populations subject to this routine manipulation is precisely to withdraw – to disregard the sphere of politics in favour of other pursuits.

Envisioning the scope for action

A crucial aspect of the ways in which agents and groups situate themselves within the collectivity will concern the scope for effective political action which might be undertaken by the agents. In the classical European tradition this has typically meant identifying historical agents: the bourgeoisie, the proletariat or more unusually an élite. In recent years the neoclassical marketeers in the guise of the postmodernists have spoken of the general social priority of the agency of the consumer as repression is replaced by seduction in a global prosperous marketplace.

On these issues we could talk about first, the types of action implied by the formulations lodged within political-cultural resources, typically the agents identified or assumed; second, those agents and lines of action which have figured within classical tradition – bourgeoisie, proletariat and so on; and third, the recent claims in respect of the loss of the agent within the sphere of the available consumer lifestyles of the contemporary global system.

In all these cases, a general position in respect of the possibilities of action will constrain the action which is attempted. On the last noted area of concern, the postmodernist celebration of marketplace lifestyle choice, it is clear that political mobilization is hindered – there is nothing for anyone to be mobilized for. One might see this as a further rehashing of the familiar 1950s 'end of ideology' thesis, but it does usefully underscore the key point – unless action is taken to be possible and useful then it will not be undertaken, and the ideological battle around the establishment of an effective politics will revolve most clearly around these sets of claims.

Engaging in action

The logical end-point of all self-conscious political-cultural reflection on the scope of action is, precisely, action. The story here begins to shift from political-cultural identity towards patterns of action where self-image is risked in practice. Arguments about ourselves entail action on behalf of those selves or, in other words, political-cultural identities involve schedules of ethical commitments and may require action. At this point we could talk about local-level community politics, social movements, regional politics, national politics, international politics, transnational politics (of MNCs) and supranational politics (of, say, the EU). However, I will not pursue these matters because at this point the debate shifts away from political culture and into the realm of the mainstream analysis of political action.

Conclusion: the multiplicity of political-cultural identity

In this chapter the concern has been with the ways in which agents come to understand themselves as members of political collectivities, how thereafter such understandings are expressed in routine practice, and how such understandings are institutionally embodied and thereafter formally legitimated in the public sphere. The ways in which individuals or groups construe their relationship to extant political-cultural structures will affect the extent to which such agents take themselves to be able to react creatively to structural change. And the ways in which such agents understand their power will feed into their routine practical actions. In respect of the notion of political-cultural identity, we can safely conclude that it is learned; that it expresses the relationship of agent to collectivity; that it identifies the scope for action; that it is always contested; and that it is multiple in its resources, articulations and expressions.

5

Global Changes and New Political-Cultural Identities

The discussions of political-cultural identity pursued thus far have concentrated on the detail of the ways in which agents might understand their situations and subsequently act to pursue particular goals. In this chapter we will consider the business of making structural arguments and look at the patterns of change being discussed now at the most general level. We turn our attention, therefore, to the very broadest structural changes which are likely to impact upon agents in the years running up to the millennium and try to indicate the outlines of their developing responses. In the three subsequent chapters we will consider in more detail the patterns of change within the three regions of the tripolar global system. The changes can be grasped in terms of the broad dynamics of structural change and the responses which agent groups make.

As global patterns of power shift and are reconfigured familiar political-cultural identities will also change. A series of levels of analysis present themselves. At the regional scale there will be changes within the three main areas of the global system as existing patterns of power within the regions alter. Then, at the nation-state level the familiar political projects of extant state regimes will be called into question as élites look to reposition themselves within the constraints of shifting global patterns, order their populations accordingly and disseminate reworked schedules of legitimation. Thereafter, at the subnational or local level, the routine practices and ideas of ordinary life will find these structural changes flowing through them, perhaps flagged by the arrival of new industries and workplaces, new social organizations (as people respond to new circumstances) and new patterns of political-cultural reflection and expression (new ideas, media and politics). And in each of these situations the agents in question will read their circumstances in different ways.

In order to grasp the broad dynamics of these patterns of complex change we can make reference to the analytical strategies of structural international political economy (Strange, 1988), which can be understood as a contemporary expression of the classical European tradition of social theorizing. On this basis we can note the present discussion of changes within the three broad areas of the interdependent tripolar global industrial-capitalist system. The common context for agents within these three regions is the shift from bipolarity to a new tripolarity, the occasion of the recognition/acknowledgement of this shift being the changes within the European state-socialist bloc over the period 1989–91.

The scale of the changes under consideration is vast and while I will endeavour to present a sketch of shifting political-cultural patterns in the light of the theoretical remarks of the earlier chapters, it will be impossible to present any very great detail. The presentation of the relevant detail is a matter for more specialist analyses. And finally, it should be noted that the analysis of patterns of change at a very broad level presents quite particular problems of synthesizing vast ranges of data within the compass of a coherent theoretical framework. I shall understand the exercise, in line with my remarks about the classical tradition, to be essentially interpretive-critical; I wish to make plausible interpretations rather than pursue exhaustive descriptions.

However, in line with the preference for ethnographic/biographical detail affirmed in the text, this chapter will begin by recalling the great surprise experienced in Europe and the West as the post-Second World War settlement dissolved away. It seems to me that this is the inevitable starting-point for all European and Western intellectual reflection on these issues. The post-Second World War global system, with its two great powers, the USA and the USSR, a divided Europe and a marginalized Third World, was definitively superseded in the period 1989–91.

The end of the comfortable certainties of the cold war

In the post-Second World War period in Europe and the West political-cultural identity had one overarching framework, the idea of the free West. In the countries of the Second World the ideological counterpart was socialism. And in the countries of the Third World there was a series of ideological positions which all looked to the pursuit of development. The period of the construction of the hegemonic Western ideology lay in the years immediately after the Second World War, when competition with the USSR declined into cold war and the formation of two military and economic blocs. Orthodox historians argue that this was a defensive move on the part of the West, while revisionist historians say the whole apparatus of the cold war was made primarily in the West and largely as a strategy of domestic political control (Walker, 1993).

The key elements of the ideology affirmed the distinction between the realm of free market-carried individual freedom and the realm of state-carried totalitarian unfreedom. The delimited-formal ideology offered a political-cultural identity for the political élite who were given a role and a set of slogans to legitimate that role (and, of course, they had many institutions through which they could pursue their own career paths). It also offered a political-cultural identity for the masses who were enjoined to support the defence of freedom.

The received delimited-formal ideology was destroyed over the period 1985–91. A series of steps encompassed the collapse. The first was taken by Gorbachev, who unilaterally withdrew from cold-war competition by initiating moves towards disarmament and *détente*. The second steps were taken when the West was slowly drawn into dialogue as the USA moved to support German concerns to advance *détente* against the narrow protests of the British state regime. The third series of steps were taken over the period 1989–91 as the Eastern bloc progressively dissolved itself. It is clear that over this period the central element of the Western official ideology of cold-war bloc-time, the object of ideological hostility, simply disappeared.

There has been considerable confusion among political élites in the subsequent period. The confusion has been acute in Europe, the West and the old territories of the Eastern bloc, but the implications for reading the global system and construing patterns of relationships within it go much wider. At the most general level of political discourse in Europe and the West there seems to be no replacement for the comfortable certainties of bloc-time in view. It is also clear that the end of the cold war has underscored the importance of existing debates about the character of the global system and a new salience has been accorded to debates surrounding claims to a new interdependent tripolarity.

Making structural arguments: the reconstruction of global industrial capitalism

In recent years a series of patterns of change within the global system has been identified, and debate continues in respect of the ways in which these changes should be construed. A number of tendencies within the global system can be sketched as patterns and styles of production change. First, in the First World the intermingled upgrading and hollowing out of the metropolitan core economies (flexible specialization and the new international division of labour). Second, the collapse of the Second World state-socialist bloc and its confused shift towards market-based political economies (a mixture of political collapse and thereafter general reconstruction in the USSR and Eastern Europe, and authoritarian market reforms in China and Indo-China). And third, the further partial dependent integration of certain areas of the Third World in Asia, Latin America and the oil-rich Middle East, and the slow drift of other areas of the Third World into a situation of apparent semi-detachment from the global system (much of Africa south of the Sahara).

These patterns of broad change have been met with a series of theoretical interpretations. On the one hand the increasingly integrated character of the global system has been addressed in terms of the development of a new international division of labour as First World industries move offshore and new areas of industrial development outside the traditionally industrial areas mature into world-class centres. This line of enquiry opens up a series of questions which revolve around the economic, social and political implications of what is read as a further stage in the expansion of the industrial-capitalist system. On the basis of this broad view the collapse of the Second World of official state socialism can be addressed and so too can the apparently semi-detached position of large parts of the Third World. However, on the other hand, this line of enquiry has found a vigorous fashionable counter-statement in the work of the celebrants of market liberalism. One line of argument reads the situation of the global system in terms of the putative triumph of political liberalism, a position eloquently announced by Fukuyama (1992), and a related line of analysis looks to the supersession of the entire Western tradition of political and social thought on the basis of a political economy of marketplace-carried abundance (Harvey, 1989).

I will argue that we can best grasp patterns of structural change within the global industrial-capitalist system using the strategy of structural international political economy and that within the analytical frameworks thereby established we can go on to consider the political-cultural projects of particular state regimes as they attempt to read and react to shifting enfolding structural circumstances (Preston, 1994a). It is within this double contextualization that, finally, the level of detail pointed to in the opening theoretical sections of this book might be adduced as ordinary people continue, as does everyone, with the routines of their everyday lives (Worsley, 1984).

The First World: flexible specialization and the new international division of labour

As the pattern of political-economic activity associated with the post-Second World War Bretton Woods system began to alter in the 1970s as problems mounted, a new pattern of industrial production began to be noted, and two aspects were often cited, particularly by commentators in the First World: the shift to flexible specialization and the global dispersal of production.

One line of analysis focused on the industrial sociology of contemporary society and considered the nature of technology, the organization of the workplace, the demands of the labour force and the interaction of the place of work with the wider society. Piore and Sabel (1984) argued that the familiar pattern of geographically concentrated large-plant Fordist mass production of standard products had given way in the 1980s to the geographically dispersed small-plant post-Fordist innovative production of individualized products. The mass production of similar products had given way to the large-scale production of a diversity of products. The shifts in demands for labour implied a diminution of concern for either familiar mass-production skills or unskilled labour in favour of a new imperative to flexible working on the basis of high and routinely upgraded skills. In a similar fashion there were expectations of a continuing process whereby familiar relationships of employment and wider social networks would change. The sharp division between work and home/leisure would soften as individuals worked more flexibly. In this situation, of course, some groups within the workforce would prosper, those with high skills, and some groups would experience severe problems.

It was suggested that there were two reasons for the problems of Fordist mass production: first, a series of external shocks to the system, including labour problems and the oil crises of the 1970s, which issued in the problems of inflation and slump and provoked an attempt by firms to ameliorate these difficult circumstances; and then second, the internal needs for reform of a mass-production system which could no longer respond to the increasingly sophisticated demands from consumers. On the basis of this analysis, there were two ways in which the problems of the breakdown of Fordist mass production could be addressed: first, an increase in global demand such that the system was reinvigorated, and this could be achieved after the suggestion of the Brandt Commission in 1980, which looked to an international Keynesianism which identified the Third World as a potential marketplace for the First World in a mutual interdependence (Preston, 1996); and second, a shift to new patterns of production which were knowledge-based, small-scale and oriented to an individualized product spread. In brief, this is the flexible specialization of a post-Fordist system of production.

A related analytical concern has been with the changing geographical pattern of production within the global industrial-capitalist system. On the basis of the theoretical machineries of world system analysis (Wallerstein, 1974) it was pointed out that in the 1970s a new phase of the development of world capitalism could be identified (Frobel and Heinrichs, 1980) in the form of the relocation of certain industries to the Third World and the establishment of some new industries in that region rather than in the First World. Over the late 1970s and 1980s some areas of the Third World saw rapid export-oriented industrial growth and the export goods produced served the demands of the First World consumer markets. The new global market for goods and the rise of the multinational corporations (MNCs) favours the new international division of labour (NIDL).

The upshot of these analyses has been to see industrial-capitalist production becoming increasingly dispersed across the global system as industries relocated from the metropolitan cores of Europe and North America to various bases in the Third World periphery. At the same time new patterns of production have been established which radically alter established patterns of working and the social positions of those engaged in these industries. A new pattern of flexible specialization has been identified and in significant measure has been pioneered outside established industrial areas. Finally, entirely new industries have grown in recent years; they are located not in the old metropolitan core economies but in the newly burgeoning economies of Asia. In all, the continuing drive of the industrial-capitalist system to intensify and extend its sphere has found recent expression in the form of the new international division of labour and the rise of flexible specialization.

The Second World: collapse and partial renewal in the socialist bloc

The dramatic reform movements in the Eastern bloc started with the democratization and liberalization moves within the USSR initiated by the Gorbachev government in the 1980s and the most dramatic upheavals took place in 1989–91. The depth of the problems facing the new leaderships are clear. In the Eastern bloc territories of Europe, in the case of political reforms, the generally peaceful shifts from command political economies to variants on the Western model was completed with elections throughout 1990. However, it has become clear that many tensions within these countries will have to be resolved. The reappearance of nationalism is one problem (Ignatieff, 1994), and it has been suggested that the crucial distinction in respect of the development of Eastern European polities will be between backward-looking nationalists and European modernists (Glenny, 1990). In regard to economic matters the situation is more obscure; an initial enthusiasm for models of *laissez-faire* capitalism is giving way to a dawning appreciation of the difficulties of securing economic reform, and of the problematical nature of the pure market schemes advocated both by intellectual groups within Eastern Europe and by Western experts in the guise of the IMF or the World Bank (Keegan, 1992).

All these changes have been claimed by market liberals, and commentators have spoken of the West having won the cold war, with the consequence that further development within the global system would necessarily follow the Western model, a celebration of the ethico-political end of history (Fukuyama, 1992). However, it was the people of Eastern Europe who made their revolution (Garton-Ash, 1990), led by intellectuals, trade unionists, church groups and artists. The final resting-point of these upheavals is yet to be established, but overall it seems that the real battle is not about which model of development Eastern Europe should adopt but the shape of an emergent Europe as reforms continue in Russia and Eastern Europe, and as the European Union moves towards some sort of unification.

It is clear that the situation of the Eastern bloc countries, as they move to reassert local political-economic, social-institutional and cultural models in the wake of the abrupt ending of the conformity required by the cold-war bloc system, is difficult and problems are legion. A series of conclusions can be presented: first, the political-cultural framework of bloc-time with ideas of socialism and talk of Middle Europe are all now disregarded; second, related to these changes, there are ambiguous new cultural idea-sets being drawn upon, in particular, varieties of nationalism; and finally, the most often cited new political-cultural notion is that of a return to Europe, where this is neither left nor right and counts as some sort of coming home.

In the other great area of official state socialism, the People's Republic of China, there has been a rather different process of reform which began in the late 1970s as Deng Xiaoping inaugurated an economic policy turn towards the marketplace. Over the period of the 1980s China has taken its place within the burgeoning Pacific Asian region. The patterns of political-economic and social-institutional change within China have been extensive and suffused with conflict (Howell, 1993; Goodman and Segal, 1994). However, the overall success of the Pacific Asian region and the lack of any political reform has meant that the changes have not been widely remarked, and the changes in China have been read in the First World as one further episode in the very slow renewal of the state-socialist sphere.

It is clear that the events of 1989–91 in Eastern Europe, and the market reforms inaugurated earlier by Deng, have begun a sequence of complex change where the final equilibrium point of the emergent system is unclear. Overall, a transition is in process from the command economies of state socialism towards a more market-based system and differentiated polities.

The Third World: dependent integration and semi-detachment

The experience of the countries of the Third World in the post-colonial period has shown a diverse mix of advance, drift and stagnation. It is clear that there has been a sharp process of differentiation within the Third World.

In the case of Asia, while areas of southern Asia have developed only slowly, large areas of what might a few years ago have been called countries in the Third World have experienced relatively rapid development. In particular, some of the Pacific Asian countries have been drawn into the Japanese orbit within the tripolar global system. The basis for economic success of the countries of Pacific Asia is elusive. In the 1980s the New Right claimed that the success of the area proved the correctness of market-oriented development policies; however, the countries of the area have all pursued state-directed development. The core regional economy has been Japan, which industrialized in the late nineteenth century and which has subsequently played a key role in the development of the Pacific Asian countries. The pace of development in the region as a whole over the 1980s has been so rapid that the countries of Pacific Asia are now spoken of as one of the three major economic blocs within the global economy.

It is the case for other areas that they have experienced dependent capitalist development. It is possible to point to the states of the Middle East where it is clear that the basis for economic success is primary-product exporting, in particular oil, but these countries have also invested heavily in industrial development. At the same time the progress of what has been called westernization, the introduction of modern social patterns, has been deeply problematical.

In the case of Latin America the extent of success is even more problematical as social inequalities, environmental problems and political instability work against economic successes. However, Latin America and the Caribbean fall within the ambit of the USA-centred sphere of the global capitalist system, and in 1993 the NAFTA agreement was inaugurated, which looks to a free-trade zone within the Americas.

In contrast to the countries of Pacific Asia, the Middle East and Latin America, the countries of Africa have experienced little progress. The share of world production and trade accounted for by African countries is shrinking and is now slight, and there is a process of slow detachment from the mainstream of the global industrial-capitalist system. In Africa the initial legacies of the colonial period included state administrative machineries, legal systems, and educated and mobilized populations. However, all these have slowly run down. In Africa there have been problems of political corruption, incompetence and instability, and the role of the military has increased. At the same time, African countries experienced interference from the two great powers as they pursued a series of overt and covert proxy wars. In the case of Africa, development specialists tend to speak of the 1980s as a lost decade.

If we try to summarize the post-Second World War experience of the Third World as a whole, then we can say that by the mid-1970s the orthodox optimism of the immediate post-war period had dissipated and was beginning to be replaced by those fears about debt, instability and failure which were to come to the fore in the 1980s. It is also true to say that the unease about the post-Second World War settlement which underpinned the discussion about development also became acute as First World economies suffered economic slow-downs and the societies saw rising problems. In the First World the intellectual and political confusion of the period saw the emergence of the New Right. In the Third World the New Right sponsored a counter-revolution which aimed to sweep away the developmental role of the state in favour of the marketplace. The overall impact upon the Third World has been to reinforce the diversity of the area's patterns of integration within the global system, producing a mixture of dependent development and semi-detachment.

The postmodernist theory of the global marketplace

Postmodernism presents a novel analysis of the global system, and it has been suggested that three particular cultural trends came together to fashion the approach (Callinicos, 1989). The first involved a shift from the austere and functional aesthetics of modernism to the heterogeneity and expressivity of postmodernism. The second involved the epistemological shift from a rationalist structuralism to the diversity and relativism of post-structuralism. The third involved a representation of the 1950s thesis of the rise of post-industrial society. The fusion of these elements generates the postmodernist position.

In formal terms, postmodernism argues that the two great metanarratives of progress constructed alongside the rise of science-based modernity, the French-inspired ideas of the Enlightenment and the German-inspired systems of speculative idealism, have undergone a dual process of decline: intellectually they have undermined themselves in shifts towards either state-linked bureaucratic control or abstract, formalized and finally empty disciplines of learning; and in practical terms the political-economic systems in which they operate have become dominated by the pragmatics of the power of technical means, and the ends of action, the points of orientation of the metanarratives, are no longer of any great concern (Lyotard, 1979). The process of decline has allowed the expression of a new form of life.

In substantive terms, postmodernism suggests that the global political economy is now dominated by flows of information produced by a natural science oriented to discontinuities and novelties rather than the task of uncovering a single coherent truth, and within these flows a new form of life emerges. The theory of postmodernism details the transformation of industrial capitalism such that the system is now knowledge-based, geared to consumption in the marketplace and global in its reach. The routine experience of persons within this system is one of a freely chosen consumer lifestyle and political concerns with ideology have dissolved away into expressive consumption. As regards those who are too poor to join this consumer paradise, the theory assumes that their objective is to belong just as soon as possible; it is only a matter of time before the consumer culture of postmodernity becomes entirely global in its reach. The structure of the postmodernist analysis can be elucidated in terms of the posited political-economic structure, social-institutional forms and associated cultural patterns.

The political-economic changes involve a shift from Fordist to post-Fordist modes of production as mass production, extensive state regulation, corporatist industrial relations and mass consumption of essentially common products gives way to flexible production, restricted state regulation, market-based industrial relations and personalized schedules of consumption from a varied menu of consumer goods. Historically, the 1930s saw the construction of the Fordist system in the USA, and thereafter in other Western countries. The essence of the productive system was the mass production of standardized products for a mass consumer market. The technologies, patterns of industrial organization, patterns of political ordering and expectations in regard to consumption of the output all took time to fix in place. Indeed, the shift to a widespread use of Fordist modes of accumulation and regulation belongs to the post-Second World War period of Keynesian demand management and the economic long boom. It was the episode of inflationary pressures compounded by the oil-price hike of the early 1970s which tipped the Fordist system into crisis. The post-Fordist mode of production involves a new rapidity in technological innovation and patterns of production which are decentralized, multi-plant, multinational and which adopt a flexible specialization strategy such that a wide range of products can be made with designs quickly changed. The new pattern of production requires an educated, adaptable and complaisant workforce, coupled with government deregulation of the market, and the restructuring of production takes place on a global scale.

The shift to a postmodern world entails reordering the institutional structures of modern industrial capitalism, away from the machineries of the state towards the mechanisms of the marketplace. In this shift two broad changes are evidenced: first, the sharp diminution of the role of the state in ordering the affairs of people across the range of their social lives (family, kin, work and leisure) as the machineries of supervision and control associated with the state are steadily closed down; and second, the related rise of personal initiative, provision and contracted relationships.

The culture of postmodernism centres upon the pre-eminent position in contemporary life of the commercial consumer marketplace (Jameson, 1991). All that is available to humankind are the consumption opportunities offered by global capitalism. The individual exercise of choice within the marketplace is the basis of arbitrarily constructed lifestyles. In this vein, those earlier cultural schedules which distinguished high culture from low culture are dismissed. In postmodernist culture any product offered in the cultural marketplace is as good as any other. Indeed, in the context of the marketplace-centred non-aesthetic and non-ethic of postmodernism, the production and consumption of novelties becomes prized simply because they are novelties. Overall, there are key characteristics of postmodern culture: first, depthlessness, as in place of structural analyses and understandings the surface image is stressed; second, ahistoricism, as in place of analyses and understandings that place events and processes in history, the present is stressed; third, intensities, as in place of considered ethics and aesthetics, subjectivist emotionality is stressed; fourth, technologies, as in place of a view of technology as servant the power of technology is stressed; fifth, pastiche, as in place of realism the play of invention is stressed; and finally sixth, episodicity, as in place of the coherence of sequential discourses, the broken nature of discourse fragments is stressed (Harvey, 1989).

The theorists of postmodernity argue that a process of globalization of culture is slowly taking place as patterns of consumption across the global system grow ever more similar. The theorists of the emergent markets of the Second and Third Worlds point to the growth of consumerism among those groups able to take advantage of the new opportunities within the marketplace. However, critics have suggested that these patterns of consumption are available only to a narrow group and that the poor who lie outside the consumer sphere are subject to severe control. In First World consumer capitalism the poor are subject to the control of the bureaucratic welfare system. And similarly, the citizens of the Second World state-socialist systems prior to the revolutions of 1989 inhabited a culture which resembled the bureaucratic welfare control system (Bauman, 1988). And, at the present time, the poor who make up the majority of the populations of the countries of the Third World are excluded. In the context of the patterns of power within the global system these groups are merely aspirant consumers (Featherstone, 1991).

One important aspect of the postmodernist material is its insistence that received patterns of social-theoretical argument are now in need of radical renewal. In place of the experience of continuous intelligible progress, the experienced world of postmodernity has become one of partial truths and relativistic subjective perspectives. In our ordinary lives we are invited to select from proffered consumer alternatives in order to construct a lifestyle, and in the realm of social theorizing we are similarly enjoined to reject received traditions aspiring to universal knowledge in favour of the local, the partial and the contingent. However, against the theorists of postmodernity, critics have argued that it is not clear that the system has changed fundamentally (Harvey, 1989).

New strategies for analysing complex change in the global system

Within the core line of the classical European tradition of social theorizing there is a long-established concern with analysing complex change, those periods when inter-related change takes place in the economy, society, polity and culture of a people. Such periods are often somewhat traumatic as clarity in regard to sequences and end-points is not readily available to those caught up in the processes. The classical tradition of social theory concerned itself with trying to grasp the dynamics of the shift from traditional agrarian-feudal society to modern industrial-democratic society. Gellner (1964) presents the transition to the modern world as one continuing episode of pervasive change, where we have a rough idea of its end-point (that is, it will be industrial rather than, say, agricultural), and which we needs must analyse from the inside, using the sceptical techniques of classical sociology (the heir to classical political philosophy). In my terms, the analytical core of the received classical tradition comprises the political-economic, social-institutional and culture-critical analysis of structures and the elucidation of related patterns of meaning, and the task for social science is to grasp the continuing dynamics of the developing industrial system.

The work of international political economy offers a simple way of approaching the analysis of structures. Strange (1988) argues that the global political economy must be thought of as a network of structures of power within which agents (usually states) manoeuvre for position. Strange distinguishes between structural power (which sets the broad agendas within which agents operate), relational power (which focuses on specific exchanges between agents) and bargains (which are the compromises agents make within a given situation). The received structures shape the actions of agents, and in turn the actions of agents modify structures.

Strange identifies four key structures of power in the global system: the security structure (which embraces matters relating to the deployment of force, plus attendant bilateral and multilateral regulatory linkages); the production structure (which embraces matters relating to the extent to which any country is effective in the production of goods and services); the financial structure (which embraces matters relating to the ability of countries or other organizations to obtain or create credit, the necessary condition of development); and the knowledge structure (which indicates where new ideas and technologies are generated). The first noted structural sphere is the familiar realm of state–state relations, the following pair note the crucial role of economic power, and finally the importance of the subtler sphere of culture is acknowledged. It is with reference to these four basic power structures that agent groups manoeuvre, primarily but not exclusively state machines, and the practical out-turn of such manoeuvrings thereafter modifies the received structures.

The security structure comprises the networks of relationships between states which revolve around and order the use of force. These structures are extensive and cover diplomatic, military and security linkages. In regard to the second pair, the production structure, the sphere of the military overlaps in the history of the development of the modern First World-dominated global system with the rise of industrial production and global trade. The related financial structure comprises an integrated global network, with major centres in Europe, the USA and Japan. This network is the source of credit, and the ability to generate credit confers significant power. Finally the knowledge structure is one of the underpinnings of the entire system, the production not merely of scientific and technical knowledge but also social technologies of management involved in the business of putting knowledge to work.

These networks of power constitute the underlying structure of the global system. While resources of power, production, finance and knowledge are unevenly distributed they provide the starting-point for the activities of any extant state regime. The strategy of analysis points to the axes of structural power which necessarily constrain/enable the actions of state regimes (as agents). In place of state–state relations we have a picture of many states within the global system enmeshed in a network of power relations. Most broadly, the international political-economy approach offers the model of a world system comprising a variety of power structures within which agent-groups move and where the specific exchanges of agent-groups and global structures generate the familiar pattern of extant polities.

One problem with the international political-economy approach is that it reduces the business of the internal make-up of any state regime to a reflection of trans-state flows of power. A corrective to this can be found within the regulationist school which has offered not dissimilar analyses that do pay attention to the internal dynamics of state regimes within the shifting patterns of power of the global system (Aglietta, 1979). The literature centres on the identification of patterns of accumulation and regulation within state regimes and across wider sweeps of the global industrial-capitalist economy.

Reprise: structural analyses of the global system

The theorists of the classical European tradition were concerned with elucidating the dynamics of complex change within the developing industrial-capitalist system. In the later years of the 'long nineteenth century' (Hobsbawm, 1994) the system expanded/intensified widely and in the wake of the ending of the short twentieth century there has been a new phase of expansion/intensification. However, while it is clear that something is happening, it is not at all clear what that something is in practice and, as in the case of the nineteenth-century classical social theorists, commentators and theorists are attempting to understand broad processes of change which encompass and run through the societies of which they are members.

In the interpretive-critical elucidation of complex change a mixture of analytical and ethical elements is used to produce prospective and engaged work. As we characterize the putative emergent system so we specify the likely key agents of change and make tentative statements in respect of the general identities of the denizens of these new structures and the likely political-cultural identities they will embrace. Three broad characterizations could be sketched: first, if the world is an increasingly integrated market system, then we are consumers and will understand ourselves as members of consumer-choice lifestyle-based groups within a global system – the story of the postmodernists; second, if the world is an increasingly integrated economic and political system where polities reflect underlying cultural/ethnic identities, then we are all first and foremost carriers of cultural traditions (we are Western Christians or Asian Muslims or whatever) and will understand ourselves as members of exclusive cultural/ethnic groups, the story of US conservatives (Huntington, 1993); and third, if the world is an increasingly integrated industrial-capitalist system, then we are subjects of a powerful and dynamic system and we can understand ourselves as rational yet bound by circumstances, and we will understand ourselves in terms of the patterns of response contrived by the groups to which we belong – the story of the international political-economy specialists.

Overall, out of this present confusion, it seems to be the case for analysts working within the classical European tradition of social theorizing that the industrial-capitalist system is becoming significantly more integrated at a global level while also adopting a distinctly regional aspect, and at the same time, areas of the global system seem to be falling away from the mainstream.

The shift from three worlds to a tripolar world

It has been customary within the confines of European social scientific analysis to work in terms of a distinction between First, Second and Third Worlds (Worsley, 1964, 1984). The characterizations of the industrial-capitalist First World and the state-socialist Second World were routinely cast in oppositional terms, simply because the rhetoric of the cold war washed over the work of scholars, but in practice both the forms of life and ideological debates in respect of them evidenced familiar European themes of progress. The circumstances of the postcolonial world were read in related terms and countries were seen to be allied to one or other bloc and to be pursuing either capitalist or socialist strategies of development (progress). However, it is clear that the end of the cold war has removed a long-familiar style of reading the dynamics of the global system and a new pattern has been discerned. The global system no longer comprises three worlds whose distinct characters revolved around the classical models of development lodged within the work of the nineteenth-century social theorists of modernity, but instead an integrated tripolar world. In the integrated tripolar industrial-capitalist system the pattern of global relationships is different, and a new agenda of questions has come to the fore (Thurow, 1994).

The new tripolar global system

In the wake of the end of the short twentieth century and the related collapse of the received certainties of the cold war which had shaped the understandings of European and American thinkers, it has become clear that a new integrated global industrial-capitalist system is taking shape. On Hobsbawm's arguments, this is an unstable system which recalls the equally unstable global system of the later years of the long nineteenth century. On the arguments of the theorists noted above, the construction of a global system is a rather more recent accomplishment. However, setting the issue of the overall evolution of the global system to one side, it is the case that the end of the short twentieth century has seen not merely debate in respect of the creation of an integrated system but also a concern for an apparently deepening tripolarity.

At the present time the global industrial-capitalist system shows a number of cross-cutting tendencies: first, to integration on a global scale, with a financial system that is integrated across the globe and extensive increasingly denationalized MNC/TNC operations; second, to regionalization within the global system, with three key areas emerging where intra-regional linkages are deepening; and third, to division on a global scale, with areas of the world apparently falling behind the regionalized global system.

In these matters it is the second issue, regionalization, which will most directly concern us in the subsequent chapters of this text. The structurally derived arguments presented in the following three chapters point to new patterns within the global system to which agent groups will have to respond as they order their various political projects. The issue of political-cultural identity which was addressed in detailed terms in the opening chapters of this text is dealt with here, at least in the first instance, in a more schematic fashion. The two lines of analysis – structural and ethnographic – together point to a richly developed grasp of the ways in which inhabitants of territories within the global system understand themselves as ordered collectivities (Worsley, 1984). The results of such enquiries have been anticipated in broad terms in recent polemical debate on the divergent nature of the forms of life of the peoples living within the three regions of the tripolar global system (Thurow, 1994). It has been argued that the pattern of the USA should be characterized as liberal-market, while the pattern of the European Union presents a social-market system, and both are to be distinguished from Pacific Asian developmental capitalism. At this point the terms of this often polemical debate will provide a useful entry to the wider scholarly issues in respect of the regional character of the tripolar system.

*Regional structural change and agent responses in the European
Union, Pacific Asia and the USA*

EUROPE In the post-Second World War period Europe was ordered at
the macro-structural level in terms of the ideas, institutions and power
relationships established by the Bretton Woods agreement. However, in
the period of the last third of the short twentieth century this system
came under great pressure, and has slowly subsided. The outlines have
emerged of an insecure and novel tripolar global industrial-capitalist
system. Confronted with these patterns of structural change, the
countries of Western Europe slowly moved towards a closer union.
These ideas and institutional mechanisms were in place when the
extent of global structural change finally became unequivocally clear
with the collapse of the USSR, and the idea of the European Union was
pushed to the fore in discussions about the future of the continent.

The core of the European Union lies in north-western Europe. In
Germany the end of the cold war meant the end of post-Second World
War division. It meant an unexpected movement to the centre of
Europe as the largest country with the strongest economy. The commitment of the core countries of the European Union was affirmed in the
Maastricht Treaty, and Germany, the Netherlands, Luxembourg, Belgium and France maintain a pro-Union stance, as does Italy. In recent
years the Scandinavian countries, with the exception of oil-rich
Norway, joined the Union, as did Austria, and the newly independent
countries of Middle Europe have announced their intention of joining
as soon as possible. And in Mediterranean Europe there has been a
similar strength of commitment: in Spain, Portugal and Greece the
European Union has been the institutional space within which post-
military liberal-democratic regimes have developed. The project of
European unification begun in the wake of the Second World War
shows no sign of faltering, and notwithstanding tensions, confusions
and the apparent doubt of some governments (Britain, Denmark) the
established institutional machineries look set to provide the vehicle for
a distinctive European region.

PACIFIC ASIA   The Pacific region over the post-Second World War period
has been divided by cold war institutions and rhetoric into a Western-
focused group and a socialist bloc. The Western-focused group has
been subject to the military, economic and cultural hegemony of the
USA. However, the Western-focused group is undergoing considerable
change and, in brief, this may be summarized as the beginnings of a
political-economic, social-institutional and cultural emancipation from
the USA. At the same time, the countries of the socialist bloc which had
spent decades following autarchic state-socialist development trajectories are now opening up to the Western-focused group.

The key exchange in the post-Second World War period has been that of the Japanese and the Americans. The countries of the inner periphery of East Asia have prospered over a long period of economic development in the political and military shadow of the USA and the economic shadow of Japan. Thereafter the countries of the outer periphery of South-east Asia have recently reoriented themselves towards the economic model of Japan. We can note the related turn of the countries of Australasia towards the Pacific Asian economies, a turn that is routinely expressed in terms of a commitment to open regionalism, thereby arguably implicitly granting a continued political commitment to the West in general and the USA in particular. Finally we have the ongoing process of the reorientation of China and Indo-China. One key contemporary public issue concerns arguments to the effect that the pattern of change in Pacific Asia is such that we can talk about a Pacific Asian model of development, where this is taken to be a particular variety of industrial capitalism distinct from the American or European models.

THE USA   The Second World War saw the emergence of the USA as the world's premier economic, political and military power. The USA established the Bretton Woods system within the sphere of the West and engaged in cold war military/diplomatic confrontation with the Second World. The position of the USA was unchallenged until the middle 1970s. The period of the late 1970s saw inflation and economic dislocation within the Western sphere. In the 1980s the military build-up inaugurated by Reagan led to the USA becoming a debtor nation. In addition, the USA was the major sponsor of the doctrines of economic liberalization which have further undermined the order of the global system.

The end of the short twentieth century has seen the USA continuing to press for an open global trading system, but these arguments are now made within the context of a tripolar system and without the convenience of the existence of the Second World, which provided an excuse for US hegemony within the sphere of the West. The influence of the Washington-based IMF and World Bank is extensive in promoting liberalization and free trade, and recent expressions of these concerns have been the establishment of NAFTA and APEC.

Analysing the tripolar global system

It is quite clear that at the present time the global industrial-capitalist system shows a number of cross-cutting tendencies. The movement towards integration on a global scale, with a financial system that is integrated across the globe and extensive increasingly denationalized MNC/TNC operations, continues rapidly and may be read as the most recent expression of that dynamism which Marx originally identified as the product of the core logic of capitalism. At the same time it seems to be the case that there is movement towards regionalization within the global system, with three key areas emerging, and the issues of the nature of this regionalization within the system (inclusionary/ exclusionary) and the extent of any internal integration remain open. It is here that commentators begin to speak of divergent models of industrial-capitalist development. And finally, it is clear that there is increasing division on a global scale, with areas of the world apparently falling behind the regionalized global industrial-capitalist system. Out of all this debate, in order to bring a preliminary order to the vast spread of possible empirical material in a fashion which acknowledges the preference for detailed analysis signalled in the opening chapters, this text will look to the confluence of structural and ethnographic argument around the claim that the three regions do evidence discrete forms of life, different versions of industrial capitalism.

Conclusion: changing global structures and agent responses

The discussions of political-cultural identity which we have thus far pursued have concentrated on the detail of the ways in which agents have understood their situations and subsequently acted to pursue their goals. In terms of the familiar distinction between structure and agency the stress has been on the later. In this chapter we turned our attention to the very broadest structural changes which are likely to impact upon agents in the years running up to the millennium. The post-Second World War global system with its two great powers, a divided Europe and a marginalized Third World was superseded in the period 1989–91. The 1980s saw the emergence of a tripolar global system. The ways in which a series of agent groups understand themselves and their place in the global system is at present undergoing significant change.

In the following three chapters we will attempt to characterize the broad patterns within each region, noting the complex internal differences as well as similarities. However, the material addressed in these chapters is vast and in a text of this length the most that can be attempted are general-level comparisons of political cultures. The utility of such comparisons is restricted, but might include: first, an appreciation of the general dynamics of the histories of the regions; second, an indication of the particular confusions attending the end of the bipolar global system within the regions; and third, a general outline of the political-cultural forms of the regions in the context of a recently achieved/acknowledged global tripolarity. The comparative analyses therefore serve both as a framework within which more detailed ethnographical/biographical material might be lodged and as a strategy for highlighting certain contemporary anxieties in respect of relationships between the elements of the developing tripolar global system.

6

Changing Political-Cultural Identities in Europe

In the post-Second World War period the peoples, organizations and government machines of Europe understood themselves within the overall framework of global bipolarity. In Eastern Europe matters were cast in terms of the achievement of a socialist polity and the sphere was ordered from Moscow. In Western Europe matters were understood in terms of the notion of the free world, and the sphere was ordered from Washington. All the other areas of the world were either assimilated to this model as allies or clients of one or other bloc, or read as marginal, as in the case of the newly independent countries of the former European and American colonial empires. However, the collapse of the cold-war bloc system in the period 1989–91 sharply undermined the familiar political-cultural identities of Europeans. In the wake of these changes it made no sense to talk in terms of East and West, it made no sense to look to Moscow or Washington for ideas and leadership, and it made no sense to suppose any longer (if it ever had) that the ritualized clash of two formulaic delimited-formal ideologies constituted the crucial axis of intellectual debate within the modern interdependent global industrial-capitalist system. The short period 1989–91 reopened the issue of political-cultural identity for Europeans, and new debate has revolved around the future of the initially Western European project of the European Union.

In this chapter I will consider the following themes: first, the European shift to the modern world; second, the period of US hegemony in the years of the cold war; third, the implications of the collapse of the institutions and rhetorics of the cold war for the European élite and popular political self-images; and finally the likely spread of changes which are running at present through the European body politic.

European routes to the modern world

The recent processes of structural reconfiguration which have enfolded Europe have occasioned a series of responses, élite and popular, which range from enthusiasm through to deep disquiet. It can be suggested that the spread of present reactions have a common starting-point in an arguably rather conservative view of Europe's recent history. The

arrangements of the long post-Second World War period of US hegemony had come to be seen as likely to endure indefinitely, with the
western half of the continent assimilated into an Anglo-American
market-based capitalism while the eastern half of continental Europe
pursued a state-directed socialism. These divisions found emphatic
expression in the ideological rhetoric of cold war. However, it is clear
that the patterns of life, economic arrangements and broader regional
institutional structures were quite particular to the post-Second World
War period. More broadly, the history of Europe can be seen to
comprise a series of political-economic, social-institutional and cultural
configurations.

The historical and comparative social theorist B. Moore (1966) addressed these matters in terms of the historical trajectories followed by
particular countries as they made the awkward and often deeply
problematical shift to the modern world. In the case of Western Europe
it is possible to point to broad patterns of structural change and to
detail the ways in which political élites read and reacted to these
changes in order to establish political projects which would offer them
some sort of route to the future. The history of Europe can be read as a
series of structural patterns, carrying a diversity of political projects,
which in turn issued in the creation of a variety of political-cultural
identities which were finally assimilated to the routines of ordinary
people. On this basis it is possible to analyse the present reconfiguration of Europe as one more episode of complex change, a further
period of structural change which will oblige political élites to formulate a coherent response in concert with their populations and
thereafter, in time, new patterns of political-cultural identity might be
expected to emerge.

Moore (1966) is concerned with the relationship of class groups in
the extended episode of the shift to the modern world. As the pre-
modern European world of agrarian feudalism dissolves under the
impress of the economic, social and cultural processes whereby
the modern industrial system of states and nations emerges, it is the
particular sequence of exchanges between ascendant and descendant
classes that shapes the route to the modern world taken by particular
countries. In the core countries of Western Europe, France, Germany
and Britain, it is possible to identify a series of variants of the
process.

THE ENGLISH LIBERAL REVOLUTION AND THE INVENTION OF BRITAIN   It is the
seventeenth-century English Revolution which marks the decisive
break with the agrarian and hierarchical past in order to establish a
liberal political order as the basis for further evolutionary change in the
eighteenth, nineteenth and twentieth centuries. Moore calls attention to
the role of violence – not merely the episode of the Civil War but also
the later suppression of the democratic impulse of nineteenth-century

Chartism – in establishing the English system with its preference for evolutionary and incremental change.

It was on the basis of this seventeenth-century English polity that further changes were made. Colley's (1992) analysis of the rise of the political project of 'Britain' makes it clear that this was a rational prospective response to changing circumstances. Over the period from the 1707 Act of Union through to the defeat of Chartism in the early nineteenth century a series of external anxieties involving wars and religious conflicts, coupled to internal reforms as UK ruling groups responded to defeat in America, isolation from mainland Europe and an influx of Scots, issued in the political-cultural project of Britain, essentially an outward-looking trading nation ordered by an oligarchic liberal polity where power continued to be the effectively exclusive preserve of a narrow rural, financial and industrial élite. The project attained extensive nineteenth-century success and reached its apogee in the years before the First World War, the end of the 'long nineteenth century'. Once established, the model of Britain is available thereafter to other mainland European countries as sets of ideas, the work of the Enlightenment, are exchanged across Europe (and the Atlantic).

THE FRENCH ASPIRATIONS TO REPUBLICAN DEMOCRACY   In France the relationship between the monarchical centralized state, its aspirant bourgeoisie and exploited peasantry collapsed in a process of revolutionary change (Moore, 1966). Yet the shift to the modern world in France was long-drawn-out and the country remained relatively economically and politically underdeveloped until well into the nineteenth century. In the early nineteenth century the theorist Saint-Simon offered the UK as a model to which those concerned with development in France could look. Later the social theorist Emile Durkheim presented an influential functionalist sociology and was committed to the establishment of a modern socialist/corporatist polity in France (Zeitlin, 1968; Hawthorn, 1976). The slow development of a modern industrial and financial bourgeoisie and the simultaneous persistence of an agrarian heartland meant that political development was slow, with rural and clerical influence persisting for longer than was the case in the UK. In the early years of the twentieth century the political confusions between liberalism, socialism and corporatism deepened in the drift towards the catastrophic 1914–18 war with Germany. However, notwithstanding the problems of development within France, the model of the French Revolution quickly came to stand for the ideals of the Enlightenment in respect of the spread of political virtues associated with republican democracy.

THE GERMAN EXPERIENCE OF MODERNIZATION FROM ABOVE   In Germany in the closing years of the century the shift to the modern world was engineered in an authoritarian fashion. The years of Bismarck's leadership secured the integration of the multiplicity of small German princely states and inaugurated a series of economic and social programmes. The intellectual and policy approach came to be associated with the German Historical School of economic analysis oriented to national goals. These goals were the concern of a quite particular pattern of power-holders in the country, with great influence being wielded by the Prussian landed aristocrats, the German army officer corps and the state bureaucracy. The experience of late development was a particular concern of the social theorist Max Weber, who devoted much of his work to arguing the case for the leadership role of the German bourgeoisie (Giddens, 1972). The German achievement of nation-statehood and economic success was not matched by the attainment of a similar political stability. The disintegration of the Hohenzollern monarchy in 1918 was followed by a socialist uprising/revolution which was rapidly extinguished by the right-wing *Freicorp* which in turn became the recruiting ground for the later National Socialists. The familiar European political Left associated with trade unions and the middle classes, who had developed along with the growth of industrial capitalism, were simply overwhelmed in the violent process of establishing a fascist regime (Shirer, 1960). After this collapse it was the episode of war which finally saw a variant of modern liberal democracy implanted with subsequent outstanding success.

THE PERSISTENCE OF THE OLD REGIMES   The shift to the modern world achieved by these key European countries was repeated across Europe over the period of the nineteenth century. It is in this period (coupled with the further changes secured after the First World War) that the present familiar pattern of European nation-states takes its shape. The process is characterized by Anderson (1983) as the second great wave of nation-state formation. The complex episode of the shift to the modern world was, as I have argued earlier, the central preoccupation of the classical European social theorists. The work of these theorists included elaborate models of change and explicit expectations of progress; however, it is clear the overall project advanced rather more slowly than is usually supposed (Nairn, 1988).

The American and French Revolutions presaged the disappearance of Europe's *ancien régime*, but there was nothing quick about the process. The whole period from 1914 through to 1945, the first catastrophic third of Hobsbawm's short twentieth century, can be seen as the process of the dissolution of Europe's old regimes. Nairn comments that industrial capitalism and its associated bourgeois society have secured their position much more slowly and awkwardly than the proponents (and critics) writing in the nineteenth century ever supposed. Nairn, like Mayer (1981), thinks that in reality the old world of late feudalism did not just fade away in the nineteenth century; it required active displacement. Nairn points out that the Habsburgs, Hohenzollerns and Romanovs stayed in power until the final collapse in 1917, and it might be noted that their collapse was not followed by the triumph of bourgeois democracy but instead the authoritarian developmentalism of Stalin, the ferocious reaction of European fascism and the disaster of the Second World War. It is only since the 1950s that anything like the nineteenth-century progressive theoretical picture of bourgeois industrial-capitalist democracy has come into existence. And, we should note, in Western Europe the final achievement of the initial theoretical expectations of the classical theorists of the nineteenth century was secured under the hegemony of the USA.

US hegemony and the rhetoric of the cold war

Hobsbawm analyses the short twentieth century in terms of the eclipse of the optimistic project of the European Enlightenment in a series of disasters including war, revolution, depression and, after a brief economic and social golden age, a return to drift. One aspect of this history is the changing nature of power relationships within the capitalist global system. An opening phase centred on the rise to global prominence of the UK in the nineteenth century, followed by the rise of competitors in the USA, Germany and Japan. The years of the First World War see the Europeans locked in conflict and the USA becomes the centre of the capitalist world economy. In the post-Second World War period the European powers are finally eclipsed as the dissolution of the major colonial economic blocks leaves the USA as the unchallenged leader of the West. The USA prepared for its global role as the core power of the liberal–capitalist system and the machineries of the Bretton Woods system of international economics were predicated upon the notion of open liberal trade (Kolko, 1968). Hobsbawm notes that the period from the end of the war until the early seventies was an economic golden age. However, as the post-Second World War period sees the decline of European power and the rise to pre-eminence of the USA it also sees the parallel rise of the USSR. Over the long period from 1945 to 1989 the two great powers ordered their respective European spheres and erected an elaborate apparatus of legitimation in the form of the institutions and rhetoric of the cold war.

President Truman launched the doctrine of containment in 1947 and it expressed the resolution of the USA to halt the spread of communism. The concern of the USA was initially focused on Europe in the wake of war-time upheaval, but subsequently the attention of the USA was extended to the Third World. In the period of the 1950s an intellectual package was assembled which centred on the putative demands of the logic of industrialism, which would thereafter promote convergence between economic systems, leading in due course to abundance and the end of ideology. The most explicit version of the schema was presented in the context of cold-war competition with the Soviet bloc for influence among the élites of the new nations of the Third World, who were offered 'modernization' as an alternative to socialism. The model of the modern was not merely the image of the USA writ large, but an image suffused with the demands of the 'patriotic imperative' (Caute, 1978) and the ideological position equated the interests of the USA, functioning liberal-market economies, resistance to communism and the future prosperity of the world. It was this cold-war situation which coloured the thinking of American policy-makers, political agents and scholars in the post-Second World War period and the doctrinal package was labelled the 'free world', the official ideology to which European élites and peoples have been invited to consent over the last fifty years. It was this settlement which collapsed over the period 1989–91 (Preston, 1994b).

The collapse of received political-cultural certainties in Europe

In Europe the recognition of changed circumstances was an extended process. A series of elements underlay change and a series of episodes took place which culminated in 1989–91. If we review the events of 1989 we find that a series of longer-term processes came to a climax: first, the slow relative decline of the USA in regard to Europe; second, the process of the decline of the command system in the Eastern bloc; third, the slow reworking of patterns of power within the global economy with the rise of Japan; and finally, the hesitant moves within Western Europe towards some sort of unified system. All this points to deep-seated long-term processes of structural and epochal change, finally recognized and acknowledged in common discourse with the 1991 failed coup in the USSR.

The end of the short twentieth century

Hobsbawm (1994) establishes the overall coherence of the 1914–91 period in terms of changes in economics, then politics and finally culture. The period begins at the moment of the high tide of late nineteenth-century European industrial capitalism, when the system attained global reach, and encompasses a process of collapse, partial reconstruction and renewed instability within the economic and political systems. Hobsbawm identifies three phases within the short twentieth century: catastrophe, golden age and drift.

In phase one there was a series of catastrophes, notably economic collapse, political revolution and war. The nineteenth-century liberal-capitalist drive towards an integrated global system faltered as a series of discrete blocks formed. Hobsbawm details the period 1914–45 and notes the impact of the First World War, the Russian Revolution and the Great Depression upon the expectations of people in the First, Second and Third Worlds. The rise of fascism and the descent into war is noted, as is the subsequent dissolution of the empires. Overall, the period sees the collapse of the pre-eminent 'Western world' and its surprising rescue in the war-time alliance with its putative opponent, communism.

In the second phase, the post-Second World War period from 1945 to 1973, there was a golden age of economic expansion, social welfare and liberal-democratic expansion. The economic boom of the period eventually became unstable and disappeared at the time of the 1970s oil shocks. However, the period sees massive patterns of social change in the First, Second and later Third Worlds. In the First World a consumer society develops. In the Second World there is some consumerism plus stagnation and confusion. In the Third World a period of optimistic decolonization can be noted, followed by the development of severe economic, social and political problems in Africa, Asia and Latin America.

Overall, for Europeans their experience can be summarized around a series of key ideas: first, the Atlantic Alliance, which tied the Europeans into the American political-cultural sphere; second, the related idea of the free West with its security structure centred on NATO, which embedded the Europeans within the hegemonic American ideology of liberalism and its associated military structure; third, the idea of the free market, which sought to lock the Europeans into an American liberal-market political project; and finally, cutting against these tendencies, the development of the European Economic Community as the vehicle of a distinctively European identity. It is within the ambit of these sets of ideas that we can find the elements of a wide European political-cultural identity and the core of disseminated official delimited-formal ideologies. And all of these idea-sets were to provide resources in 1989–91 when patterns of change became evident and were perforce acknowledged in public political discourse.

The third phase, from the 1970s onwards, saw the establishment of a transnational capitalist system that recalled the late nineteenth century in its integrated global extent. However, it was an unstable system, as drift in the First World, the collapse of the Second World and decline in the Third World showed. In brief, the economic system becomes global but the political structures necessary to order such a system are not created, and a wealth of social/cultural confusions and conflicts develops. By 1991 it is clear both that the economy is global and that there are no integrating global political structures.

Hobsbawm, in sum, offers a broad synoptic overview of patterns of global change in terms of the internal structure of the specified period (collapse, recovery and drift), which in turn is explained by patterns of change within the global industrial-capitalist productive system. The notion of the short twentieth century is immediately attractive. It is this sweep of history which overlaps with the local events in Europe of 1989–91, and the peoples of Europe inherit the subsequent political-cultural confusion. The project of European unification has formed the political and institutional axis around which subsequent debates about the future of Europe have revolved.

Political-economic changes in Europe

In order to grasp the broad situation of the European Union within the tripolar system it is necessary to have a general appreciation of the size of the Union's economic space. The general information provides the clue to a novel way of reviewing familiar lines of debate in respect of the dynamics of the European political economy.

The European Union economic space in the global system

It has become clear in recent years that the European Union is one of three major economic groupings within the global industrial-capitalist system (Thurow, 1994). On the basis of the standard agency data, we can note that the fifteen members of the European Union have a population of approximately 373 million with a 1990 GNP per capita ranging from US$4,900 in Portugal to US$22,320 in Germany (World Bank, 1992). The economic space of the European Union encompasses a measure of economic inequality; on a general table of wealth in Europe with a European Union index of 100, Denmark scores 138, Germany 123, France 114, Italy 102, Britain 98, Ireland 60 and Portugal 31 (Franklin, 1990). We might also note that the countries of Eastern Europe together with the CIS have a numerically marginally larger population but are economically very much weaker. Indeed, to the extent that one can rely on World Bank data, the eastern areas of the continent approach Third World levels of living, where Hungary has a 1990 GNP per capita of US$2,780, Czechoslovakia a 1990 GNP per capita of US$3,140, Bulgaria a 1990 GNP per capita of US$2,250 and Romania a 1990 GNP per capita of US$1,640 (World Bank, 1992). Overall, it is clear that within the local context of the European area the European Union is economically dominant.

The situation of Europe within the tripolar world can be illustrated by comparing the broad economic data for the three regions. The situation of the European Union within the tripolar system is discussed by Wilkinson (1990) who makes it clear that the European Union, the USA and Japan are the three major economies within the global system. The standard agency data record a 1990 USA population of 250 million, a Japanese population of 123 million and a European Union population, as noted, of 373 million (World Bank, 1992). The economic data record that in 1960 the USA GNP was US$500 billion, with a GNP per capita of US$2,500; the EEC GNP was US$270 billion, with a GNP per capita of US$1,000; and Japan's GNP was US$40 billion, with a GNP per capita of US$400 (Wilkinson, 1990: 8). At this time the USA had the world's most powerful economy. By 1989 the USA GNP was US$5.2 trillion, with a GNP per capita of US$21,000; the European Union GNP was US$4.8 trillion, with a GNP per capita of US$15,000; and Japan's GNP was US$2.8 trillion, with a GNP per capita of US$23,100 (Wilkinson, 1990: 8). It is clear that the USA had the strongest economy, but was only one of three more or less similarly powerful economies.

And further, it should be noted that the picture could be revised somewhat to include the alterations to the pattern produced by including significant peripheral areas: first, in the case of the European Union the data in respect of the economies of the three recent members, and the associated economies of Central Europe, can be added; second, in the case of the USA the data in respect of the countries of Canada and Latin America can be added; and third, in the case of Japan the data in respect of a broad sphere of economic activity in Pacific Asia can be added. In this context, the particular strength of the East Asian economies would imply that the three regions are of similar size on conventional economic measures (Abegglen, 1994); however, Thurow (1994) argues that the European Union will become the key region in the next century and will therefore 'write the rules' of the new global trading system. Of course, against the temptation to unwarranted enthusiasm, we should be careful with the business of drawing lines on maps and aggregating the data, as these are merely formal procedures with necessarily limited utility, but in the case of the three areas under discussion it is the case that there is significant inclusionary regionalism in practice.

The upshot of these data, in sum, is to point to the following: first, the three areas are very roughly the same economic size; second, they dominate the global economy; third, they are regionalized, which is to say that they trade internally to a significant extent; and finally, they engage in significant inter-area trade. So we can say both that there is some sort of interdependent global industrial-capitalist system, and that there is some sort of tripolar inclusionary regionalism within this system, where, finally, these political-economic structural patterns are the basis for related patterns of institutional and cultural change.

Received debates in respect of the European political economy

The political package of the free West was closely bound up with the post-Second World War industrial, military and political pre-eminence of the USA. In this period social scientists pursued the analysis of industrial societies, and this was the core of a set of ideas comprising industrialism, convergence, modernization and the end of ideology

(Giddens, 1979). The intellectual package affirmed that social scientific enquiry could provide the knowledge necessary for securing economic growth and social welfare. It was, in brief, the ideological counterpart to the post-Second World War Fordist golden age and therefore the vehicle whereby the post-war settlement between capital and labour was ordered. However, through the late 1960s there were increasing signs that the long period of prosperity was coming to an end, and the oil crisis of 1973 put an end to the period of economic growth. As the period drew to a close the intellectual, political and institutional vehicles of the compromise which sustained that growth also fell into decline. In recent years this compromise has broken down, and we can identify two major intellectual-political responses to this decline: the formal and substantive democratic response, and the reactionary New Right position.

In the case of the former, one response to the failure of what he would take to be the reformist-technocratic approach to the politics of the present day has been advanced by Habermas (1971, 1989). The gist of his position is that what is needed is not more technocratic planning, and certainly no attempted return to situations of less planning, but instead more democracy. The present condition of monopoly capitalism has seen the increasing rationalization of the human life-world as we have become ever more subject to the pronouncements of purported experts of one sort or another, whose cumulative impact is to withdraw control of the social world from the citizenry and lodge it in the technocratic-management systems of the contemporary capitalist system. On the basis of these analyses, a broad project of democratization is advocated.

The second line of response to the comparative decline of the post-war reformist social-democratic package has come from the New Right. In general, the ideology of the New Right centres on the purported power of the marketplace, and their particular intellectual vehicle has been a restated neoclassical economics. The celebrants of the market advance a series of claims: economically, the claim is that free markets are optimally efficient, thus we have claims to maximize material welfare; socially, the claim is that as action and responsibility for action reside with the person of the individual then social or moral worth is maximized in non-state-centred, free market systems, thus we have a claim to maximize human moral values; and politically, the related claim is that liberalism best expresses and protects the interests of individuals, thus we have a claim to maximize political freedom. And on the basis of these analyses, a broad programme of marketization is advocated.

On all this we might note, first, that reflection in the history and theory of economics, where the variety of economic approaches and their relationships to the intellectual-political world can be noted, strongly suggests both that neoclassicism be rejected, and that the sphere of the economic has to be reappropriated for social science (Ormerod, 1994). And we might note as well that there is a wealth of discussion in respect of the political theory of liberalism (Macpherson, 1973; MacIntyre, 1981); as Plant (1991) points out, the project of securing acceptance of a generally agreed set of political rules is in the end untenable. In respect of both economics and political theory, the work of the New Right can reasonably be characterized as intellectually untenable.

The European model and debate about the involvement of the state in the market

The nature of political-economic structures and the power of the state have long been discussed and there have been two main areas of analysis: those which focus on the role of the state, and those which speak of the role of the market. The arguments of the market enthusiasts are familiar; however, a new slant on this debate is generated in the intellectual context of tripolarity, where we can speak of a European model of industrial capitalism, distinct from American or Pacific Asian. In this context an interesting and influential area of debate in respect of these issues involves the idea of corporatism.

The essence of the notion of corporatism is that in the modern world it is to the advantage of all parties to come together in order to secure agreement about ordering the economy and society. The theory of corporatism points to mechanisms to secure such state-level agreements between the major players in the economy and society. In Western Europe the major players have been the government, the employers' federations and the trade unions. The notion has a history reaching back to the late nineteenth century, when it was presented as an alternative to *laissez-faire* capitalism and socialism. The idea that economy and society constituted an organic unity was stressed. In the 1930s the notion of corporatism became associated with European fascism. However, recent usage of the idea has dismissed the general theories of society and focused on the idea of expressing and resolving the interests of groups in society.

Katzenstein (1985) offers a review of the recent experience of the West, and identifies three state strategies of responding to global change: first, the liberal strategies of the USA and UK, which stress market solutions while using protection to secure a breathing space for threatened industrial sectors; second, the statist strategies of France and Japan, which stress state-led planning to adjust to global system demands, and which again have recourse to protection; and third, the corporatist strategies of the smaller European states of Sweden, Norway, Denmark, the Netherlands, Belgium, Austria and Switzerland, which seek to adjust cooperatively to demands flowing through the global system (the German model of the social market is added as a variant).

Katzenstein characterizes democratic corporatism as follows: an ideology of social partnership expressed at national level; a relatively centralized and concentrated system of interest groups; and voluntary coordination of conflicting objectives through continuous political bargaining between interest groups, state bureaucracies and political parties. Katzenstein offers a summary statement which identifies two European variants of democratic corporatism, the Austrian and the Swiss models. The first is liberal corporatism (Swiss); it has a strong internationally focused business class with weak decentralized unions, and political compromise is effected privately. It has a relatively less centralized decision-making system, but it is stable and effective. It addresses broad questions (excluding investment and employment) and bargains in a bilateral way with trade-offs left implicit. Political inequalities between actors are narrowed. In contrast, the second is social corporatism (Austrian), which has a weak nationally focused business class with stronger centralized unions, and political compromise is effected publicly. It has a relatively more centralized decision-making system, but it is stable and effective. It addresses narrower questions (including investment and employment), and bargains in a trilateral way with trade-offs explicit. Political inequalities between actors are narrowed. The situations in Sweden, Norway and Denmark tend to social corporatism; and the situations in the Netherlands and Belgium tend to liberal corporatism. Katzenstein is quite clear that the corporatist states have been more successful in adjusting to the pressures for change transmitted through the power structures of the global system. The governments of these corporatist states have pursued policies of cooperative and consensual flexible adjustment to the demands of the global system.

On these matters, Marquand, in an influential analysis of the UK, begins by noting that the political authorities have 'failed to adapt to the waves of technological and institutional innovation sweeping through the world economy' (1988: 263), and the root of this failure is traced to the 'ethos of market liberalism' (1988: 146). The strategy of market-led adjustment favoured by the UK élites declined in importance as competitors wedded to state-led strategies, as in Japan and France, or corporatist consensual strategies, as in Germany, arrived on the scene. Marquand argues that 'At the heart of that ethos lies a set of attitudes to the role of public power, and to the relationship between public power and private freedom, which is unique in Europe' (1988: 146). Where the mainland Europeans (and Japanese) repudiated *laissez-faire* economics and deployed Listian-style national economic strategies, the UK ruling class did nothing and the 'notion of a developmental state . . . met dogged and uncomprehending resistance'

(1988: 147). It is the historically received liberal individualist political-cultural disposition which blocks any attempt in the UK to identify a developmental role for the state (Preston, 1994b: 52). And it is a public and social sphere ordered by a developmental state that is in evidence in the successful polities of Germany, Austria and Sweden (Katzenstein, 1985). Marquand argues, in sum, that the legacy of the English Revolution left the UK political class unable to deal with structural change in a creative prospective fashion. In contrast, the Germans, Americans, Japanese, French and north-western Europeans managed to secure economic and social progress because in place of the celebration of the market they put in place the political, institutional and cultural bases of developmental states.

It is appropriate to note, in the context of the development of the European Union after the upheavals of 1989–91, which placed Germany at the centre of events, that there is a German variant of corporatism which has been called the social market. The notion entails an acceptance that patterns of economic production are ineluctably social and that a polity must affirm notions of common interests (social justice) in pursuit of a rational democratic strategy of ordering economic/social activity. In the German case these broad commitments find expression in a dense network of duties and obligations accepted by groups within society. The presence of these dense networks of duties and obligations finds familiar expression in a 'mixture of state-sponsored technological innovation, long-term indicative planning and social corporatism' (Harvie, 1992: 45). It is argued that there are three main reasons for success: 'finance is committed to industry; workers are highly-trained and involved in the strategy of firms; and the culture is egalitarian and work – rather than expenditure – governed. Underlying the first two is the key notion of social partnership' (Harvie, 1992: 46).

Social-institutional change in Europe

In terms of a broad characterization of the form of life of Europeans, the key elements revolve around a political-economic structure in which state and market interact, with the state having a directive role. Thereafter it is possible to point to a characteristic social-institutional structure which affirms the importance of community, workplace and social welfare. The social-philosophical orientation can be summarized in terms of a broad humanist social philosophy and a tradition of social-democratic or Christian-democratic politics.

The social-institutional forms of contemporary Europe, in all their regional variety, can be taken to have been put in place in the long period of the continent's shift to the modern world. The spread of industrial-capitalist forms of life from an initial centre in the UK throughout large areas of Europe brought in its train all the familiar features of industrialization: a shift from rural to urban living; a shift from close-knit rural communities to less densely ordered patterns of association within rapidly growing urban areas; a shift from extended family groups lodged within kin networks towards the contemporary pattern of nuclear families; the shift of the workplace, away from the home and into the newly ordered surroundings of the industrial factory; a related shift in the patterns of gender relations as a domestic sphere opened up for women while their menfolk worked elsewhere. Alongside these social-institutional changes new patterns of cultural expression developed: new patterns of mass consumption; new patterns of mass media; and new patterns of mass political involvement. All these structural changes found intellectual expression in the work of the classical social theorists of the late nineteenth century (Nisbet, 1966) and in various ways European social theorists have routinely addressed these issues (Hawthorn, 1976).

It is clear that these general patterns of change found local expression in the separate nation-states of Europe, and the particular form of social-institutional arrangements expressed local patterns of power (Moore, 1966). It is possible to sketch out a broad series of distinctions: first, in the UK the shift to the modern world was made early and read in liberal terms as established patterns of power adjusted to novel demands, thereby maintaining a large measure of continuity with earlier patterns of life; second, in France the shift was made in the form of a revolutionary upheaval, the construction of a self-conscious republic and thereafter a slow process of embedding these ideals in the routines of everyday life; third, in north-west Europe a series of prosperous social-democratic-style nation-states emerged, albeit in the shadow of larger neighbours; fourth, in Germany the shift was made in the form of an authoritarian revolution from above which failed to secure a broader social base and declined thereafter into a variant of fascism, with a modern European social democracy being a product of post-Second World War reform and reconstruction; and fifth, in southern Europe the shift to the modern world was later and routed through further variants of fascism (Anderson, 1992). However, against this diverse experience the catastrophe of the Second World War acted both to impose a model of social-institutional development upon the continent (a mix of the influence of the UK and most especially the USA) and to spur élites into cross-national cooperation. Thereafter, it can be said, again at a very schematic level, that the subsequent dynamic of European life has been convergent. The social-institutional pattern of contemporary Europe is, broadly, social democratic or Christian democratic and finds institutional and popular expression in a schedule of commitments to work, community and social welfare.

Political-institutional change in Europe

Strange (1988) argues that the transnational systems of political, productive, financial and cultural power are the appropriate frame within
which the actions of states can be read. This position replaces the idea
of the state as a unit interacting with other similar units with the idea
of state machines as concentration points within wider power systems.
In the case of Europe the present pattern of states is in process of
dissolution (Wallace, 1990), and the European future seems in outline
to be a federal system with a common 'multiple' citizenship (Meehan,
1993).

Marquand (1988) has suggested that there will be a long process of
state deregulation coupled to supra-state and regional-level reregula-
tion of socio-economic formations. It may be that a complete layer in
the structure of political authority is to be remade and left with a much
diminished role. It is clear that this broad expectation of change
generates a lengthy further set of questions. In the first place, we could
ask how the reform of extant political structures will be accomplished,
and which sets of institutionally embodied powers/authorities will
have to be relocated to the European level. A related question concerns
the distribution of new institutionally embodied powers/authorities at
European level, old nation-state level and regional level and raises
important issues. And a broad concern at the back of all these matters
will be the extent to which the law promulgated by the old nation-
states will be superseded by European-level law. It is clear that the
juridical and institutional pattern of the European Union is an increasingly important arena of debate and negotiation among member
countries. And whatever the decisions reached by political élites, a
crucial question remains how emergent structures of power will be
legitimated in terms of electoral and parliamentary mechanisms at the
regional, old nation-state and European level. It might be noted that
these issues have been a part of ongoing debate in respect of the
development of Europe. The Treaty of Rome established a transnational organization, and this implied a transfer of power to the new
centre. This was confirmed and advanced by the Single European Act
(in particular with qualified majority voting in regard to a spread of
economic issues), and further transfers of power to the centre were
effected by the Maastricht Treaty.

The overall trend of European Union institutional and political
development is towards federalism, and the details of the evolving
pattern of reforms of the European Union have been discussed by
Lodge (1989) who considers a series of points. First, institutional
perspectives, where Lodge notes that the machinery of the European
Union has developed slowly over many years. It is only in recent years
that national governments have regarded the European Union machine
as anything other than marginal. Now there is much manoeuvring in

the process of reform and advance. A major problem is that of the 'democratic deficit'. The existing European Union is essentially an intergovernmental arrangement and the extent of direct democratic input is low. Second, internal perspectives where, around the business of the completion of the single market, Lodge takes note of the extensive implications in various fields of policy. Power is shifting towards the centre. Rule-setting is increasingly European in orientation, as the single market implies, rather than merely intergovernmentally aggregative. Third, external perspectives recall that until very recently the European Union has not acted on the international stage as a unity; however, it is a member of many international organizations and is increasingly important as a player. Finally Lodge concludes that the organization is changing fast, and that the changes are very dramatic for the political élites. The European Union is increasingly important for national-level governments/politics, at the European level and also in the international sphere, and debates in regard to the futures of European countries are increasingly conducted with reference to the European Union.

The political expectations of 1991, when the Maastricht Treaty was agreed, were optimistic, yet the post-Maastricht phase has been much more problematical and it is possible to note the spread of tensions which will shape how the treaty is translated into practice (Preston, 1994b). In brief, we can posit a process whereby diverse national understandings of the relationship of agreed theory and its relation to practice will be mutually negotiated over a long-drawn-out period. A speculative outline of these interactive dynamics can be offered in terms of a series of scenarios which can be constructed around a 'rational model' of the outcome of these dynamics, namely a republican democratic federal system.

The optimistic rational model affirms the goal of a federal Europe; however, there must be some doubt as to the likelihood of this model being generally affirmed at a European level, and to that extent it is a much less emphatic dynamic than might be expected. It might be thought that a more likely route to securing the rational model, particularly after the shock of the first Danish referendum, which in part was an affirmation of local-level democracy against the developing intergovernmental élitism of the European Union, would entail more citizen involvement to supplement the existing technocratic style. One variant of this sort of route to the future has been characterized in terms of an uneven and multi-tracked style of development, where the community continues to move towards some sort of union but also continues to be *sui generis* in terms of political institutions.

Other ways of imagining the future of the community revolve around notions of breakdown and the reassertion of nationalism. An outright withdrawal into nationalism implies that Europe's economic, political and cultural future would be primarily shaped by the

Americans, the Japanese and the Germans. In particular, Germany would in fairly short order come to dominate Europe. Another possibility is of a somewhat more restricted form of conflict, an economic nationalism as competition between extant states becomes the order of the day. Such economic nationalism would leave each agent to read and react independently to global structural pressure. In terms of global structures, America, Japan and Germany would increase in importance. A further, related possibility has been noted by those associated with the project for a federal Europe who have spoken of a variable-geometry strategy, with a core group going ahead with union and a periphery of weaker economies or politically uncommitted countries forming a second tier. The likely core would include Germany, Austria, France and the Benelux countries. The periphery might include Italy, Spain, Portugal, Greece, Sweden, Finland and Ireland, all of whom might be expected to join with the core at a relatively early stage. The detached periphery would then be the UK and perhaps Denmark. In this scenario the expectation is of an essentially piecemeal advance among a variety of institutional spheres towards a unitary political-economic and cultural space. However, it is clear that when one comes to speculate about how the post-Maastricht pursuit of further European Union integration might work out in practice, these scenarios are of some utility in sketching ranges of broad possibility but they cannot be an effective substitute for the attention to the detail of economic, political and cultural processes.

Cultural changes in Europe

The foregoing material has dealt primarily with the structural aspects of complex change. I turn now to the matter of agency, not so much in terms of institutional forms and active groups but rather in terms of those sets of ideas which individuals, groups and institutions will draw on to order their activities.

Available cultural traditions

Confronted with the demanding business of grasping the nature of complex change, those concerned will draw automatically on stocks of available ideas. Hawthorn (1976) has pointed out that there are distinct national variations among social-scientific traditions, and variations in concern for general theory flowed from the differential relationships between national intelligentsias and their states. It seems appropriate therefore to raise the matter of differences of intellectual-cultural tradition within Europe in so far as these might be taken to bear upon theorizing, lay or professional, for example: nationalisms; regional particularisms; ethnicities; religious traditions; and informal traditions of class. If these can be taken as possible occasions for reading the world differently, then, following Hawthorn, what will thereafter shape these ideas will be their institutional possibilities of expression.

A condition of process-centred interpretation is a grasp of the detail of particular histories as these condition theorizing. In respect of formal knowledge claims, this might involve rediscovering cultural resources already available and reaffirming them. This could include noting that Europe has a rich common history and that this will have to be read out of power-bloc-dominated national frameworks and read into a common history. A part of such a common history would be the affirmation of the world-historical role of post-Renaissance Europe, both as a world power (only recently eclipsed by the USA in the wake of two world wars) and as the originators/inventors of the modernist project.

Such interpretive constructs will be used by various groups in the formal political struggle surrounding change in Europe, and crucial debates will involve federation in respect of the European Union, and the creation of new patterns of exchange with the old Eastern bloc, in all, debates about the shape and character of an emergent new Europe. This is, in a way, the familiar territory of party statements, political writing, newspaper and media debates, but formal organizations are also involved, and employers' groupings, labour organizations, myriad research groups within Europe, existing institutional centres (state, para-state and supranational) and so on are all engaged.

It is clear that explicit programmatic delimited-formal ideological statements in regard to European development have been made; indeed, they have a distinguished history. Arguing that a federal system was needed both to address global-level problems and to overcome residual nationalism, Brugmans (1985) went on to specify four basic questions in regard to the project of building a united Europe: the matter of identity; the problem of defence/security; the social dimension of welfare; and the political issue of democracy. Thereafter, in a marvellous overview, Brugmans rehearses the outline of a series of specific debates, concluding broadly that a federal Europe is the route to a reaffirmation of Europe's place in the developing global system.

And, of course, all this business of reading the shift towards European unity has a common-sense version, the sphere of pervasive-informal ideology. The present pattern of complex change is not a matter solely for élite inspection, as broad citizen responses constrain formal political programmes and extant thinking is itself shaped by political struggles, that is, hegemonic and counter-hegemonic idea-sets. If we ask how common sense has variously regarded the project of European unity, and how it might read the emergent European unified system, with its seemingly dominant role for Germany, then it is clear that this will be a crucial area of political struggle over the years.

Reinventing Europe

The notion of Europe is not straightforward. It has taken several forms over the centuries. It can be read as a contested concept. Delanty (1995) argues that the notion of Europe which we most directly and unself-consciously inherit, where Western Europe is read as the centre of civilization in contrast to the Eastern worlds of the Orient, as the vehicle of the universalist truths of the Enlightenment which found conservative modern expression in discrete nation-states, is both unsatisfactory (in its ethical Eurocentric narrowness) and arguably in process of an unfortunate representation in the guise of the nation-state writ large of 'fortress Europe'. In place of this project, Delanty proposes a post-national European identity built around notions of citizenship which would be tolerant of the diverse cultural styles of those inhabiting the geographical space of Europe. In the light of these remarks it is clear that it is important to note that the political-cultural project of the European Union is fluid and open. However, it is not clear how the available stock of cultural resources will find expression as agent groups read and react to enfolding global structural patterns. It does seems clear that one aspect of these processes will be the attempt to sketch the essence of a European identity.

It has been argued earlier that the key to identity and political-cultural identity is the mix of locale, network and memory. It has also been argued that the public sphere of collective memory has been shaped by official ideologies. In modern Europe these have been nationalisms. It seems clear therefore that in the process of the invention of a new European political-cultural identity, familiar claims about nation – in both delimited-formal and pervasive-informal guise – will be a key starting-point for reflection upon the nature of a new European identity.

The invention of national identities has taken place in phases over 200 years, with the USA as the first specimen of a modern nation-state (Anderson, 1983). The late nineteenth century saw the apogee of nation-statehood. However, it seems safe to assert in the wake of the Second World War, which was rooted in part in nineteenth-century nationalism, and the subsequent long period of US hegemony that the idea of nationalism is in decline in the European Union countries. In the post-Second World War period it has been suggested that decline in European nationalist sentiment has been evidenced in fewer nationalist flags, parades and anthems. It has been suggested that more non-national popular imagery has been made generally available. Here it may be that the role of the media-given cultural example of the USA was important initially, and subsequently what is now dubbed consumerism played a part. Personal identity becomes bound up with freedom to consume, lifestyle and so on, everything now theorized under the fashionable heading of postmodernism. Overall, national identity is neither a central element of state-level political activity, nor is it as important as it was in constituting the identity of individuals as citizens. The growing movement towards the creation of the European Union merely reinforces long-established trends. On both global structural and historical grounds, both centring albeit for different reasons on the notion of interdependence, nationalism is flowing out of the routine experience of Western Europeans.

However, it is clear that nationalism and its relative ethnicity can be created and used by élite groups to secure their political goals. As the idea of Europe comes to challenge that of nations, we might expect a lengthy period of establishing new identities, new contested compromises. Recent trans-system changes thus generate challenges at the level of the legitimating ideas of the state-level structure. Official ideologies, with their approved nationalisms and ethnicities, are deeply implicated in given patterns of internal state arrangements. When the trans-state system changes so as to occasion internal state changes, then established contested compromises are radically disturbed and the process of re-establishing such compromises is likely to be difficult and lengthy. Kearney (1992) asks if Europe can reinvent itself and its traditions in the wake of 1989–91, and notes that the problems include diverse state forms, sometimes antagonistic national traditions, and the legacies of religion and history, all of which have found violent expression in the former Yugoslavia (Ignatieff, 1994). However, in general, on all this Taylor (1992) affirms a notion of dispersed and tolerant nationalism. Identities can be multiple and it is possible to live in inclusive and tolerantly diverse federations.

Complex change in the regions of Europe

The dynamics of change in post-bloc Europe are a matter of great contemporary concern. I will sketch out the patterns of change in the sphere of political-cultural identity in order to illustrate some of the themes discussed in the earlier chapters. The remarks offered here are very brief but perhaps they usefully recall that in terms of the strategy of enquiry adopted in this text there are two major substantive concerns to address: first, the responses to the collapse of cold-war bloc-time and associated official ideologies; and second, the response to the project of the European Union.

The core areas of north-western Europe

In the core areas of Scandinavia, Benelux, Germany, Austria, France and northern Italy, the end of bloc-time has generally modulated into the programme for a federal European Union; however, the business of translating general commitment into practice will be drawn-out and fraught. In Scandinavia there is concern with the democratic deficit of the Union. In the Benelux countries there is concern with the size and power of neighbouring Germany. In northern Italy, the industrial heartland of the country, there is strong support for the project, and a disposition to distinguish themselves from southern Italy. In France there is continuing élite commitment to the original ideals of the European Economic Community's founders in terms of moving beyond the wars between nation-states of Europe. The relationship between France and Germany is often made central to the development of Europe.

In Germany the end of the cold war meant the end of post-Second World War division. The citizens of the Federal Republic lost their small, comfortable and prosperous country, while the citizens of the former German Democratic Republic lost their country altogether. The newly reunified Germany immediately moved to the political centre of Europe (the largest country with the largest economy, located in the heart of the continent) and the long-standing commitment of the Federal Republic to the European Union was put to the test (Fritch-Bournazel, 1992). On this, Ignatieff (1994) finds confusion in Germany in the wake of the reunification. A series of processes are under way: East Germany is being absorbed; returnees are coming from Russia and the old Eastern bloc; and asylum-seekers are received. In the context of modern Germany the historical legacy comprises romantic nationalism, a civic nationalism (liberal, democratic and social-democratic variants are noted) and a state-centred nationalism derived from the Bismarckian developmental state of the late nineteenth century. And to this must be added the legacies of the period of Hitler and thereafter, the post-nationalism of West Germany. In general, Ignatieff takes the view that, while the comfortable Federal Republic is no more, it is not clear what has replaced it.

The southern areas of the Mediterranean

In the southern areas of Spain, southern Italy and Greece, the end of bloc-time has generated problems and the shift into the project of European unification has not been smooth.

In Italy the end of bloc-time generated a collapse in the authority of the political classes. Here the end of the cold war meant an end to excuses for the continuing power of the corrupt political system dominated by the Christian Democratic Party. A revolt on the part of pro-European Union professionals led the attack on the established alliance between politics and business. Thereafter the project of the federal European Union received support.

In Spain the European Union has been the vehicle of its emergence from fascist regimes established in the 1930s (Anderson, 1992). The record of post-Second World War economic and social change has been remarkable. The authoritarian regimes inherited from the 1930s proved adept at generating growth, but eventually their political structures and ideas proved unsuited to further development. Anderson (1992: 315) suggests that the upsurge of interest in Eurocommunism was an early symptom, but it was the establishment of social-democratic regimes in the wake of fascism which genuinely ushered in the new European period of development.

The western areas of the Atlantic coast

In the western areas of Europe the collapse of bloc-time ideology has had a dramatic impact on one country in particular, and its response to the project of European unification, but for the other western territories matters have been much smoother.

The development of the European Union has been the vehicle for reform in Portugal (Anderson, 1992). The end of bloc-time is not particularly relevant in the context of post-fascist development. The end of bloc-time for Ireland makes little difference and its commitment to the European Union remains strong (Kearney, 1988, 1992). Ignatieff (1994) sees Northern Ireland loyalism as a cargo cult, a borrowing and remaking of an identity, in this case Britishness, yet even here there are signs that a European dimension to the debate has been recognized.

However, in contrast, in Britain the end of the comfortable certainties of the cold war caused consternation among the political classes as they lost their role and self-understanding (Preston, 1994b). As the project of the European Union came to fill the void, it threatened them directly, not merely a loss of role, rather active abolition in a dual process of Europeanization and democratization. Thereafter, there have been three broad reactions. First, in England the political classes are bereft and the population confused. There is the possibility of reaction from disappointed nationalists and/or marginal groups. The fraction of the UK ruling class which rallied to Thatcher in the 1980s is appalled at recent events in Europe, and there are small right-wing reactionary nationalist groups in other Western European countries. Second, the situation of Scotland in relation to contemporary history is different. Harvie (1992) suggests that its inhabitants must acknowledge their fellow Europeans and the various legacies they can draw upon. In the case of the Scots there is the tradition of the Scottish Enlightenment, with figures such as Smith, Ferguson and Hume. In all Harvie diagnoses a legacy of civic humanism, an appreciation of the 'small knowable polis existing within loose structures' (1992: 19) which resembles the Eastern European civic forum notions of discourse. It is a tradition that is quite distinct from Anglo-Saxon marketism, with its economic liberalism and minimum state, and more closely approximates the model of the Germany's *Länder* system where power is regionalized. Harvie is confident both that Scotland, thus understood, could contribute to a new notion of Europe, and that to secure this future for Scotland requires the removal of the centralizing hand of London, in other words, independence. And finally, in Wales the European Union might rescue the local culture. Williams (1989) has argued that the emergence of a supranational Europe would constitute a last chance for some of Europe's regions; thus the Welsh, for example, could be rescued by Europe from a final decline by assimilation.

The areas of Central Europe

In the Central European countries of Poland, the Czech Republic, Slovakia, Hungary and Slovenia there has been enthusiasm for the end of bloc-time and a declared intention to join the European Union, often cast in terms of 'returning to Europe'. However, in the countries of the Balkans, in particular the former Yugoslavia, there has also been an atavistic resurgence of ethnic nationalism.

Ignatieff (1994) draws a distinction between civic nationalism and ethnic nationalism. The former is traced back to the ideals of the French Enlightenment – a rational rule-governed community – and the latter is traced back to the German romanticism of the early nineteenth century, which reacted to the expansionism of Napoleonic France by stressing that the core of nationalism was the people – a community of language, descent and culture. Of these, civic nationalism has a better claim to sociological realism as most nation-states are multi-ethnic and indeed most are rule-governed; civic nationalists are ironists, sceptics and cosmopolitans. In terms of the historical development of nationalism, Ignatieff links it to an unexplicated notion of achievement, a notion of civilization as a historical achievement. The cosmopolitans are lucky because they inhabit societies which are rich enough and sophisticated enough to permit their position. It is a historical achievement, an achievement secured against human nature. And on the other hand, Ignatieff argues that ethnic nationalism has a more immediate psychological appeal, to an idea of the natural given-ness of identity. The link to identity is made psychologically, and ethnic nationalists are supremely sentimental; their art is kitsch.

Ignatieff tries to illuminate matters via a series of journeys. In Croatia and Serbia he discovers the 'narcissism of minor difference' and the cherished memories of earlier wrongs. The violence is extreme; as the Yugoslavian federal state structure has fallen away the warlords have returned. The social hierarchy is reversed, the young male becomes important – purveyors of violence – and the educated middle classes are lost. The rhetoric of nationalism is taken to be rationalization after the fact, and in the Ukraine he traces the move from USSR to naïve nationalism. In a general conclusion Ignatieff returns to the level of ideas, psychology and violence and argues that ethnic nationalism is the language of fantasy and escape, a route out of banal reality into a heroic situation. The rhetoric is routinely inauthentic (in the end

Ignatieff thinks no one really believes it) and most of the violence that accompanies ethnic nationalism is the product of young men (a psychological reaction against the order of the state/father). As against ethnic nationalism, civic nationalism is an achievement of civilization, at present under some pressure.

Ignatieff prefers to operate in the sphere of ideas and psychology, and the political-economic and social-institutional patterns of change which occasioned the recourse to nationalist violence are not pursued. On this, Rieff (1995) records the events of the collapse of Yugoslavia in terms of the slow decline of the Titoist project, the broader implications of the collapse of the Eastern European bloc, and the response of political agents in Belgrade, which was to reinvent Serbian ethnic nationalism. In sum, against the position which reads the conflict in Bosnia as a civil war occasioned by irrational nationalism Rieff (a) details the political manoeuvres of the Belgrade political élite which turned to ethnic Serbian nationalism as a deliberate post-communist strategy to keep power, (b) notes that the war in Bosnia was inspired and orchestrated from Belgrade (at least at the outset, though the relationship between Belgrade and Pale became more complicated later), and (c) details the way in which a multi-ethnic Bosnia saw division into ethnic enclaves. Here the key point is that it was not a spontaneous expression of suppressed or otherwise latent ethnic identity; rather it was orchestrated and fuelled by extreme violence. In other words, the present ethnic divisions are not the cause of political action; they are the product of political action.

The further development of Europe

It is not possible to predict how the diverse groupings of people within the territory of the European Union will come collectively to plot a route to the future. It is possible to analyse the situation. A rational model of the development of the European Union can be presented in terms of the project for a federal solution. All other plausible scenarios lead to the view that Germany will come to dominate Europe and would inevitably take the lead in discussions with the USA and Japan (both of whom would be content with a squabbling Europe which would thus remain a large accessible market for their goods) (Preston, 1994b). However, against this pessimism, it is safe to predict that the global structural pressures for European unification within the tripolar world system will continue to bear down upon actors.

Conclusion: a new Europe in the making

The collapse of the cold-war bloc system sharply undermined the familiar political-cultural identities of Europeans. As we try to decipher those processes which enfold us we can identify some broad key elements of this structural reconstruction: first, change in the European Union towards a more unified system; second, change in Eastern Europe and the CIS towards economic and political reform; and finally, change in the broader global system. A clue to deciphering this pattern of complex change is given by the overall line of change which would seem to be towards some sort of unification of the countries of Europe within a tripolar system.

7

Changing Political-Cultural Identities in the USA

In respect of the sphere of the Americas it seems clear that the core economy is that of the USA. In the wider Americas the reduction in influence is slow, but it is implicit in the idea of a more integrated region, a set of rules binding all participants. In Latin America the uneven pattern of development continues, as does the ambiguous relationship with the USA. In Canada the economic integration with the USA continues, and there is increasing concern for independence in Quebec, as a group reading itself as culturally distinct and politically secondary to English-speaking Canada tries to extricate itself from the federation (Ignatieff, 1994).

At the present time the USA is in slow relative decline within the global system as its overwhelming post-Second World War economic strength expressed in the Bretton Woods settlement is reduced. Inside the USA regional changes have been extensive, with population movement from north to south and from east to west. The public politics of the USA has moved away from the post-war preference for dispersed state intervention in pursuit of a unified community, the declining legacy of the New Deal, and towards an emphatically market-based and fragmented population, a circumstance recently theorized as postmodernity (Woodiwiss, 1993). In reviewing these materials, as with the other chapters dealing with the three regions of the global industrial-capitalist system, we need to begin with the ways in which received political-cultural identities have been disturbed in recent years. It is with present confusions that reflection upon identity and political cultural identity begins.

In respect of the political-cultural identities of the people of the USA, at the general level of public discourse we can point to two streams of ideas which are overlapping and cross-cutting but distinct: on the one hand, the ideology of Americanism, which we can take to be a product of the economy and society of the late nineteenth century (Anderson, 1983); and on the other, the sets of ideas associated with the assumption by the USA of a global role in the years following the Second World War, in sum, the spread of ideas and institutions which comprised the construct of 'the free world' (Kolko, 1968; Aron, 1973). These materials underpin the subsequent confusions of the suggestions of the inevitability of the decline of great powers (Kennedy, 1988) and the recent claims of an end to history (Fukuyama, 1992). At the present time the citizens of the USA must confront an unexpected tripolarity within the global system (Thurow, 1994).

The end of the short twentieth century has seen the USA continuing to press for an open global trading system, but these arguments are now made within the context of a tripolar system and without the convenience of the existence of the Second World, which provided an excuse for US hegemony within the sphere of the West. The influence of the Washington-based IMF and World Bank is extensive in promoting liberalization and free trade, and recent expressions of these concerns have been the establishment of NAFTA and APEC. The key elements of the American model of industrial capitalism might be taken to include: (a) a commitment to an open market economy; (b) a popular tradition which celebrates the achievements of ordinary people; and (c) a cultural tradition of liberal individualism along with a public commitment to republican democracy. Overall, in the wake of the collapse of the post-Second World War settlement the general public sphere of the USA is beset with confusion in respect of the character and opportunities of the emergent tripolar global system. In this chapter I will review in a very broad fashion the recent shifts within American political-cultural identities.

The shift to the modern world: structural patterns and agent responses in the making of the USA

The classic tradition of European social theory has been concerned with elucidating the dynamics of complex change in the shift to the modern world. Within the schedule of questions which go to make up this engaged and prospective interpretive-critical agenda is lodged a concern for the nature of personhood, both individual identity and political-cultural identity, where this expresses the relationship of the individual to an ordered collectivity.

The business of the shift to the modern world can be discussed in general terms dealing with the nature of the development of political-economic structures, social-institutional arrangements and patterns of culture; however, in practical terms the shift to the modern world has been a matter of particular groups of people in particular places at particular times. In other words, we can speak of a variety of routes into the modern world where these are both distinct and lay down a particular spread of cultural residues – ways of going about things – which subsequently form the basis of the forms of life of subsequent generations, in brief, the dynamics of structures and agents run down through time. In this section we can note both the way in which the USA made the shift to the modern world and the spread of cultural forms bequeathed to subsequent generations.

The colonial period, the War of Independence and the Civil War

Moore (1966) presents a comparative historical analysis of the relation-ship between class groups in the complex shift to the modern world which indicates that particular sets of relationships could constitute particular routes to the modern world and issue in different sorts of polities within the modern world. In respect of the USA the broad history is one of European colonial expansion, the displacement of native populations and the eventual expulsion of the metropolitan colonial powers in the process of the establishment of an independent republican democracy.

The American Revolution or War of Independence (1775–83), Moore notes, effected few social and economic changes within the USA. The economies were primarily agricultural and remained so after inde-pendence. However, the revolution did lead to the political unification of the various colonies. It seems clear that the radical political currents present were ambiguously lodged within the developing political culture. Anderson points out that 'many leaders of the independence movement in the Thirteen Colonies were slave-owning agrarian mag-nates' (1983: 51). However, Anderson goes on to add that the 'success of the Thirteen Colonies' revolt at the end of the 1770s, and the onset of the French Revolution at the end of the 1780s, did not fail to exert a powerful influence. Nothing confirms this "cultural revolution" more than the pervasive republicanism of the newly independent com-munities' (1983: 53).

Moore argues that the Civil War of 1861–5 did effect changes – political, economic and social – and was a revolution which saw the industrial north establish its pre-eminence. However, the war need not have taken place because there was no deep-seated functional misfit between north and south and, for example, the US could have devel-oped like Bismarckian Germany with its powerful Prussian land-owners. Moore argues that the war had the political objective of establishing bourgeois capitalist democracy. And in a similar way, Anderson comments that American nationalism was flexible enough in its claims upon those who lived in the territories in its early years to encompass a civil war almost a century after independence (1983: 64). It was only in the late nineteenth century that notions of an American identity became somewhat more robust in their grip upon the population.

Moore argues that there were three forms of American capitalist growth. It is noted that by 1860 the US had developed in three distinct ways: first, the plantation south, with its justificatory ideology of southern gentility which pointed to 'courtesy, grace, cultivation, the broad outlook versus the allegedly money-grubbing outlook of the North' (1966: 122); second, the northern industrial regions, with their commitment to bourgeois democracy; and third, the western lands of increasingly prosperous small farmers, with their ideologies of in-dividualism and responsibility. Each sector had particular economic and political interests; they did not mesh smoothly, nor did the linkages between the regions stay fixed. In the years before the Civil War the north and west came to find it easier to accommodate each other; the perhaps temporary northern need for tariff protection, which the south as a primary-product exporter did not want, was the final precipitating reason for the war.

The differences between north and south, Moore suggests, were cast in terms of different forms of life leading to irreconcilable views on slavery, which became the overt trigger of conflict between the two ruling groups/factions within the US. Any revolutionary impulses in the form of a broader progressive aspect of the war were drawn off by the open lands of the west. The industrialists of the east could ally themselves with the more plebeian small farmers of the open lands of the west. Moore comments that the meaning of the war was that it established the path of American capitalism, industrial and liberal-democratic. If the south had remained unchanged, then the US would have developed more like Latin America with its *latifundia*. The war was a decisive political step in directing the whole system into a particular line of historical advance, a particular route to the modern world. It was only after the Civil War that a distinctively American political-cultural identity was formed.

Of the Americas generally, Anderson notes

> Out of the American welter came these imagined realities: nation-states, republican institutions, common citizenships, popular sovereignty, national flags and anthems, etc, and the liquidation of their conceptual opposites: dynastic empires, monarchical institutions, absolutisms, subjecthoods, in-herited nobilities, serfdoms, ghettoes, and so forth. (1983: 78)

In the case of the USA, as elsewhere, what follows next is the manner in which sets of ideas find expression (or not) in routine practice. In this vein, Hawthorn notes the intellectual debts of Americans to the work of Locke and argues that the 'radical rhetoric of the European Enlightenment was . . . deployed for what were literally conservative ends' (1976: 192). A series of consequences follow. First, that Americans attended to private property on the one hand and the state (as rule guarantor) on the other, and the broad sphere of social structure and its constitutive role in personhood falls away into the background. Second, the stress on property/individualism entailed a social conformity for, as no person could lay claim to superiority in respect of another, so too was a spurious equality affirmed. Third, the experience of progress has been narrowed down, in a country taken as exemplify-ing Enlightenment virtues and thus in essentials neither needing nor admitting improvement, to the accumulation of material novelties. Hawthorn argues that each of these three deep-seated traits within general US political-cultural identity have restricted intellectual life because the pervasive liberalism blocks the possibility of rational criticism of US society except in terms of pointing to technical means to improve the functioning of a system taken as perfect in essentials. The debate is narrowed and the critical intellectual reflection familiar in Europe is less evident. Moreover, the claim to perfection cuts against criticism in so far as it lends credence to a pervasive anti-intellectualism (if the system is fine, then it does not need intellectuals criticizing it and when they do they must be guilty of self-indulgence).

In a similarly general way, Jaffe (1995) identifies a broad political-cultural style which can be summed up as an 'anti-politics'. Jaffe looks back to the appropriation by American political agents of Hobbes and Locke, with their stress on individuals and contracts, and notes that these claims could be read into the experience of those colonizing an effectively empty continent in an unusually direct fashion. In practical terms there is a stress on people, on the local level, and on deal-making, and the federal government exists as a distant and suspect sphere, a source of possible interference. In ideological or political-philosophical terms, these experiences resonate with ideas of the priority of persons and the civil sphere. The realm of government is a necessary evil. The social world is given in individuals and the political realm is a subsequent contrivance.

Jaffe notes that the historical experience of the development of the USA, when read through the imported philosophy of liberalism, has generated a fundamentally anti-political culture. It is supposed that the civil sphere of individual persons making contracts is both funda-mental and pre-political. The sphere of formal politics has no core role and becomes merely the arena for the resolution of the conflicts of individual or aggregated group material interests. The idea of politics is reduced to politicking. There is no public good to be identified, debated and pursued. The repository of agreed rules which structures exchange is the constitution and here is one sphere of debate, but again it is ritualized debate. Reducing politics to quasi-theological disputes about the intentions of those who drafted the constitution and the precise manner of its present-day interpretation is an escape from genuine political debate precisely because the difficulties of political debate are elided in favour of the entertainments of technical quasi-theology. Overall, Jaffe argues that the general cultural style is domi-nated by the mentality of the marketplace.

An American political-cultural identity established

The pace of political-economic development in the final years of the nineteenth century following the Civil War was very rapid. The years running up to the start of the short twentieth century saw a spread of changes in technology and business organization which began what has subsequently been tagged 'Fordism' with mass production for mass markets (Lash and Urry, 1987).

The process of industrialization also saw the construction of a more unified American identity from the elements favoured by each of the three regions identified by Moore (1966). All of this took place within the essentially republican democratic official ideology established in the War of Independence and restated after the Civil War. It is in this period that we can locate the construction of the familiar pattern of American exceptionalism with its four elements of claims to equality of opportunity, a strong economic individualism, a preference for political liberty and an institutional style of republican democracy.

It has been argued by Hawthorn (1976) that this set of ideas does not cohere as the claim to republican democracy is formal/ritual and the polity is thoroughgoing liberal. In this system of ideas progress is possible only in material terms. As the society/polity is already perfect (republican democratic) there is no scope for progressive reform and consequently the possibilities of the future are reduced to the material. And against the espoused commitment to democracy, we might also want to note that the late nineteenth century saw a phase of US imperialist expansion with wars in Mexico, Cuba and the Philippines, and patterns of trade-centred expansion in other parts of Asia. It was the 'black ships' of Commodore Perry which obliged the Japanese shogunate to open its territories for trade, thereby precipitating the Meiji Restoration. And the late nineteenth-century movement of American settlers and traders into the native Indian lands of the western regions of the continent can now be seen to have been an episode of genocidal colonial expansion. On Hawthorn's view the polity of the USA is liberal, and it has pursued a spread of material concerns in a familiar way.

The first period of the short twentieth century

The First World War disrupted the economies of Europe and allowed the already powerful USA to move forward to a position of pre-eminence within the global system. However, the upheavals of the war and the loss of financial pre-eminence by Britain meant that the late nineteenth-century liberal world system identified by Hobsbawm (1994) fell into a pattern of separate economic spheres which practised protectionism. The inter-war period saw a collapse in international trade and the economies of the major countries contracted sharply.

It was in this period that the politics of Wilsonian idealism found expression in the establishment of the League of Nations. It was also in this period that the reaction of isolationism was pursued, as the US Congress declined to pass the bills establishing US membership of the organization. None the less, with the economic reconstructions of the programmes of the New Deal and the economic boom generated by war production in the period of the Second World War, the USA attained a global position. However, it was not until 1945 that the pre-eminence of the USA was finally established within an economically devastated global system and given institutional and ideological articulation in the Bretton Woods agreement (Harrison, 1967).

In the period 1914–45 we can note three major developments: first, the establishment of the political economy of Fordism; second, the impact of the depression years; and third, the impact of the 1917 revolution in Russia and the subsequent early success of the planned economy, which provided a marked counter-example to the inter-war failures of free-market capitalism. It was against this backdrop that political life proceeded. In sum, in the first period of the short twentieth century the Fordist economy of the USA came to underpin a polity which became hegemonic over large parts of the global system in the years after 1945 (Van der Pijl, 1984; Overbeek, 1990).

The rise of Fordism

Harvey (1989) remarks that the symbolic start of Fordism should be 1914, when the new car plant at Dearborn, Michigan, was opened. However, the roots of the Fordist style of production go back to the railway boom of the late nineteenth century. Ford built on the models available and moved matters forward:

> What was special about Ford (and what ultimately separates Fordism from Taylorism), was his vision, his explicit recognition that mass production meant mass consumption, a new system of the reproduction of labour power, a new politics of labour control and management, a new aesthetics and psychology, in short, a new kind of rationalized, modernist, and populist democratic society. (Harvey, 1989: 126)

Harvey notes that the mix of capital/labour relations, industrial strategies and state intervention roles took a long time to establish – and there were many partial attempts to get the mix right (from utopian solutions through to fascism) – and it was not until after the Second World War that the package found full expression in the open trading system established at the behest of the USA at Bretton Woods. It lasted until 1973 when Nixon effectively undermined it and ushered in the period of both domestic and international industrial restructuring which has led to the present interdependent tripolar global system.

Along with the development of the economic form of Fordism, the USA saw the rise of a mass culture carried by the increase of the popular media. In the early years of the modern period it was a reading public which helped establish the idea of national communities (Anderson, 1983). In the period of the nineteenth century the reading public expanded, along with the commercial sphere of the printed word, with popular newspapers and magazines of all kinds. In the inter-war period a new community took shape, based around the new technologies of sound and vision, and the epitome of this new listening/viewing public was the world of the Hollywood movie. These developments also saw the rise of the critiques of that mass culture which suggested either that popular taste was aesthetically degraded or that the mass media were instruments of oppression (or both).

The depression years

The great depression was a major crisis for the global industrial-capitalist system. Hobsbawm argues that it was triggered in the USA, whose financial sectors had assumed a worldwide importance but not a worldwide vision. The collapse began in the USA and was exported around the globe; it destroyed the intellectual and institutional pretensions of economic liberalism for fifty years (Hobsbawm, 1994: 94).

The period gives us the politics of the New Deal. In the late 1930s the presidency of Roosevelt attempted to alleviate the distress of the unemployed in the USA by running a series of public-works programmes. These programmes were considered very contentious and were challenged by the political Right in terms of their being ideologically socialistic and unconstitutional. It was not until the demands upon productive industry rose in order to meet the needs of war that unemployment finally disappeared.

In general, the response which the great depression provoked among governments (albeit with much debate and opposition) was to look to state intervention. The intellectual vehicle of the establishment of the role of government in regulating market-economic systems was established in outline over this period and translated into practice in the construction of the Bretton Woods system by politicians, policy analysts and academics whose thinking had been profoundly marked by the experience of the depression (Dorfman, 1963; Kolko, 1968; Graham, 1976). The intellectual routes to the interventionist role of the state were various, but in general they have come to be associated with the work of J.M. Keynes; in brief, it can be said that Keynesianism became the handmaiden of Fordism.

American unease at the rise of the socialist bloc

The Russian Revolution was a political shock to the élites of the USA. The economic success of the USSR in the inter-war period was also in sharp contrast to the depression. The conflict between American ideals of rugged individualism and the collectivism of socialist doctrines can be dated to this period and it is clear that the conflict has coloured subsequent US political life (Caute, 1978; Chomsky, 1991; Walker, 1993).

The period saw in the realm of politics a ferocious reaction to the Russian Revolution. The US political style of 'red-baiting' in the electoral realm and the routine attempts to suppress trade unions all date from this period. The strategy of red-baiting was an available tactic during the years of the Second World War, when the extensive involvement of the state in the war economy was paralleled by a concern to order the post-war world, which critics on the political Right viewed with great unease. The presidency of Roosevelt had overridden these anxieties and the attacks which flowed from them, but this was not to be the style of Truman. Indeed, Truman was apparently happy to give ground to the political Right and by 1947 was inaugurating the cold-war confrontation with the USSR (Kolko, 1968). In the years of the Reagan presidency this style found renewed emphasis in the designation of the USSR as the 'evil empire' and the pursuit of the related 'star wars' programme of exotic military defence technologies. The rhetoric of anti-communism has been deeply embedded within the public politics of the USA for some seventy-odd years, and the collapse of the USSR in 1991 removed a key defining element of it.

Some cultural residues of the years to 1945

The entire period can be regarded as a series of agent responses to changing structural circumstances. The period can be taken to have left cultural residues, that is, memories lodged in institutions, practices and official and folk ideologies. In this context the enduring features in the American polity include a commitment to an open market economy, a positive valuation of the achievements of ordinary people and a cultural tradition of liberal individualism, along with a public commitment to republican democracy.

However, in this context there is also a political fragmentation within the state machinery (McKay, 1994) and an aversion within the population to all encompassing ideologies except the long-established ideology of Americanism (anti-statism, freedom, equality, democracy). And it is true that the idea-set of Americanism has survived many social and economic upheavals over this century. At the present time the polity faces three challenges: first, the hegemonic role which has been embraced since 1941 is now declining; second, there is a growing state machine dealing with the economy, military and welfare whose presence needs to be acknowledged and rationally considered (McKay, 1994); and third, there is a new social fragmentation which makes coalition-building in the political system difficult.

The USA in the post-Second World War period

Analysed in terms of patterns of structural change and agent response, we can identify a series of broad phases: first, the immediate post-Second World War period of political-economic, military-diplomatic and cultural hegemony, which saw the invention of the free West; second, the internal problems of the 1970s – war, race and youth – and the slow decline in position and influence when these were added to external changes like the rise of Japan and the EEC; third, the phase of postmodernist theorizing; and fourth, the problems of the end of the short twentieth century and attempts to comprehend the present.

The USA and the post-Second World War settlement

The episode of the Second World War saw the emergence of the USA as the premier economic, political and military power in the world. The power of the USA was used to establish and underpin the Bretton Woods system within the sphere of the West. The power of the USA was extensively deployed in the military/diplomatic confrontation with the Second World.

American political-cultural identities in the period 1945–75 took on a new energy. After the triumph of the Second World War the USA attained an unparalleled cultural influence in the West. In the sphere of economics American know-how was celebrated in the evident pre-eminence and dynamism of an economy which was able to underpin unprecedented levels of mass consumption and affluence. The prosperity was so remarkable and such a deep contrast with pre-war problems that critics spoke of the affluent society and called for a reconsideration of the prioritizing of personal consumption (Galbraith 1958). At the same time the social institutions of the USA were celebrated in contrast to the conservatism of Europe and the colonial repression of their overseas holdings. The US notions of pluralism, individualism and democracy were advertised, and in the related sphere of culture the diversity and opportunity of the USA were stressed.

The position of the USA was unchallenged until the middle 1970s, when the financial burdens of the war in Vietnam occasioned the first changes within the Bretton Woods system. The period of the late 1970s saw inflation and economic dislocation within the Western sphere. At this time the relative position of the US political economy began to change – in particular with the rise of Japan and European Union. And in the 1980s the military build-up pursued by Reagan led to the USA becoming a debtor nation. In addition the USA was the major sponsor of the doctrines of economic liberalization which have further undermined the order of the global system. Krieger (1986) points to the period when the benefits of the Bretton Woods system to the USA begin to fall away as the inauguration of the politics of decline.

McKay (1994) details the elements: first, a relative economic decline parallels the decline in order within the global system and, as the USA is more involved in the global trading system than has historically been the case, so the relative economic decline causes problems; then second, open markets and protectionism cause problems because, where the US took the lead in making the post-war system open, others have used trade protection; thus the Europeans and Pacific Asia have protected home markets while looking to the US market as a destination for their exports, and this has had impacts on the US (trade deficits and job losses); and finally, the US role as military/diplomatic leader of the West has become much more problematical with the rise of other centres (the European Union, Japan) and the shift beyond simple cold-war certainties.

Changing American identities in the period 1975–91

McKay (1994) argues that, notwithstanding the myth of the unchanging essence of America, the ideology does change and there is ideological debate. The pattern of political thinking shifts along with changes in the underlying political-economic structures. It can be argued that up until 1917 US industrial capitalism needed little government involvement because it was dynamic and successful. However, after 1917 the USA became involved in the First World War and then suffered the long period of the depression, and over the period the state did act to secure economic growth. It is also clear that the state continued to act after 1945 within the newly established Bretton Woods framework. The US federal state machinery became increasingly involved in regulating the economy and society. And over this period, the population of the US became familiar with the role of 'big government' and the programmes which it could run.

It was the New Deal period which was historically novel in terms of the very rapid growth of the machineries of an interventionist state. The machineries set in place over this period served the subsequent Bretton Woods period with its sustained economic growth, what Krugman calls the 'magic economy' (Krugman, 1994: 3). However, as the 1970s wore on it was clear that the political economy, social-institutional forms and politics of the USA were changing. A series of problems was addressed within the context of overall relative decline and the upshot was the rise of the New Right whom Krieger (1986) suggests pursued a policy of disregarding reality in favour of posturing.

THE DECLINING IMPORTANCE OF SOCIAL CLASS   Over the 1970s, as the economy prospered and then drifted, the old patterns of economy, society and class changed. As industries established in the earlier parts of the century declined or closed (creating the 'rust belt') there was a complex shift of population and industry. The elements of these shifts included a movement of population from the old city centres to the suburbs, with the suburbs prosperous in comparison with declining poor inner-city areas. At the same time there was a geographical movement from the older established areas of the north and the east to the growing ones of the south and west. The upshot of these changes is that settled industrial populations have been disturbed in favour of newer and less settled patterns of life. The old patterns of class became less important, as did older patterns of religion and ethnicity; however, in these changes the situation of black America continued to divide the population. As class declined the old machine politics went, and over time the Democrats' New Deal coalition went. The broad affluence of the system underscored the preference for the material lodged in received culture and a pervasive consumerist materialism was established. An optimistic theory of postmodernism celebrated a consumer lifestyle, but social and economic problems remained and got worse (the 1980s saw the coining of the expression 'macjobs') but American ideology and the New Right disposition militated against state action.

THE RISE OF SINGLE-ISSUE AND POPULIST POLITICS The class-based democratic New Deal coalition declined in line with the large shifts in the social and economic structure of the USA. In the late 1970s the New Right moved into power, yet the new Republican coalition built around Reagan seemed impermanent. The socio-economic structure of the country was more fluid; at the level of the machinery of the federal state Reagan controlled the White House but the Senate and House of Representatives more often than not were controlled by the Democrats. In this situation McKay (1994) argues that a new politics emerged in the form of single-issue programmes and populist mobilization against the centre.

McKay (1994: 36) points out that populism is compatible with received American ideology with its individualist preference for the ordinary man and a related distrust of intellectual/political élites. A series of examples could be cited, including tax revolts, distrust of government and suspicion of corporations, and in 1992 Ross Perot emerged as a political-cultural force. The tradition of populist mobilization has always been strongest in the south and west, precisely the newly prosperous areas of the USA. One strong theme of post-1970s political discourse has been the strong suspicion of the federal state, and a turning away to individual or group-level solutions to political problems.

The patterns of socio-economic change which occurred over the 1970s have led to a pervasive cultural fragmentation. It seems to be the case that acknowledgement of the common concerns of those sharing particular social categories has replaced class-based affiliations as the basis of political actions. It would seem that people are mobilizing along lines of age, sex, race and so on. In particular, the race issue, which has been a continuing theme of US politics in the modern period, and most particularly since the civil rights movement of the 1960s, became polarized in a more complex way as middle-class blacks were joined by new and successful immigrant groups, while at the same time a largely black underclass formed in the declining cities. All these changes underpin the rise of lifestyle politics concerned with consumption and explicit single issues (environment, tax, abortion, prayer, ethnicity, the deficit and so on).

SOCIAL FRAGMENTATION AND CONFLICT   Overall, in economics the USA experienced a relative decline in the 1970s as Japan and Europe recovered from war-time disruptions. In international debates there were new concerns with learning from Japan and sharing the military burden with the Europeans. And in the social-institutional sphere the period saw the beginnings of a reaction to the influence of the 1960s civil rights movement, the debates around the Vietnam War and the influence of the counter-culture as politically retreating social liberals were pursued by disingenuous right-wing critics denouncing an alleged preoccupation with 'political correctness' in respect of the sensibilities of ethnic and other minority groups (Hughes, 1993). In general, in the cultural and media realm the sphere of expressive consumption grew and slowly modulated into a self-referring realm celebrated as postmodern culture.

THE POLITICS OF DECLINE   Krieger (1986) places the political-cultural changes of the period into a broader context and argues that the Reagan presidency was a particular reaction to relative economic decline. The crucial context of decline was the falling away of economic predominance, a slippage which was then accelerated by domestic decisions and thereafter necessitated a strategy of decline management. In the case of the USA Krieger notes the slow relative economic decline of the post-Second World War advantage of the USA as Europe and Japan recovered. Domestic decisions centred on government spending. Krieger notes that the 'policy package of international liberalism inaugurated at Bretton Woods and mild Keynesian welfarism at home was jeopardized by the budgetary excesses of the Vietnam war' (1986: 12). A little later the oil shocks of the early 1970s presented problems which the Carter administration was unable to deal with and the post-war package collapsed. The response was the market-centred project of the New Right whose success required both the destruction of extant social coalitions and a strong centralized state direction. The New Right in the USA over the 1980s confronted decline with systematic denial and the pursuit of market-based economics conjoined with conservative social policies which have generated social division and accumulated large debt burdens.

The particularity of the ideology of the USA

On the ideology of the USA, it is clear that it is quite particular. McKay (1994) argues that if we distinguish between political culture (the pluralist line which sees ideas pervading society and informing state/ government) and dominant ideology (the Marxist line which sees an élite disseminating ideas to serve its interests) then neither seems all that appropriate, because the USA has no visible ruling élite and yet does have a coherent set of ideas (which act in effect to maintain a status quo which disadvantages many, thus a poor welfare system and recent economic insecurity).

The notion of hegemony has been deployed, McKay notes, to try to grasp what is going on, and it has been suggested that there is a pervasive ideology of Americanism, the supposition that the USA is an exception to the general rule among industrial societies in being uniquely modern, advanced and free of the ideological problems of other similar areas. The ideology of Americanism has four elements; in the first place, the commitment to equality of esteem and opportunity but not of result. There is a deep aversion to privilege and deference. All the objective inequalities of class are there, but they are not recognized as such and instead a myth of opportunity and the possibility of self-advance is affirmed. Then second, a commitment to the ethic of economic individualism, so that success is taken to flow from individual effort and failure is taken to flow from a lack of such effort. Again, we have the myth of opportunity. State provision is poor, and the idea of collective responsibility for a person's success and failure is absent. In fact state equates with government and this is seen as a rule-bound arena for sorting out interests, not the vehicle of common concerns. The third element involves a commitment to liberty. The US is celebrated as an open society, but liberties are read as natural rather than the outcome of political creeds and institutions, and again the ideology slides towards a myth which collapses US and liberty, so there is no space for criticism, and opponents are seen as necessarily anti-American or un-American. And the final element is a commitment to democracy, where there are many elective offices, many elections, and democracy is seen as evidenced in majoritarian elections. It is a narrow liberal notion rather than the substantive ethic of European social philosophy. McKay makes the final point that the belief in the USA as a model of liberty and an example for others is deeply held.

With McKay we can record the changing nature of American exceptionalism. In the pre-war period US exceptionalism was moralistic and isolationist, but after the war the USA presented itself as the model for others to copy. The position found general expression in modernization theory (Preston, 1982, 1996). However, this version of American ideology lasted only a few years because it collapsed in the confusions of the war in Vietnam and the failures of the domestic campaigns against racism and poverty. The optimistic celebration of the position of the USA was revived by Reagan but in the late 1980s this too began to fade as US economic performance began to slide and relative decline (economic, trade, diplomatic) became obvious. And when the USSR dissolved, Reaganite exceptionalism was left without its key negative defining object. The result has been the sense of fragmentation discussed earlier. In all, it has become more difficult to get the state working in the USA just at the time when it is most needed to face problems of decline. McKay (1994) argues that the details of the weak state and fractious society-based politics reinforce the overall conclusion: a stronger state is needed but is not in prospect and further drift might be expected.

The idea of postmodernism read as an ideological exercise in active and creative forgetting

Woodiwiss (1993) discusses the rise of social modernism, a dispersed economic and social reformist interventionism presented as the epitome of the modern and the American (Fordism and the Bretton Woods system), from the 1930s until the 1960s when it finally failed to deliver on its promises and underwent a process of active forgetting (with the symbolic collapse being conventionally identified as 1971) such that the discarded elements of the project were available to be reworked as postmodernism. In this judgement Woodiwiss recalls Callinicos (1989) who argues that postmodernism should be seen as the disappointed consciousness of Left intellectuals turned yuppies. And in this judgement Woodiwiss also presents postmodernism as the third response to the collapse of the post-Second World War settlement, the others being Habermasian democracy and New Right marketism (in other words, postmodernism is not the same as New Rightism). The political-cultural package of postmodernism is not the dawning of a new epoch but the period after the collapse of optimism in the USA. The whole process of the invention of an optimistic social modernism, its collapse and subsequent forgetting in postmodernism is particular to the USA. In Europe and Japan this sequence was never run through and optimism in respect of industrial capitalism and possible alternative futures continues to animate public political discourse.

The New Deal is treated by Woodiwiss as the formal political initiative around which a whole spread of new ideas and associated social and economic groups coalesced, as a new discourse was established, which was committed to growth and welfare, but in an American fashion with the individual stressed and the collective aspect suppressed as much as possible. In the 1950s there was a period of great prosperity which was, however, not channelled by any European-style social democracy, but which simply allowed market-based success for some, less success for others and no success for some neglected ethnic groups; in all, success plus increasing market-based social division. The growth of the economy and the affirmation of social modernism led to increasing state intervention. In the Kennedy years social modernism was relatively successful but never directly acknow- ledged; therefore it could not be sustained, it was always somehow a partial commitment.

The growth of the economy came increasingly to rely on the state with military Keynesianism, and the class compromise enshrined in social modernism slowly began to fall apart. It never lived up to its promises and its supporters and addressees became its critics. The narrow focus of the dissidents – unions, students, women and blacks – on the particular failures of social modernism did not address funda- mentals (that is, the nature of American industrial capitalism) and they both helped to undermine social modernism and encouraged the rise of an equally futile New Right. The economic, social and political dislocations occasioned by the Vietnam War are also implicated in the collapse, as are the problems of the war on social want (maximally expressed in the Great Society programme); the upshot was that in the 1970s capital slowly reasserted itself while the critical discourse of social modernism collapsed.

In this context, the intellectual turn to postmodernism is read by Woodiwiss as an active forgetting of social modernism. The continuing problems of the US polity are noted because the New Right are as useless as the discarded residues of social modernism which are recycled as postmodernism. The USA faces a continuing crisis of self- understanding and thereafter societal direction. In sum, Woodiwiss argues that the putative theory of the new epoch, postmodernism, is the specifically US response to the specifically US failure of the specifically US version of interventionist modernity, that is, social modernism. As such it represents a particular pathology. It does not hold for Europe or Japan. Woodiwiss argues that a necessary condition of its supersession within the USA is that it first be acknowledged as pathological.

The period in retrospect

The period of US hegemony within the West ran from 1945 until the 1970s, when the pressures of financing war production led to the slow collapse of the Bretton Woods system and ushered in the New Right. The active celebration of the sovereign remedy of the marketplace has been particular to the USA (and one or two other Western countries, in particular, the UK). It has not been a general movement. The slowly emerging distinctions within the global system were thereby encour- aged. In the wake of the collapse of bipolarity, the USA found that the model of industrial capitalism it favoured and which it had assidu- ously fostered over its hegemonic period was not the sole model available and that henceforth the USA would have to deal with the social-welfare variant of industrial capitalism in Europe and the developmental industrial capitalism of Pacific Asia.

The impact of the end of the short twentieth century on the USA

In respect of the collapse of the received post-Second World War certainties which have shaped the political-cultural identities of the people of the USA at the more general level of public discourse, we can point to two streams of ideas including the ideology of Americanism and the sets of ideas associated with the assumption by the US of a global role in the years following the Second World War, the spread of ideas and institutions which comprised the construct of the free world. The two lines reveal internal patterns of decay which run together in the recently fashionable doctrines of postmodernism.

The ideology of Americanism

The ideology of Americanism has been widely discussed. It comprises a set of intellectual/ethical commitments – equality, individualism, liberty, democracy – which both celebrate the pattern of life of Americans as essentially/uniquely satisfactory and present this pattern of life as a model for others to emulate. Inside the USA these ideas/ethics both find expression – for example, in the widespread preference for individual effort and the disinclination to organize state provisions – and routine refutation in the actual practices of an inegalitarian capitalist society which has perforce a strong state machinery. In terms of the styles of reasoning found within the classical European tradition of social theorizing, the ideas/ethics which comprise Americanism are uncritical. If the arrangements of the US polity are in essentials satisfactory then fundamental criticism is not needed and only restricted particular problems can be dealt with. It has been argued by commentators that this fundamentally uncritical ideology militates against the rational public discussion of the nature/problems of the US polity (Hawthorn, 1976).

Outside the USA the presentation of the form of life of the people of the US as a model for others to emulate has not been generally accepted. The economic, political and cultural influence of the USA in the post-Second World War period has been extensive but it has not overridden other cultures which have taken elements of the model and remade them as necessary (structural change and agent response). It can be argued that the uncritical presentation of the USA as a model has militated against more dialogic exchanges with other cultures. It has been argued that the post-Second World War expression of this American ideology took the form of the theory of modernization, presented both to the home population and to the rest of the world. It is also argued that the theory of modernization has clearly been seen to fail and that the experience of failure coupled to an essentially un-critical set of ideas has left Americans at some loss as to how to proceed. It has been argued that postmodernism is precisely an in-choate expression of this confusion. However, there has been one recent line of positive argument which relates to the end of the cold war, and we can come to this debate after first noting the business of the construction of 'the free world/West'.

The ideology of the free world

The central positive strands of the ideological construct of the free world can be taken to revolve around the system of open and regulated trade which found institutional expression in the Bretton Woods system. The system comprised a set of institutions – the IMF, the World Bank, GATT and the International Bank of Settlements – which, to-gether with the UN, provided the organizational vehicle for the US-sponsored reordering of the global industrial-capitalist system in the wake of the confusions of the preceding years of depression and war. The sets of ideas/ethics which found expression both in these institu-tions and in the debates within the public sphere revolved around a general commitment to the pursuit of growth and welfare.

In Europe and Japan these commitments found expression in either a social-democratic corporatist style or developmental polities. In both cases there was a deep-seated state-centred commitment to the rational ordering of economic, social and political development. In the USA the ideology of Americanism with its strong commitment to individualism read state provision and state intervention negatively; such inter-ventions were taken to be un-American and socialistic, and conse-quently the extent of post-Second World War self-consciously reformist economic and social reconstruction was more restricted and problem-atical in the USA than in Europe or Japan.

The central negative strands of the ideological construct of the free world revolved around the institutional and military opposition between the blocs of the West and the East. At the outset, in institu-tional terms the two spheres were separated. The USSR in the after-math of the war years was denied access to the Bretton Woods system except on terms which would have entailed dismantling its political economy (Flemming, 1961) and economic links were systematically discouraged, in particular, for high-tech equipment through COCOM. The competition in respect of economic and social order was extended in a proxy fashion through the newly politically independent territories of the old European and Japanese colonial empires. Against the offers of socialism proffered by the socialist bloc, the USA and its allies made the offer of modernization as a route to catching up and joining in with the free world. And in military terms there was a global network of treaties and alliances. Thereafter, in ethical/social theoretical terms the Western bloc was characterized in wholly positive terms (free economies, free polities, free speech, free choice, freedom in general) and the Eastern bloc was characterized in wholly negative terms (unfree planned economy, unfree state-dominated polity, unfree speech dominated by state-policed restrictions, unfree choice specified by state bureaucrats from among the limited goods their unfree inefficient economy did manage to produce, and unfreedom in general). Overall, the whole construct comprising institutions, military and ideology was summarized under the label of the free world and the USA was taken to be its exemplary core.

Against the claims of the ideology of the free world, there are two problems which are pointed to by commentators: first, the Bretton Woods system has declined in the years following Nixon's 1971 decision to float the dollar, and second, the bloc system has collapsed. As a consequence, the new situation of the USA comprises geo-strategic fluidity and a post-bloc dispersal of negative attention (there is no longer a useful convenient enemy to be 'the other' against which 'we' are defined). Add to this the influence of the fundamentally uncritical nature of the official ideology of Americanism and there is a recipe for unclearness of direction, a loss of political-cultural clarity as regards what it is to be, in the general realm of the public sphere, an American.

The inevitable decline of great powers, the clash of civilizations and the end of history

The present situation of unclearness has seen some partial replies. In this period of confusion it is not easy to identify crucial areas in terms of particular debates/issues; rather, what we have is a series of symptoms of underlying unease. The focus of the unease shifts but as yet it is difficult to uncover any broad resolution of these matters. It may be, of course, that in the wake of the collapse of the Manichean simplicities of the bipolar period that the new tripolar world, with all its complexities, is offering commentators an unusual occasion for restricted engagement with problems and issues which admit of no easy resolution. In other words, the unease may be merely an artefact of the removal of the previous spurious confidence.

In the late 1980s the historian Paul Kennedy (1988) caused consternation by arguing that powerful empires have their own rhythms and that, as they rise, so inevitably they decline. Kennedy added that the USA looked as though its power was on the wane. A long period of decline was implied as the economic situation of the USA *vis-à-vis* other powers, in particular Asia, altered in line with long-term trends. A related subsidiary debate could be pointed to in terms of the proliferation of literature concerned to learn the economic/managerial lessons of the Japanese experience (Vogel, 1980; Eccleston, 1989). It might be noted that this literature had a more conservative aspect in that some commentators were concerned with removing the unfair competition of the Japanese and other East Asians via programmes of liberalization (Eccleston, 1989). A stronger version of the conservative line suggested not that the USA needed to react against the East Asians but that these economies were either converging on the model of the USA (*The Economist*, 1994) or were exemplifying precisely those fundamental economic logics which animated the US system (World Bank, 1993).

The political scientist Samuel Huntington entered the debate in an apocalyptic fashion with the proposal that the future would see a clash between West and East (Huntington, 1993). However, the ideology of Americanism recently found a restatement in the work of Fukuyama (1992) who argued Hegelian-style that the tenets of liberal democracy represented the social-philosophical end-point of the historical development of ideas/institutions within the West in respect of the matter of ordering political communities. Again, the USA was the model and again there was no intellectual space from which to make critical commentaries on the situation of the USA.

In sum, in the wake of the collapse of the post-Second World War settlement the general public sphere of the USA is beset with confusion.

The USA in the tripolar global system

The exposure of the USA to the flows of power within the global system is now significantly higher than at earlier periods in the country's history. The USA is now the core economy of one of the three regions within the world industrial-capitalist system. And trade relationships with Japan and the European Union are now important issues – witness the conflicts with both in the period of the World Trade Organization negotiations and witness the continuing debates with Japan which have been extensively discussed in the USA (Thurow, 1994). Within the Americas there is a new drive for economic cooperation – NAFTA is symptomatic – as the new politics of geo-economics comes to be a central concern of élites.

In terms of the ethnographic/biographical notion of political-cultural identity which was canvassed in the earlier chapters of this text, it is clear that the patterns of change within the global system will impact on the thinking/practices of ordinary Americans. The end of bipolarity and the new concern for economic relationships, which are already a concern for élites, will slowly come to effect local-level action. One symptom may be the turning inwards which commentators have read as an aspect of the attractiveness to the electorate of the Republicans. Another symptom may be the spreading impact for many blue- and white-collar workers of the relative decline of the US economy. The familiar American preoccupations with individualism, material progress and race coupled to the new spread of single-issue concerns will continue to feed into the learning/acting of individual political agents, but they will do so within the increasingly salient enfolding structures of the changing global system.

Conclusion: changing identities in the USA

At the present time the USA is in slow relative decline within the global industrial-capitalist system as its overwhelming post-Second World War economic strength expressed in the Bretton Woods settlement is reduced. As structural circumstances shift, the ways in which agent groups read and react takes on new forms. Inside the USA regional changes have been extensive, with population movements from north to south and from east to west. The public politics of the USA has moved away from the post-war preference for state intervention in pursuit of a unified community and towards the single issues identified piecemeal by a socially and economically fragmented population.

In respect of the political-cultural identities of the people of the USA, at the general level of public discourse we can point to the ideology of Americanism, which we can take to be a product of the economy and society of the late nineteenth century (Anderson, 1983) and the sets of ideas associated with the assumption by the USA of a global role in the years following the Second World War (Kolko, 1968; Aron, 1973). These materials underpin the subsequent confusion of the suggestions of the inevitability of the decline of great powers (Kennedy, 1988) and the recent claims of an end to history (Fukuyama, 1992). At the present time the citizens of the USA must confront an unexpected tripolarity within the global system. The end of the short twentieth century has seen the USA continuing to press for an open global trading system; the influence of the Washington-based IMF and World Bank has been extensive, and recent expressions of these concerns have been the establishment of NAFTA and APEC.

8

Changing Political-Cultural Identities in Pacific Asia

The post-Second World War period has seen the dissolution of the European, American and Japanese empires in Asia, the rise in influence of China and the spectacular recent economic success of Japan. In the late 1980s and early 1990s it was argued that Pacific Asia had become a coherent and distinctive region within the global industrial-capitalist system. The arguments in respect of the nature of Pacific Asian industrial capitalism were given added interest in the wake of the collapse of bipolarity, which had arguably acted to conceal the success of the Pacific Asian region. In this chapter we will consider the ways in which the territories of Pacific Asia entered the modern world and assumed their present and changing forms. The crucial territory in the overall tale of the region's shift to the modern world and subsequent partial integration as Pacific Asia has been Japan.

Pacific Asia: routes to the modern world

The modern history of Pacific Asia, encompassing North-east Asia, China, Indo-China and South-east Asia (Shibusawa et al., 1992), centres on the nature of the region's shift to the modern world. In schematic terms this can be taken to include in turn, first, the pre-contact period and the process of absorption within the Western colonial system; second, the post-colonial pursuit of effective nation-statehood; and finally the rise of Pacific Asia centred on Japan. It is the complex pattern of exchanges between Japan and its Asian neighbours, on the one hand, and the region and the global system, on the other, with Japan as the key country, which has shaped the modern history of Pacific Asia.

The shift to the modern world to 1945

Worsley (1984) argues that the modern world can be understood as a particular cultural form. It is a way of organizing the relationship of people to nature and to other people. The inhabitants of modern societies construe their lives and societies in material and individual terms. The cultural form of modernity originated in Europe and has slowly spread to cover much of the world. In this long-drawn-out and continuing process existing local cultures have been slowly drawn into the modern system and their patterns of life variously altered. It can be described as a process of absorption and reconstruction as existing cultural resources are more or less radically remade in line with the expectations and demands of modernity (Sachs, 1992). The cultural form of modernity comprises the general celebration of the power of human reason, the extensive development of natural science and an economic system dedicated to material progress via science-based industry. This cultural form developed in Europe over the period 1500–1900, and in this time it both refined itself internally, that is, it became better organized and penetrated through the social world, and expanded externally, that is, it grew geographically. In this context, the broad period of pre-1945 Pacific Asian history can be encompassed in a series of points: first, the pre-contact forms of life of the peoples, that is, patterns of livelihood, government, social organization and belief; second, the process of the irruption into the region of the capitalist West, with traders, missionaries and empire-builders; and third, the colonial period.

The general characteristics of the pre-contact forms of life of the peoples of Pacific Asia can be seen to have taken two broad forms. On the one hand, the East Asian sphere was typified by the closed, bureaucratic, feudal, agrarian society of imperial China, with a similar society in Japan. And on the other hand, the South-east Asian sphere was typified by the riverine agrarian empires of Indo-China and the maritime trading empires of South-east Asia. It should also be noted that Asia's third major cultural area, South Asia, centred on India, has exerted considerable influence on the other two areas (with, for example, Islam, Hinduism and Buddhism) (Evans, 1993: 9). It was this spread of long-established civilizations and the simpler peasant forms of life lodged within their bounds which the carriers of the expanding global capitalist system encountered in the sixteenth century (Grimal, 1978).

The expansion of European- and American-based capitalism moved through a series of phases: first, the early trade journeys involving very few traders and specializing in exotic luxury goods; second, the later linkages involving relatively settled factories whereby the trade in luxury products was regularized, albeit still at a very low level of numbers of traders and quantities of goods; third, the shift towards much more extensive trade links as the competing incomers looked to establish exclusive spheres; fourth, the shift towards colonial holdings; and finally, the establishment of colonial holdings alongside the new schedule of demands made upon the resources and peoples of the region by industrial capitalism. In the case of Pacific Asia, the European traders had little impact on existing societies in the early years of contact. In the mid-sixteenth century, when these traders first arrived, they did so in small numbers and with trade expectations confined to small quantities of exotic and luxury products. This pattern of exchange persisted and slowly expanded through the seventeenth and eighteenth centuries. It was in the nineteenth century that the depth of the involvement of the Europeans and Americans in the territories of Pacific Asia deepened significantly when, as a result of the dynamics of metropolitan industrial capitalism, the schedule of demands for trade goods in the region expanded and at the same time the rapidly increasing technological superiority of the West in respect of the ruling regimes of the region allowed them to insist that their requirements be acknowledged. The upshot was a slow but steady movement to take control of areas within the region in order to facilitate their integration within the industrial-capitalist system. The final stage of this process involved the imposition of formal colonial regimes on large parts of the region, the quasi-colonization of China and the effective resistance of Japan. In the twentieth century it was against the empire systems that the nationalists of the colonized territories were to organize their resistance as the political-cultural resources of the colonizers were turned back against themselves (Barraclough, 1964; Anderson, 1983).

Japan's route to the modern world

The nature of the shift to the modern world effected by Japan was conditioned by two sets of anxieties on the part of the Japanese political élite: the first concerned their relationship with the technologically superior Western powers, whose concerns for trade and colonial expansion represented direct threats to Japanese autonomy; and a related anxiety concerned their relationship with the countries of East Asia, whose weakness in the face of Western expansion represented a broad threat to Japanese interests. The Japanese ruling Tokugawa shogunate was unable to formulate a response to these twin problems and it was overthrown.

In Japan the 1868 Meiji Restoration saw political power shift from the controlling family within a land-centred economy and polity which resembled the European feudal system to an oligarchic developmental state, and a creative strategy of authoritarian modernization from above was inaugurated. The Meiji state proceeded to borrow from the model of the developed West and in a relatively short period restructured the Japanese economy. However, social and political change was controlled and changes in received cultural ideas and patterns of authority were held to a minimum. The episode constituted an authoritarian modernization from above (Moore, 1966). It is true to say that the links of Japan and Pacific Asia in the late nineteenth and early twentieth centuries may be taken as being shaped by the experience of the Japanese in regard to their own shift to the modern world.

In the late nineteenth and early twentieth centuries the economic development of Japan was very rapid. A key aspect of this ordered and rapid renewal was a deep anxiety in respect of the possible further intrusive demands of the West. The authoritarian modernization from above was undertaken within the context of this real anxiety and, as success was achieved, it found expression in imperialist terms taken from the West. The Japanese saw a legitimate sphere of interest in North-east Asia, within which they could remedy some of the resource-poor aspects of their domestic economy. At this period the European powers and the USA were extensively involved in China and the whole territory was regarded as a trade resource open to exploitation.

There was early Japanese activity in the area of the Russian Far East, in the Korean peninsula and in China. All these areas were geographically contiguous with Japan and thus, given contemporary notions of empire and interstate relations, obvious places for the expansion of Japanese interests. The process involved two significant wars. The first, the Sino-Japanese War of 1894–5, lasted nine months, in which time the Japanese armed forces expelled the Chinese from Korea and captured Port Arthur and the Liaotung peninsula. In the peace treaty Taiwan was in addition ceded to Japan. However, the triple intervention by Russia, France and Germany obliged the Japanese to withdraw from Liaotung and Port Arthur (Watts, 1993). As the Europeans and Americans had at that time very extensive colonial holdings, this generated resentment within Japanese ruling circles and helped foster a reactionary conservative nationalism (Dale, 1986). Thereafter, the second episode of hostilities, the Russo-Japanese War of 1904–5, saw success for the Japanese who gained influence in Manchuria and Korea, which was made a protectorate in 1905 and formally annexed in 1910. In general, all this seems to have attracted the passive sympathy of the Europeans (and, in regard to the naval victory over the Russian navy, a strong measure of approval from Asians (Barraclough, 1964)). However, when Japan began to make demands on China a few years later, in 1915, Western sympathy rather tended to fade away. It is argued that this early rebuff by the Western powers to Japanese borrowings of the notion of empire had the effect of encouraging an aggressive Japanese nationalism which subsequently modulated into the fascism of the inter-war period.

In the 1930s the Imperial Japanese Army had become the dominant force in Japanese politics (Beasley, 1990). The army staged an incident at Mukden on 18 September 1931 and began the seizure of Manchuria. In 1932 Tokyo officially recognized Manchukuo and in 1934 Henry Pu-yi was made emperor. The incident at the Marco Polo bridge outside Peking in 1937 led to a general war with China. However, it would seem that the various elements of the Japanese military were never entirely clear about their war aims and with whom they might deal at the local level, and the upshot was a long-drawn-out conflict. It turned out to be fatal to Japanese military expansion, as it was involvement in China which drew the criticism of the USA and Europeans, and in due course led to the Pacific War (Ienaga, 1978; Thorne, 1985).

China's route to the modern world

The slow decline of the Qing dynasty as a result of internal decay and European and American incursions accelerated over the second half of the nineteenth century in the wake of the Opium Wars of 1840–2 and the resultant treaty-port system, which acknowledged and firmly established the European and American trading presence. Inside the Chinese ruling class there was considerable debate about the appropriate strategy of response to these incursions. The established Chinese world-view placed the Imperial Court at the centre and ranged all others in circles of descending importance around this core. The culture was inward-looking and disinclined to begin the business of learning from outsiders. However, the military defeats of the Opium Wars and the routine evidence of European and American commercial vigour did encourage the pursuit of modernization by some groups within China, but they received no support from the imperial centre, indeed they were discouraged, and overall, reports Moise (1994), there was little real grasp of the extent of changes required within China if the country were to respond positively to the arrival and demands of the Europeans and Americans.

In 1899 the Boxer Rebellion, which had the tacit support of the Empress, began to attack foreigners and laid siege to the foreign legations in Beijing. The rebellion was quickly suppressed by a combined expedition of Europeans, Americans and Japanese forces. It was in the wake of the failed rebellion that the Qing dynasty finally began a serious programme of modernization. The structures of administration were reformed and constitutional reform was begun. In 1909 provincial assemblies were elected and in 1910 a National Assembly was convened, half elected and half appointed by the imperial court. There were reforms to the military and to systems of education. And there were also attempts to renegotiate the terms of the treaty ports and tariff systems in order to reassert Chinese control. Moore comments 'The pattern of her [the Dowager Empress's] actions strongly suggests that her real goal was the establishment of a strong centralized bureaucratic government over which she would be able to exercise direct personal control, roughly along the lines of a Germany or a Japan' (1966: 184).

However, in 1911 the Qing dynasty central government experienced one more crisis (over railway construction) and there was a widespread revolt among provincial gentry; two-thirds of the country quickly fell into the hands of Sun Yat Sen's revolutionaries, who declared him President in the provincial city of Nanjing. However, the Qing authorities asked the regional army commander, General Yuan, to suppress the rebels and in the ensuing confusion both the dynasty and the newly established republic gave way, first to the brief rule of General Yuan and subsequently a series of regional warlords. Thereafter, up until

1937, there was a battle for power between the Koumintang (KMT), Sun's nationalist party, led since 1925 by Chiang Kai-shek, the Communist Party of China (CCP), which had been founded in 1921, and the still powerful regional warlords. Chiang Kai-shek slowly broadened his power and established a unified Chinese state with a military government in Nanjing in 1927. Moore (1966: 188–201) regards the KMT government with its landlordism, gangsterism, opportunistic commercial factions, backward-looking nationalism and militarism as a variant of the familiar European model of fascism. Further, the effective collapse of central authority in China, and the political and social chaos which followed, left the country open to the demands of foreign powers. The Western colonial powers expanded the spheres of influence they had established in the late nineteenth century, and the Japanese became involved, with open warfare raging from 1937.

Moore (1966), reflecting on the shift to the modern world undertaken by China, argues that the Qing dynasty was incapable of formulating a response to the incursion of the West. The Qing dynasty system comprised five key groupings: the central authorities, who dispensed laws of property, but whose power was relatively weak; the crucially powerful scholar-bureaucrats who administered the regions of the country; the powerful local gentry who were important landowners; the peasantry, who had little scope for independent action but whose work carried the system; and the merchant groups whose activities were not encouraged but which were becoming more important within the overall economy.

The scholar-bureaucrats administered the dynastic system of law, tax gathering and public works. They were recruited by merit in examination but their activities overlapped with the family- and clan-based networks of the landowning gentry. The country was very large and central control was always relatively weak so that local scholar-bureaucrats could establish mutually beneficial relationships with local powerful landowners. The system was designed to extract resources from the peasantry. Finally, the merchant, manufacturing and trading groups were not directly involved in this political-economic system. They existed, so to say, off to one side. The scholar-bureaucrats acted to keep them in check and they did not establish themselves as an independent socio-economic grouping (as had been the case in Europe). However, the equilibrium of the system was fatally disturbed by the arrival of Western traders and the hitherto weak Chinese traders now had access to powerful trading partners. After the Opium Wars of 1842 the Chinese merchant groups began to prosper, in particular along the coasts where they traded as *compradores* with the Europeans and Americans.

Moore argues that the initial reaction of the dynastic centre to the incursions of the West was wholly inappropriate to the threat which they posed. There was no effective centrally sponsored attempt to modernize. In the early years of the twentieth century the dynastic centre did attempt to establish the institutional machineries of a developmental state, but Moore notes that there was no social group available to support such mobilization, 'the social basis for such a regime was lacking in China' (1966: 184). The dynasty was unable to read and react to the developing demands of the global system in the nineteenth century and slowly it decayed until the regime collapsed in 1911 and thereafter drifted into the chaos of warlordism, civil war and world war.

The post-colonial pursuit of effective nation-statehood

Overall, in this process of industrial-capitalist expansion, the demands made by the system deepened, and the territories were slowly remade in line with the schedule of needs of the metropolitan centres. The upshot was the pre-1941 situation of colonial Asia, where the Dutch and British controlled South-east Asia, the French ruled in Indo-China, the Americans occupied the Philippines, the Japanese occupied Korea and Taiwan, and all these powers competed for advantage in China. At this point the entire sphere of Pacific Asia had been drawn one way or another into the Western-centred industrial-capitalist system. Thereafter, the Pacific War altered the situation irrevocably as the confusions of war-time swept away the colonial systems.

The episode of decolonization in the post-Second World War period saw the withdrawal of foreign powers and the beginnings of a process of recovery of indigenous balance in the countries of the region. Three broad aspects of this complex process can be noted: first, the dissolution of the European and American empires; second, the revolution in China; and finally, the involvement of the USA in anti-communist alliances in the region.

The military victories of the Japanese armed forces in 1941-2 destroyed the European and American colonial power structure and through the chaos of the period laid the basis for post-war independence throughout the region. The disruption of familiar economic, social and political patterns left a space open for indigenous nationalist movements. The post-war formal withdrawal of the colonial powers was accomplished relatively quickly, although in many cases it was attended by violence, with the encouragement of the newly dominant USA.

One significant aspect of the post-war situation was the victory of the Chinese communists in 1949 and the consequent pursuit by the USA of a policy of containment in Asia. The USA sought allies among the countries of the region, and the US presence, plus their spending on the military, were significant in the maintenance for many years of a divided region, the recovery and subsequent development of the

Western-oriented parts of the region and the (re)emergence of Japan as the most influential regional economy.

The rise of Pacific Asia

The post-Second World War period has seen the rise to regional pre-eminence of Japan and this process could be elucidated around a series of key issues: first, the Meiji Restoration and the particular nature of the modernization of Japan (Moore, 1966); then second, the routine and deep-seated Japanese concern for East Asia (Rix, 1993); third, the inter-war period of fascism and expansionism (Beasley, 1990); and finally, the post-war phase of reconstruction and the establishment of the regional core economy (Cronin, 1992). Overall, it is clear that Pacific Asia now constitutes the third major political-economic grouping within the developing global system. This observation raises a series of issues which centre upon the nature of regionalism within the global system, the linkages within Pacific Asia and the implications of the rise of the region for the USA and Europe.

The relationship of the Japanese economy to Pacific Asia

The Japanese empire did not survive the war-time exchange with the USA and its allies; however, the occupation of Japan by the USA was distinctly idealistic, somewhat right-wing, arguably inept and relatively benign (Buckley, 1990). The occupation powers made relatively limited changes to the political-economic, social-institutional and cultural structures of Japan, and the rehabilitation and rapid reconstruction of the country began with the outbreak of the Korean War in 1950 and the US drive against world communism. Thereafter the general business of reordering the global system around its new US centre, with decolonization, the establishment of the Bretton Woods settlement, the related founding of the UN and the pervasively deployed US conservative ideology of anti-communism, gave the Japanese a framework within which they could rebuild the economy and, along with this, their links to Pacific Asia.

It seems fairly clear that the episode of post-war reconstruction involved a great measure of continuity with pre-war patterns of economy and society (Johnson, 1982; van Wolferen, 1989). More broadly, because the history of Japanese involvement with Pacific Asia is longer and deeper than the wars of the twentieth century, an available theme within Japanese commentaries characterizing the relationship generates the view that the unique and gifted Japanese are able to lead the rest of Pacific Asia in development (Rix, 1993). It seems that this is a major source of thinking in regard to Pacific Asia and development aid, thus it is seen as a matter of responsibility and duty, and the actual narrowly pragmatic nature of the links is glossed over

(Orr, 1990); none the less, the ideas are available and help underpin the role of core regional economy.

The question of the relationship of the Japanese economy to economies of Pacific Asia remains crucial and it has often been answered by non-Japanese commentators in a fashion which implies the existence of an ordered grouping. These social theorists have spoken of the Japanese core being surrounded by an inner periphery (the NICs) and an outer periphery (ASEAN), to which a new circle has recently been added in the guise of a reforming socialist block (Nester, 1990; Phongpaichit, 1990; Cronin, 1992). It is clear that the history of modern Pacific Asia can be told in terms of the series of exchanges between Japan and the territories of Pacific Asia on the one hand and the exchanges of the region with the Western-dominated global system on the other.

The anxieties of the USA and the European Union

Within the USA and the European Union some concern is voiced in respect of the evolution of the global capitalist system; in particular, it is argued that the world economy should not be left to fragment into three regions. Yet it does seem that there is increasing pressure towards such an arrangement. The debate has been sharpened in the wake of the ending of the cold war. In this context the significance of the cold war was multiple: first, it provided a broad set of themes which ordered interstate exchanges both within and between the blocs; second, it provided the overarching rationale for a split within the Pacific Asian sphere as between the 'free world' and the 'socialist world'; third, it provided a general framework for Japanese and American relationships, such that the Japanese adherence to the tenets of the Western bloc overrode any problems with economic exchanges; and finally, it provided the occasion for US strategic activity which offered opportunities for economic growth to the countries of the region, in particular in East Asia. It is clear that with the end of the cold war the nature of the relationships between the various countries of Pacific Asia and their relationships with the USA are in question for the first time in nearly fifty years. However, these issues are now raised in a radically different situation. In place of a spread of war-ravaged economies and polities we have a series of economically prosperous countries. In other words, where the immediate post-Second World War period of confusion and disorder saw the unchallenged establishment of the economic, military and political hegemony of the USA, with socialist Asia locking itself away within an inward-looking grouping, the present period of change involves a group of much more equal players.

One way in which change has manifested itself is in a concern for ordering the interstate relationships of the Pacific Rim countries. There has been a series of new organizations founded or old organizations revivified or redirected. In contemporary discussions of the development of the Pacific region new acronyms abound – APEC, AFTA, EAEC and so on. It would seem that this concern for semi-formal groupings in the post-cold-war phase has been prompted by the success of the project of the European Union. However, these political manoeuvres are responses to fundamental changes within the global economy, which in the wake of the end of the cold war are having to be addressed directly. In brief, there has been both a measure of globalization in production and exchange (although consumption is still skewed towards the DCs), and a drift towards regionalization.

The contemporary global system is sustained and ordered through a number of institutions and novel technologies: first, formal intra-governmental organizations such as the IMF, the World Bank and the WTO; second, the interstate system of treaties; third, the presence and activities of global economic organizations (TNCs) and practices (the twenty-four-hour financial markets); and fourth, the surprising capacities of new technologies (communications via many channels, some outside the control of state governments, thus satellite television or the Internet, and the related extensive human movement on the basis of long-haul airlines). At the same time the givens of geography and history, coupled to present economic and political imperatives, are pushing the global system towards a set of regional groupings (Thurow, 1994). In other words there are contradictory pressures within the global system, where on the one hand the exigencies of geography, history and culture point in the direction of the regionalization of the global system, while on the other there is a continuing concern to protect the concept of an open trading system.

Changing political-cultural identities in Pacific Asia

A central theme within the classical European tradition of social science is the analysis of complex change, and one aspect of this general concern is the matter of identity. The ways in which individuals and groups understand themselves is taken to be a matter of reading changing circumstances in the light of available ideas and present urgent problems. In the post-cold-war period, with the comfortable certainties of confrontation gone, and Japan ever more obviously the regional core economy, the issue of identity can be raised in the context of Pacific Asia. In particular, it can be asked whether the ideal of a Pacific Asia region, which would inevitably centre on Japan, could offer the disparate countries of the area an overarching theme around which more local identities could be ordered.

The Pacific Asian region over the post-Second World War period has been divided by cold-war institutions and rhetoric into a Western-focused group and a socialist bloc. The Western-focused group has been subject to the economic, political, and cultural hegemony of the

USA. The countries of the socialist bloc have spent decades following autarchic development trajectories. However, the Western-focused group in Pacific Asia is undergoing considerable change and, in brief, this may be summarized as the beginnings of a political-economic and cultural emancipation from the hegemony of the USA. At the same time the socialist bloc in Pacific Asia is undergoing rapid change. In the period since the early 1980s there have been economic, social, political and diplomatic changes. In total these may be summarized as an opening-up to the wider world of a capitalist system. We can look at these ongoing processes of change within Pacific Asia and consider how patterns of change within the region are linked to changes within countries. We can begin with the key exchange in the post-Second World War period, that of the Japanese and the Americans.

The central role of Japan in Pacific Asia

The Plaza Accord of 1985 which revalued the yen upwards against the US dollar had the unforeseen consequence of further accelerating the development of the Japanese presence in the countries of Pacific Asia as home industries were relocated to low-cost parts of the region. The region now displays a significant measure of internal integration and new questions have emerged in respect of the depth of such integration and the likelihood of the Japanese assuming an overt leadership role. In all, the deepening particularity of the Pacific Asian region within the tripolar global system is evident and now commands increasing scholarly and policy-analytic attention.

THE PERIOD OF US HEGEMONY IN JAPAN   The war in the Far East came to an end in late August 1945 and the Allied occupation forces arrived in September. The occupation was nominally an Allied matter but in fact was almost entirely an American affair. General Douglas MacArthur was made Supreme Commander for the Allied Powers (SCAP) and pursued an ambitious reform programme.

The Japanese military machine was dismantled. Installations and equipment were destroyed all over Japan and the armed forces were demobilized. Many soldiers from overseas were repatriated, as were civilians, as all Japan's territorial gains since the Meiji Restoration were removed. Thereafter, in the economic sphere, the power of the old urban and rural élites was broken. The industrial conglomerates which had enjoyed great power in pre-war Japan were broken up and new labour laws were introduced to allow trade unions. There was an important land reform and large agricultural holdings were broken up to create a rural small-farmer class. In the sphere of social institutions there was an important educational reform; a US pattern was introduced and the pre-war stress on nationalism removed. In society the 'continuing family' was abolished in 1947; a spread of general social

152 Political/cultural identity

rights were affirmed and the suffrage was broadened to include
women.

In the political sphere there were extensive reforms. There was an
extensive purge of the machineries of the state to remove potentially
anti-democratic forces. The emperor was left in place, having re-
nounced his divinity and embraced a Western-style notion of 'constitutional monarchy'. This was a matter of some debate at the time and
critics asked why the figure on whose behalf the Japanese had waged
their wars should be left in place. In the early occupation period the
existing political system was used and the bureaucracy came to have a
greater role than in pre-war days simply because its competitors were
no longer present (Johnson, 1982). A new constitution imposed by
SCAP, and brought into force in May 1947, established a US-style
system with extensive devolution of powers to regional prefectural
governments, while the central government machine was modelled
after the British system of a cabinet reporting to parliament. In 1952 a
peace treaty was signed and a part of this was a defence agreement
which made Japan a military protectorate of the USA.

The Japanese resisted quietly and all American-sponsored reforms
had to be put into practice through the agency of the Japanese
bureaucracy. Other than displacing the military, the depth of the
changes to Japanese political economy, society and polity accomplished
by SCAP have been the subject of much subsequent debate. The
political reforms, rural reforms and education reforms were all taken to
have had significant effects. However, the familiar criticism of SCAP is
that it did far too little. The perceived failure is considered to have
flowed from two factors: (a) an initial *naïveté* in the matter of making
reforms; and (b) a later desire to have Japan become an ally in the
American anti-communist crusade. The central directorate of SCAP
comprised a mixture of New Deal liberals and anti-communist conservatives; as time wore on the latter group came to have the greater
influence with the key figure of MacArthur. Buckley (1990) comments
that one key criticism of MacArthur is that he did far too little and that
the issue of reforming Japan quickly gave way to a preference for Japan
as an ally in the containment of communism. Overall, a series of
elements, which included the limited nature of the SCAP reforms, the
use of Japanese bureaucracy to effect reforms specified by SCAP, the
start of the cold war, the US/Japan defence agreement and active US
sympathy for the Japanese political Right, came together in order to
lodge in power in a conservative-dominated US-oriented Japanese
ruling group bringing together political, bureaucratic and business
interests.

In total, the reforms undertaken by SCAP were in retrospect arguably rather modest. At the time many of the reforms were viewed
unfavourably by the Japanese political élite, and aspects of SCAP rule –
such as the war-crimes trials were resented even at a popular level

(Tsurumi, 1987). None the less, the SCAP period brought a conservative business-dominated Japan firmly into the American sphere of interest. The relationship of the Japanese state with the USA is now the key foreign relations concern for the Japanese. At a popular level, the influence of America has been strong in the post-war period, in the media, in popular culture and in slowly changing patterns of behaviour attendant upon the development of an insistent consumerism.

THE LEGACIES OF JAPANESE EXPANSIONISM IN PACIFIC ASIA   The relationship of Japan and the countries of Pacific Asia is coloured by memories of Japanese colonial expansion and war. The historical legacy of Japanese colonialism in Pacific Asia is complex and involves a mixture of long-established rule, war-time violence, and some political and economic reforms. It took a different character in each of the various territories.

In the 'inner periphery' the legacy of colonialism is complex. In Korea the colonial episode saw harsh treatment of the indigenous population. It would seem that there is a legacy of bitterness down to the present day, and while it is initially difficult to see any positive legacy, it was the case that the colonial period saw a measure of industrialization (Beasley, 1990). However, at the present time pragmatism and geographical proximity underpin economic linkages (Koppel and Orr, 1993). In Taiwan the colonial episode was very broadly similar to that of Korea, but is perhaps recalled more positively, and the present linkages with Japan are extensive (Hamilton, 1983).

In the 'outer periphery' the story is rather different but no less complex. In the Dutch East Indies the early period of war and exertion of Japanese control gave way to a measure of cooperation. An army of indigenous people was formed, as was an organization of political representation led by Sukarno. In this sense the Japanese had a role to play in fostering an eventually successful nationalist movement (Jeffrey, 1981). And in Burma a similar situation held, with Aung San's army and political organization (Pandy, 1980). In a rather different way this organization modulated into the independence movement which in due course secured this goal. In Malaysia, where the Japanese encouraged Malay nationalism while treating the Chinese harshly (Watson-Andaya and Andaya, 1982), the Japanese interregnum has had a lasting impact in the form of communalist politics, which may in part be traced to the war-time period. And in Singapore the war-time episode was harsh and is remembered as such by the largely Chinese population (Turnbull, 1977); however, as with other areas of Pacific Asia, there is a pragmatic focus on economic cooperation. Finally, in the Philippines a similar pattern is visible in that the Filipino élite cooperated with the Japanese and ideas of independence were floated; however, the return of the USA saw the re-establishment of the status quo ante, leading to a pattern of American-dependent crony capitalism that culminated in the era of Marcos. It is difficult to identify a positive legacy of Japanese colonialism; current determinants of the relationship are the pragmatics of economic growth coupled to geographical proximity. And it should also be noted, finally, that if the political impact of the period of Japanese colonial rule for the outer periphery was ambiguous, then it must be said that the economic impact was severe but of short duration; these territories were absorbed as materials-supplying elements of a war economy that in turn quickly collapsed. It is also clear that this continues to be a key interest with trade, investment, resources and security in general for the Japanese.

In the 'reformed socialist bloc' there is now a growing linkage to contemporary Japan. In China one might suppose that the record was one of simple violence, remembered with hostility by the victims today and unacknowledged to date by the Japanese government save for ritual apologies. In such a case it would be difficult to see a positive legacy in this episode; however, notwithstanding the disruption of the war years there was considerable Japanese investment in Manchukuo and China, and the war-time legacy included a significant measure of industrialization (Beasley, 1990). At the present time contemporary economic links are well established. It would seem that a mix of historical/cultural similarities plus delicacy over the Second World War provide the base for pragmatic links whereby the Chinese secure a source of capital and the Japanese markets plus regional stability (Koppel and Orr, 1993). And finally, in French Indo-China the eventually successful nationalist resistance movements involved the Vietminh, Khmer Rouge and Pathet Lao. After the war-time occupation the drive for independence in Vietnam began and an attempt to re-create the status quo ante by the French failed, as did the subsequent US attempts. There were similar post-war conflicts in Cambodia and Laos. It is difficult to identify a positive legacy of Japanese colonialism; once again we note the overriding influence of present economic power. With the end of the US boycott announced by President Clinton in February 1994, Japanese firms are investing in Vietnam.

It can be suggested that the manner of withdrawal from colonial holdings has an impact on the subsequent relationship of ex-colony and ex-colonial power. In the case of the dissolution of the Japanese empire in Pacific Asia we have an abrupt ejection occasioned by war, and the continuing legacies of the episode have been noted. However, the manner of the ejection of the Japanese was quite particular, and we can note the relatively brief period in which the ejection was accomplished, with military defeat becoming obvious by the middle of 1944 and the Japanese armies defeated by late 1945 and withdrawn shortly thereafter. We can also note the relatively ordered nature of the withdrawal of the Japanese from South-east Asia, China and Indo-China (in contrast to the general débâcle which befell Germany in 1945). And finally, we must note the use by Europeans and Americans of Japanese soldiers as 'police' in parts of East and South-east Asia, and Indo-China, for the temporarily recolonized territories in the inter-regnum between the collapse of the Japanese empire and either the return of the civilian/military powers of the various pre-war colonial powers or the establishment of post-Japanese colonial era regimes. In brief, the military defeat was total but the subsequent pattern of withdrawal was something less than utter débâcle; a measure of order can be identified. In contemporary Japan the episode of war is either ignored, taken as the occasion for a ritualized pacifism or seen as essentially unproblematical in the sense that states have wars and the Japanese state had a war which it happened to lose (Buruma, 1994).

CONTINUITY AND CHANGE IN JAPAN   One theme which runs through the available discussions of Japan's role in Pacific Asia is the matter of leadership. Commentators ask whether Japan wishes to exercise leadership and, if so, whether Japan is able to do so. All agree that this implies reforms within Japan and the following issues are often mentioned: reforms of Japanese politics; reforms of the Japanese economy; reforms of Japanese society; plus reforms of Japanese culture, and an extensive reworking of Japan's relationships with Pacific Asia, in particular, via reforms to Japanese ODA programmes.

A general diagnosis of the problems of Japanese politics is given by Buckley (1990), who notes that there are problems with political and business corruption, a pork-barrel style of local politics, a secretive and powerful bureaucracy and, most broadly, a general inability of the political system to articulate effectively and thereafter deal with a spread of domestic and international policy problems. Similarly, van Wolferen (1989) argues that the political system centred on the bureaucracy is 'results focused' by which he means that it attends not to matters of principle and policy but to the pragmatic resolution of immediate problems. Within a dominating overall commitment to economic expansion, problems are tackled on an ad hoc basis. It means both that the system is hugely successful within its own terms and that it is unable to formulate responses to problems that fall outside its routine frame of expectations. In stronger terms, van Wolferen argues that, strictly speaking, the system is so flexible and pragmatic that it amounts to an absence of a formal state, and instead there are shifting patterns of alliances between the various important players in bureaucracy, business and politics; in this it recalls the system established at the time of the Meiji Restoration. It is a system running mostly out of the control of its beneficiaries/victims.

The general nature of the criticism of the Japanese economy is that the system is in some way a victim of its own success and that reform is urgently needed to redirect the energies of the system away from production, and the expansion of production, towards consumption, in particular, both private and public consumption for the benefit of the ordinary people of Japan. Eccleston (1989) notes that the state is routinely interventionist and works in a corporatist fashion. It takes no large equity shares because it does not have to in order to secure control. The state invests in industry and infrastructure. The state holds down social consumption (of schools, hospitals, transfer payments and the like). The state encourages savings and uses them for economic development. The state oversees business activity with MITI offering 'administrative guidance', and in any case the line between administration and business is blurred (thus civil servants retire and shift into the private sector). In all, Japan has a corporatist developmental state. And all this generates a series of issues that are hotly debated and involve: first, the nature of the role of the state (where debate revolves around the costs/benefits of such interventions (World Bank, 1993)); second, the nature of the economic structure (where debates revolve around the costs/benefits of the dual structure with a large-firm sector and a small-firm sector); third, the nature of employment patterns (where debate revolves around costs/benefits of life-time employment and small-sector employment); fourth, the nature of the costs/benefits accruing to the Japanese consumer of the present system, for example, the controlled retail sector; and finally, the costs/benefits of the production focus of the system to Japan's trading partners.

The schedule of reforms canvassed in respect of polity and economy is lengthy, and their interactions various; the proposals all have widespread implications for the nature of Japanese society. The practical problems which are routinely cited include poor housing, poor public facilities, long hours of work (and commuting), inequality between genders, excessively examination-centred schooling, a lack of leisure time for families, overstressed habits of conformity and the problems of an aged population. In all, the Japanese people are presented as the unwitting victims of the successful corporatist system which they have created and from which they receive restricted benefits. Thereafter, if we consider the Western commentators, excluding the over-anxious nationalists, then theorists of the right propose the liberalization of the Japanese economy in the expectation that consumer benefits will follow, while commentators of the centre Left propose a more consumer-friendly democratic system. In this way one can see a broad similarity in the approaches of the two groups as both are concerned to enhance the position of the Japanese consumer at the expense of currently dominant producer interests. Yet if we consider the debate among Japanese, Sheridan notes 'there still has been surprisingly little popular public debate in Japan about the future directions of economic development and national purpose' (1993: 3).

After an exhaustive review of the development experience of Japan, which recalls the story told above, Sheridan argues that, while Japanese have become rich, there are problems with long working hours and long commuting times, very expensive housing costs and a lack of adequate social capital (or infrastructure). Sheridan notes that over the 1960s and 1970s there was some improvement both in quality of life (for example, with environmental standards) and a reducing inequality in wealth, but the 1985 revaluation of the yen triggered speculation on the back of asset inflation and this has done great damage (especially via land prices, which may be expected to feed through into higher housing costs). However, Sheridan does see reasons for hope in the signs that the Japanese people are beginning to shift from a politics of fear to a politics of Utopias (that is, away from reactive positions towards prospective stances). And in relation to this charge, the system does allow collective effort in respect of communal goals. Sheridan argues that the system could be shifted away from its preoccupation with economic expansion towards the provision of the social capital necessary to improve people's lives. Sheridan points out that the Japanese state is an effective activist state, and a future oriented to quality of life could be envisioned. Sheridan then goes on to unpack this overall proposal in terms of a series of policies designed to enhance the position of women, improve local and neighbourhood life, reduce inequalities and reform the land market. All of these goals are to be pursued with a Japanese strategy which would draw on the country's established strengths of cooperative collective hard work. However, any reform strategy is dependent upon action from the centre, and here the myths of marketeers and the state's prejudices against welfare spending would have to be overcome. In all, change is likely to be slow.

Japan in Pacific Asia

The relationship of Japan and Pacific Asia is bound up with trade, FDI and ODA linkages. The official rationale of Japan's ODA is helping the less fortunate. Self-help by recipients is stressed; otherwise there is no consistent view evidenced. There are cultural antecedents in Meiji ideas of self-help, and charity is not stressed. Rix (1993: 20) notes that trying to grasp Japanese motivation is not easy as MITI stresses trade, resources and markets while MOFA looks to diplomacy and security, and there are shifts and changes in emphasis over time. The focus on Asia and the stress on responsibility is noticeable and Rix comments that 'Asian development was more a means of achieving Japanese objectives than a goal in its own right' (1993: 23). In a similar fashion, Yasutomo (1986) deals with the diplomatic rationale of Japanese ODA and is clear that it is a matter of national self-advancement. The role of ODA is lodged within a concept of 'comprehensive national security' which urges that national security depends upon regional security, and in turn this is helped by economic growth in the area. Yasutomo argues that the Japanese government pursues five interrelated goals with its ODA programmes: (a) 'economic well being'; (b) 'national prestige'; (c) 'domestic support'; (d) 'peace diplomacy'; and (e) 'national security' (1986: 112). Overall, the Japanese ODA programme is relatively loosely organized and that, while it needs revising so as to encompass a Japanese ODA leadership role, this is unlikely to happen (Rix, 1993). The present system serves many vested interests and all seem content with the status quo. However, as the Pacific Asian region integrates there are wider implications for the global system. Cronin (1992) argues that Japan can constitute the core of the region but that the region's export dependency on the USA means that the region cannot become a closed bloc. Cronin offers a series of 'scenarios' for the future.

The first scenario is of the competitive globalization of Japan. Cronin argues that 'would have Japan interacting with Asia as an increasingly open economy, partially supplanting the United States as an export market for Asia-Pacific countries, while at the global level using its financial resources to undergird the present system' (1992: 107). A wider spread of concerns in respect of ODA might also be anticipated, including 'greater participation by non-Japanese firms and more emphasis on human resources development . . . investment projects would involve more participation by local subcontractors, transfer more technology, and be more oriented to the Japanese market' (1992: 107). Cronin suggests that this scenario is close to the optimistic reform position within Japan and would find support in the USA. It would mean Japan 'using its growing economic power to support the current global trading system' (1992: 107). On optimistic analyses the result would be an expanding global economy and a stable international environment. Cronin reports that an 'important theoretical basis for this scenario is the premise that Japan cannot suspend indefinitely the operation of what many see as universal economic laws' (1992: 109), and that liberalization will have to take place; however, he immediately adds that support within Japan for globalization remains 'shaky at best' (1992: 110). In sum, this scenario involves Japan building on established links with the USA and Pacific Asia in order to develop further the open markets of the region as the closed Japanese system bows to economic market logic and opens up to the global system.

The second scenario sees 'Japanese aid and investment in Asia as primarily acting to increase the competitive position of Japanese companies in world markets *vis-à-vis* the fast rising NIEs, while Japan's own markets remain relatively closed' (1992: 111). Cronin speculates that this is an unstable line of advance as trading partners might react against the lack of reciprocity. And over the longer term the Japanese relationship with the USA could wither away, and such an eventuality would call into question many ideas currently taken for granted in respect of order in Pacific Asia. A school of thought has now emerged, reports Cronin, which holds that Japan 'will not significantly abandon its neo-mercantilist policies' (1992: 112) and there are many problem areas that could tip the Pacific system towards protectionism (for example, the issue of the US trade deficit). In sum, the second scenario is one of heightened rivalry as Japan continues to build up its own position, thereby fostering conflict as other states respond to protect their economies. The implication is one of various patterns of breakdown of the established global order.

The third scenario sees 'Japanese aid and investment, and increasing access to the Japanese market by Asian exporters, as producing a Japan centred Asia-Pacific economy' (Cronin, 1992: 115). Cronin comments that this scenario could develop in a beneficial way for most non-US countries or could turn into a second co-prosperity sphere, and in both 'variants of this scenario, Asia-Pacific countries would become increasingly dependent on Japan for capital flows (both aid and investment) and increasingly tied to Japan by trade links, while US domestic manufacturers and multinationals would face increased competition both in Asian and in the US market [as would the EU]' (1992: 115). One condition required by this scenario is that the Japanese market supplant that of the US as the regional core – able to draw in the region's imports and fuel the region's need for new capital and technology. Cronin notes that there is no agreement at present on how the system is moving, and that there are arguments for and against the notion of an emerging yen zone; however, Cronin takes the role of the US as market and investment location to be of continuing importance, and thus the emergence of a yen bloc looks unlikely. In sum, the third scenario is a Japan-dominated Pacific Asia where more ODA and FDI plus trade access for Asians to the Japanese market results in the creation of a yen bloc. However, cutting against this possibility is the general extent of global integration and the particular links which Japan has with the USA.

The inner periphery of East Asia

The expansion of the Japanese state into the area of East Asia began in the late nineteenth century and came to involve large holdings in Manchuria, colonies in Korea and Taiwan, and extensive interests in China. All this may be tagged 'late imperialism'. In due course the war against China precipitated the Pacific War. In the early period of successful expansion the Japanese government looked to the formation of a Great East Asia Co-prosperity Sphere, a sphere of mutually beneficial economic activity. However, in the post-Second World War period the colonies of South Korea and Taiwan were taken from Japanese control and prospered under American protection. Halliday (1980) characterizes their extensive economic links with Japan in terms of their constituting an 'inner periphery'. None the less the relationship at both popular and governmental levels is somewhat fraught as ever-present historical memory continues to haunt otherwise successful economic exchanges (Orr, 1990).

South Korea constitutes, according to Shibusawa et al., a 'near-perfect example of a developmental state' (1992: 69) as the circumstances of independence plus the dominant role of the military fed into an authoritarian pattern of development. Yet after some thirty years of post-war success the political economy, society and culture advanced to the point of rejecting the authoritarian aspects of the system. A series of distinct groups can be identified within society; each has its own interests, and these include the world of business, an educated middle class and an energetic working class. In recent years there has been an extensive political liberalization. At the same time, South Korea has attempted to shift the focus of its development away from Japan and the USA in order to embrace a wider spread of Pacific Asian and OECD partners. The relationship with the USA which was forged in the post-Second World War period of aggressive anti-communism has been crucial to South Korea. It has always been viewed with doubt by sections of the population in Korea and in the USA (with a recent episode of 'Korea-bashing' on economic grounds) and it must be expected that it will change in the wake of the end of the cold war. In contrast, the relationship with Japan is both historically long-established, close in practical terms and deeply difficult. There is a historical memory of the colonial period in Korea and routine discrimination against Koreans in Japan.

We should note that a similar situation holds in respect of Taiwan, whose economic record is if anything even more remarkable than that of South Korea. In the late 1980s a process of reform from above was begun in the political sphere and in recent years attempts have been made to redirect the linkages of the economy with the global system. In this case it is a matter of winding back dependence on the USA and Japan in order to look to the region and the countries of the OECD. However, in the case of Taiwan a major economic linkage is developing with mainland China. In terms of patterns of identity it would seem that as Pacific Asia changes, it is the link to China which will dominate Taiwanese thinking for the foreseeable future.

Overall, at the present time in respect of the East Asian view of the role of Japan within the growing Pacific Asian region we can point to a mixture of historical memory, post-Second World War economic success and a regional situation which is slowly changing in the post-cold-war period with the relative eclipse of the USA and the rise of China. As the USA slowly reconfigures its relationship with the countries of the region in the wake of the ending of the cold war, the countries of the inner periphery face the task of maintaining a continuing relationship with Japan, where the burgeoning economy and political instability of China constitute a further and developing relevant context.

The outer periphery of South-east Asia

The relationship of Japan with the other Pacific Asian countries is often characterized with reference to the metaphor of 'flying geese' where Japan is the leader with the other countries following behind in a series of steps down (Cronin, 1992: 27). The ideal relationship implied by this metaphor is one of a regionally complementary division of labour centred on Japan. Cronin points out that the linkages which Japan has with the countries of the region vary significantly, and with the developing areas such as China and most of South-east Asia the relationship is one of 'complementary cooperation' (1992: 33) skewed in Japan's favour. Overall, Japanese ODA and FDI are a force for economic growth and regional integration, and as Dobson (1993) points out, focusing on the ASEAN case, in recent years host governments have positively welcomed such inward investment.

It can be argued that the recent wave of foreign investment in the ASEAN region was initiated by changes in the circumstances of the Japanese economy. In the 1950s through to the 1970s Japanese FDI expanded slowly and in the pre-1985 period the focus was on raw materials, cheap labour and market access (Phongpaichit, 1990: 29). A distinctive pattern of investment with the East Asian NICs favoured, and thereafter some attention to Singapore, with the rest of ASEAN coming behind. However, after the 1985 Plaza Accords, investment in ASEAN increased sharply and it was now focused on export-oriented industrialization. Phongpaichit argues that the underlying reason, notwithstanding the issues of the appreciation of the yen and the Japanese government's desire to be seen to be responding to growing US concerns about trade imbalances, was lodged in Japan's shift from an economy centred on labour-intensive heavy industry to one focused on high-technology industrial development. This structural change pushed out FDI to offshore production platforms as Japanese capital looked to escape the impact of the high yen and US restrictions via a drive to increase markets and production capacity (Phongpaichit, 1990: 33). The Japanese economic space within Pacific Asia expanded. Phongpaichit records that this expansion has had a large impact on ASEAN, and she adds that the recipient states have been active participants.

In Malaysia (Ariff, 1991; Kahn and Loh, 1992) the government instituted an explicit 'look east' policy in the early 1980s, which took Japan as the model for Malaysian development. Khoo (1992) argues that this was the policy of a group of modernizing technocrats surrounding the Prime Minister, Dr Mahathir, and that the drive for development has overridden other more traditional groups within Malaysian society. It has been a policy conducive not merely to economic growth but also extensive social conflict, which found partial expression in politically charged debates about the nature of 'Malayness' (Shamsul, 1996). And in a similar fashion the increasing prominence of the Japanese sphere within the global economy has been noted in Singapore, where Japan is a major trading partner. The government has recently promulgated a policy which acknowledges Singapore's 'double role' as partner to the Japanese and as a long-established nexus in the global system in terms of the goal of the status of 'regional hub economy' (Rodan, 1993). Thereafter, in the resource-rich areas of South-east Asia, that is, Thailand and Indonesia, MacIntyre argues that there have been 'remarkable economic developments' (1993: 250) in both countries, and that there are increasing signs that the East Asian NIC model of export-oriented development is being repeated. MacIntyre comments that there is 'little doubt that their economies have been profoundly influenced by Japan and the four NICs' (1993: 261) and that both countries have benefited from being located in a rapidly growing region. In the future it is likely that the key problems will not be economic, rather they will be political and social as the broader impacts of the recent phase of outward-directed growth work themselves through the societies of Indonesia and Thailand (MacIntyre, 1993: 267).

Phongpaichit (1990) suggests that we can distinguish between domestic capital, state capital and foreign capital and thereafter we can plot the shifting patterns of interest and how these are expressed in response to incoming FDI. In ASEAN, broadly, there was an early resistance to FDI as state and domestic capital prospered. Then, in the depression of the early 1980s, state capital ran into trouble and began to run up significant debt. At this point FDI became attractive to ASEAN governments and with the incoming investment the phase of EOI takes off. It is clear that each country has had a particular experience of FDI-assisted EOI, but in each case Phongpaichit insists the acceptance of FDI must be seen as an expression not of passive acceptance but agency. In these terms, the actions of South-east Asian state regimes over the late 1980s can only be read as a knowing acquiescence in the dominance of the region by Japan.

China and Indo-China

The reforms of the early 1980s in China have led to increasing Japanese involvement in that country's economy. Against a historical backdrop which included both centuries of exchange, where Japan was the cultural borrower, and a post-Meiji antagonism culminating in the war of 1937–45, the linkages of the recent decade have been dominated by the pragmatics of economic expansion.

Shibusawa et al. (1992) report that the 1978 reforms initiated by Deng Xiaoping looked to secure the 'four modernizations' (agriculture, industry, science and defence) in order to achieve by the turn of the century a modest level of development in China. The story thereafter is one of burgeoning success coupled to internal social and political stress. The reforms in the rural areas were initially successful and the farmers launched a variety of industrial activities. Shibusawa notes that the impact of these reforms on the images of China held in the region were positive – China looked as if it was becoming another developmental state. However, the reform process in the industrial sector turned out to be much more problematical. These industries were long-established and closely integrated in the party/state apparatus. In this sector reform was difficult and slow and, indeed, the failure of attempts to secure change coupled to the avoidance of political reform of the party/state machinery can be taken to have led to the political tensions which culminated in the Tiananmen Square débâcle.

It is clear that the reform process inaugurated by Deng Xiaoping has led to significant economic advance; however, in recent years, in addition to the tensions noted above, there have been two key features which commentators now routinely address: (a) the pronounced regional nature of the economic changes, with coastal regions experiencing rapid growth, and apparently significantly enhanced regional powers at the expense of Beijing, while the inner agricultural regions are rather left behind; and (b) the increasingly visible and vital linkages of the burgeoning coastal regions of China with the Pacific Asian region in general. In the future, commentators anticipate that the outward-directed development of China will continue, indeed, it is said to be running somewhat out of control, and that social and political change are almost inevitable. A key issue for the future will be the way in which China orders its relationships with the Pacific region in general, and that region's core Japanese economy in particular (Gipoloux, 1994). Finally, we might note that in Indo-China a similar story can be sketched out. The key aspect was the resolution of the Cambodian problem, and the related removal of the American veto on FDI and multilateral development agency assistance to Vietnam, now with its own marketization programme. The region is now rapidly reorienting itself to the global capitalist system in general and the Japanese regional core in particular.

Australasia joins Pacific Asia

In the 1980s the governments of both Australia and New Zealand have had explicit policies which point to the future of these countries within the developing Pacific Asian region. In the case of New Zealand, the accession of the UK to the EEC caused great damage to the local economy and a process of reorientation began. In the 1980s a series of New Right governments continued the marketization and regionalization of the New Zealand political economy, and with it a shift to an Asia-sensitive multiculturalism in regard to identity. In the case of Australia, we find a long-running concern with the issue of identity, and indeed many of the terms of debate pre-date the rise of Pacific Asia (Whitlock and Carter, 1992).

Walter (1992) recalls the invention of a 'British Australia' around the turn of the twentieth century where before there had been only colonies looking to the UK. These ideas of Australia were informed by notions of 'British stock' making up an immigrant community who had, given their pattern of economic life, a particular affinity with 'the bush'. The invention of this tradition can be traced to particular groups of intellectuals and journalists (White, 1992). The native people of the continent, the Aborigines, were simply written out of the story. However, in the post-Second World War period the story itself is revised and a notion of the 'Australian way of life' emerges in the context of a general Western anti-communism; this view of Australia was implicitly anti-immigrant in line with ideas of 'White Australia' (White, 1992). Overall, this general record forms the background to the deliberate 1980s turn towards Asia which has seen an explicit 'multiculturalism' in the domestic sphere linked to a concern to locate Australia in its wider geographical context of Asia. Many of the arguments which have been adduced to support this reorientation point to the country's economic linkages to Pacific Asia, yet against this it has been argued that the economic policies of the 1980s were deeply flawed and that the economic linkages to Asia have been wildly oversold (Byrnes, 1994).

An integrated Pacific Asia

It is possible to identify broad political-economic, social-institutional, political and cultural similarities among the various countries of Pacific Asia. It is also possible to point to recent economic growth and suggest that available similarities are proving to be the basis for practical exchanges which in due course might be expected to find political expression. However, two points need to be kept in mind: first, that the region is at present dependent on the USA as a market for the consumption of its exports; and second, that the region is very large and very diverse (in terms of economies, societies and cultures).

However, we can conclude by recording that it does make some sort of sense to speak of the distinctiveness of Pacific Asian political-economic, social-institutional and cultural structures. We can make a summary characterization of Pacific Asia in the following fashion: the economy is state-directed; state direction is oriented to the pragmatic pursuit of economic growth (that is, it is not informed by explicit or debated political-ideological positions); state direction is top-down style and pervasive in its reach throughout the political economy and culture; society is familial and thereafter communitarian (thus society is non-individualistic); social order is secured by pervasive control machineries (sets of social rules and an extensive bureaucratization of everyday life) and a related hegemonic common culture (which enjoins submission to the demands of community and authority); political debate and power are typically reserved to an élite sphere (and political life centres on the pragmatic pursuit of overarching economic goals); political debate and action among the masses is diffuse and demobilized (thus there is no 'public sphere'); and culture comprises a mix of officially sanctioned tradition and market-sanctioned consumption. Culture stresses consensus, acquiescence and harmony and eschews open conflict. Overall, it seems clear both that some sort of distinctive developmental capitalism is in process of formation in Pacific Asia.

Conclusion: the rise of Pacific Asia

Identity is socially constructed, carried in language, liable to revision at some cost, and routinely expressed and contested in ordinary life. Political-cultural identity can be understood as the way in which private understandings are presented within the public sphere. A political-cultural identity will express a balance between private concerns and public demands. Such private concerns are products of our own biographies and are thus likely to be idiosyncratic in expression even as there are commonalities with others in similar situations to ourselves. And public issues will be presented to us via the public sphere, in which case these matters will come to us in an already processed form (as ideology or tradition). The notion of hegemony lets us identify an interest on the part of powerful élites in ordering the way we think, as publicly presented issues can invade private concerns.

The cold-war period saw the wide dissemination of a public official ideology which imposed itself on the private thinking of many people. It offered people an overriding political-cultural identity (as free individuals enjoying the free markets of the free West with its commitment to freedom). It provided standard truths for élites to present in the public sphere. When the cold war came to its unexpected and abrupt end the familiar official truths and popular ideologies were rendered irrelevant overnight.

In Pacific Asia it would seem that the élite-level response to the sudden withdrawal of long-familiar cold-war ways of understanding the world has been an interest in the ideal of a Pacific Asian region. The enthusiasm is evident in the plethora of acronyms which now abound. However, there is a structural occasion for the élite-level discourse and it resides in the changing patterns of economic power within the global system. It is on this structural basis that we might look to the ideal of Pacific Asia as an ordering theme for the countries of the region. It would seem that a broad commonality in political economy, society and culture will be further deepened around the energetic expansion of the regional core economy of Japan. As élite groups respond to these slowly changing structural circumstances by advancing an idea of Pacific Asia – a response made more vigorous by the collapse of the available strategy of understanding delivered through the essentially American rhetoric of cold war – one might expect the emergent new identities to find both institutional and popular expression in new patterns of political linkages, new patterns of economic activity and new patterns of political-cultural understanding.

9

Locale, Network and Memory

After the Second World War the routine experience of most Americans, Europeans and (albeit in a less evidently secure fashion) Pacific Asians has been bound within the frameworks of a bipolar global system centred, for the inhabitants of the West, on the USA and ordered via the machineries of the Bretton Woods open trading system, while the peoples of the Eastern bloc looked to an uneasy double centre in Moscow and Beijing. The bipolar system found expression in a range of transnational and national institutions and official ideologies, and a spread of models of political-cultural identity received élite approval and state-sponsored dissemination. However, the dramatic events of the period 1989–91 have fatally undermined the plausibility of idea-sets derived from this period, and it has become clear that the eclipse of political bipolarity has revealed an incipient economic tripolarity. And once again, as in 1945, global structural change is running through the ways in which states, organizations, groups and individuals order their relationships to relevant collectivities.

It is the present dynamic of global restructuring, as a tripolar system takes form, which provides the context for the current concern for identity and political-cultural identity. In this text I have tried both to elucidate the theoretical aspects of the issue and to review in broad outline how the dynamics of structural change are working in practice in the three key regions of the emergent tripolar system. In this concluding chapter I will recall the key elements of the theoretical approach which I have sketched, consider the formal outlines of possible future developments in the spheres of identity and political-cultural identity in the period of high modernity and take note of the divergent patterns of life increasingly evidenced in the three regions of the global industrial-capitalist system.

Identity in locale, network and memory

In line with the arguments presented earlier, I would take the view that identity will continue to be a matter of locale (the place where people live), network (the ways in which people interact) and memory (the understandings which are sustained and re-created over time). The details of particular forms of life might alter but there seems to be little reason to suppose that humankind is going to alter the broad patterns which have characterized industrial-capitalist forms of life, a point made clearly in Gellner's general anthropology (Gellner, 1964, 1991). However, as the global industrial-capitalist system continues to extend its reach and deepen its penetration of the social world it is likely that general patterns of identity will change. We can speculate that there will be rather less confidence in respect of the fixity of identities and rather more approving involvement in the fluid nature of patterns of identity, a shift which has been called the movement to 'high modernity' (Giddens, 1991).

I have argued that if we begin with a simple idea of identity as the way in which we more or less self-consciously locate ourselves in our social world then we can make a simple schematic review of the multiple aspects of identity in the fashion of a substantive ethnographic/biographical report. I have suggested that the substantive business of identity can be unpacked in terms of the ideas of locale, network and memory, and in using this schema I am recalling the rich given-ness of ordinary experience. The trio of ideas points to the ways in which we inhabit a particular place, which is the sphere of routine activity and interaction and is richly suffused with meanings, which in turn is the base for a dispersed series of networks of exchanges with others centred on particular concerns, all of which are brought together in the sphere of continually reworked memory.

It seems clear that identity comprises a rich array of meanings. It is not an attenuated formal realm. The idea of locale points to the dense pattern of routine practices and social contexts which embrace the individual self. Hoggart (1985) grasps this point when in respect of his own childhood in the northern English industrial city of Leeds, in the days before the Second World War, he recalls the detail of the life of his family as they moved through the social landscape of the pre-war working classes. Hoggart's memory is detailed, caring and clear-eyed, and the lives he describes are richly elaborated.

It is characteristic of the work of Hoggart that the locale which he evokes in such detail is very specific to a time and place. It is the northern English working class of the pre-war and immediate post-Second World War years. At one point he remarks on the characteristic inwardness of their lives (Hoggart, 1985: 72). However, some fifty years later it would seem that individuals, groups and whole peoples are more mobile than at any time in the recent historical past and in the high modernity of the present one might point to a greater fluidity in the practical definition of the locale.

The immediate pattern of life of the individual person can be captured in terms of an idea of locale. We invest our attention in the domestic sphere, thereafter the world of work, then the formal institutional sphere and, as a loose spread of ideas bathing the whole area, the world of the media which is simultaneously present in the detail of life and superficially distant from it. An individual's locale can be regarded as the base from which wider dispersed practices and meanings are embraced. The network of practices will involve family and kin networks, employment networks, and the casual links of holiday, hobbies and consumption. These networks carry practices and meanings which are part of the experience of individual selves, and are likely to be idiosyncratic (one person's network is quite particular) and shifting (the expectations of continuity which dominate locale are softened as networks change). In terms of a simple distinction between the traditional and the modern worlds, we can say that patterns of movement, the practices which constitute networks remote from locale, have expanded in the modern period, and thereafter, as the global system becomes integrated and interdependent in the period of 'high modernity', they are becoming ever more extensive.

If we regard identity as reflexively constituted in the narratives whereby we constitute discrete events as belonging to a particular self, then memory is a crucial constituent of the process. As we move through our particular social world we assimilate events to a continuing self. We recall mundane details of family change such as lines of relationship and patterns of descent (some formalized for property reasons) and we recall changes in the community or area in which we live. We inhabit cultural traditions (and we invent them) and we invoke the past to explain and judge the present. And we affirm ideas of progress (identity is thus lodged in developing time). The idea of memory points to a creative exchange with the flow of passing events. Samuel (1994) comments, in general terms, that:

> memory, so far from being merely a passive receptacle or storage system, an image bank of the past, is rather an active, shaping force; that it is dynamic – what it contrives symptomatically to forget is as important as what it remembers. (pp. vii–x)

And, looking to systematic remembering, he remarks that

> history is not the prerogative of the historian, nor even, as postmodernism contends, a historian's 'invention'. It is rather a social form of knowledge; the work, in any given instance of a thousand different hands. (p. 8)

Thereafter, against critics read by Samuel as dismissive of the ordinary experience of people, he notes:

> A more ethnographic approach . . . might think of the invention of tradition as a process rather than an event, and memory, even in its silences, as something which people made for themselves. Rather than focusing on state theatricals, or the figures of national myth, it might find it more profitable to focus on the perceptions of the past which find expression in the discriminations of everyday life. (pp. 16–17)

In the context of the centrality of memory we can note a tension between self and collectivity, because the intersection of the personal sphere and the collective realm will be one site of possible conflict. Indeed, it has been argued that history is a zone of conflict between the subordinate and the powerful, a battle for control of historical memory.

After the analyses of Wright (1985) it is clear, in the period of high modernity, that control is a continuing and crucial issue.

I would argue that it is clear that identity has a complex structure which can be grasped in term of the notions of locale, network and memory. I would also argue that the business of identity for the individual self is typically largely unproblematical. One might say that ordinary life is just that, ordinary. The security of identity is a matter of the habits of routines taken for granted. It is true that structural change will entail reworking identities, but most of the time such change is both pervasive and slow (Gellner, 1964; Nairn, 1988). It is true that the unproblematical given-ness of identity can be taken as the occasion for claims to the fundamental given-ness of identity. A putative base in race, gender, cultural type or language can be presented as the occasion for a reductive naturalism in explanation. However, against such temptations it is clear that identity is the outcome of a complex series of social processes, it is embedded and sustained within them, and as the world changes with the progressive development of high modernity then patterns of personal identity will change in turn.

Cosmopolitanism, adulthood and scepticism

In the context of recent debates surrounding the cultural condition of the present, the influential theorists of postmodernity argue that the modernist project of a rational society has been overtaken by events, in particular, the creation of a postmodern knowledge-based society of expressive individualism (Lyotard, 1984). It could perhaps be said that the nostrums of postmodernists did have a measure of plausibility during the 1980s period of unusually high material consumption in the West. However, theorists working within the classical European tradition, most especially those who look to the material of the Marxist tradition, prefer to speak of the unfinished project of modernity (Habermas, 1989). As will no doubt be clear, this text is constructed from within the general frame of the classical tradition; however, there are two provisos which must be made. In the first place, substantively, it is clear that the industrial-capitalist system is now global in its reach and increasingly tripolar in form. As the industrial-capitalist system has become interdependent at a global level it has also taken on distinct regional forms. It is now possible to speak of a variety of forms of industrial capitalism. It is no longer possible to reduce the various styles of industrial capitalism to one model. And in the second place, formally, it is clear that any contemporary expression of the modernist project has to acknowledge the demands of reflexive self-embedding in the form of a routine scepticism about the claims which can be made within the classical tradition. In this connection, lines of argument have become available from within the sphere of social philosophy which suggest, in particular, that any attempt at intellectual closure centred on the received model of the West would be an error. The crucial lesson is drawn by MacIntyre:

> different languages as used by different societies may embody different and rival conceptual schemes, and . . . translation from one such language to some other such language may not always be possible. There are cultures and languages-in-use that one can only inhabit by learning how to live in them as a native does. And there are theories framed in different languages-in-use whose incommensurability arises from their partial untranslatability. (1994: 141)

However, against any temptation to dismiss the modernist project in its entirety (a line of criticism which MacIntyre also runs), and against the characterizations of positivistic celebrants and postmodernist critics alike, we should recall that the project of modernity was never a mono-ethical mechanico-formal pursuit of a specified end-point but was in fact routinely sceptical, reflexive and open-ended. It is also the case that the self-consciousness of modernity was always self-critical. In the present period as the global system moves to express more fully an interdependent tripolarity, it is clear both that a conception of the scope and possibilities of the modernist project must be affirmed in a sceptical guise, and that the available self of modernity will be re-worked. As the dynamics of the industrial-capitalist system become ever more subtly articulated within the social sphere, it seems to me that we can look to a parallel pattern of learning among the system's inhabitants. In general terms, as the movement into high modernity expresses an increasing systemic sophistication, then analogously the shift from the self of modernity to the self of high modernity can be construed as an exercise in learning. I will attempt speculatively to sketch the implications of these change in terms of the related ideas of cosmopolitanism, adulthood and scepticism.

THE COSMOPOLITAN NATURE OF HIGH MODERNITY The coincidence of private concerns and public issues which occasioned this text, with its central preoccupation with political-cultural identity, found brutal expression in the war in Bosnia, the first war in Europe since the Second World War of 1939–45. In the UK the reaction to the unfolding conflict was one of initial disbelief, which thereafter modulated into dismay and then scorn at the feeble, disingenuous and unsuccessful responses of the political élites of the European Union. If the élites of Western Europe signally failed to respond adequately to the challenge of the war, it remained the case that responsibility for the débâcle lay with the political élites of the disintegrating Yugoslav federation, who confronted the dynamics of post-cold-war structural change with an emphatic preference for violent atavistic nationalism.

Ignatieff (1994), in endeavouring to understand the cultural/psychological dynamic of the Balkan war, draws a useful distinction between civic and ethnic nationalism. The former is traced back to the ideals of the French Enlightenment and celebrates the ideal of a rational rule-governed community, and the latter is traced back to the German romanticism of the early nineteenth century, which reacted to the expansionism of Napoleonic France by arguing that the core of any nationalism lay in the intrinsic character of a particular people, thereby tracing community to language, descent and culture.

Ignatieff argues that the former has a better claim to sociological realism, as most nation-states are multi-ethnic and most are rule-governed. However, he grants that the latter has a more immediate psychological appeal. The character of this appeal is traced to a particular idea of the natural given-ness of identity. On the one hand, civic nationalists are ironists, sceptics and cosmopolitans and are able rationally to review the processes of the social construction of identity. In civic nationalism the contingency of identity is granted. On the other hand, ethnic nationalists are supremely sentimental and the logic of such an emotional response entails an emphatic affirmation of the truth of the sentiments expressed. In ethnic nationalism the affirmation of sentimental truth leaves no space for contingency, therefore identity must be necessary, it must be given.

Ignatieff explains:

Nationalists are supremely sentimental . . . The latent purpose of such sentimentality is to imply that one is in the grip of a love greater than reason, stronger than the will, a love akin to fate and destiny . . . Stripped of such sentimentality, what then is this belonging, and the need for it which nationalism seems to satisfy so successfully? When nationalists claim that national belonging is the overridingly important form of all belonging, they mean that there is no other form of belonging – to your family, work or friends – which is secure if you do not have a nation to protect you. This is what warrants sacrifice on the nation's behalf . . . Belonging, on this account is first and foremost protection from violence. Where you belong is where you are safe . . . the nationalists claim is that full belonging, the warm sensation that people understand not merely what you say but what you mean, can only come when you are among your own people in your native land. (1994: 6–7)

And, contrariwise:

For many years, I believed that the tide was running in favour of cosmopolitans . . . There were at least a dozen world cities – gigantic, multi-ethnic melting pots which provided a home for expatriates, exiles, migrants and transients of all kinds . . . Cosmopolitans make a positive ethic out of cultural borrowing . . . There was nothing new in itself about this cosmopolitan ethic . . . Two features, however, distinguish the big city cosmopolitanism of our era from what has gone before. First of all its social and racial diffusion . . . The second obvious change is that the global market we live in is no longer ordered by a stable imperial system . . . Globalism in a post-imperial age only permits a post-nationalist consciousness for those cosmopolitans who are lucky enough to live in the wealthy West. It has brought chaos and violence for the many small peoples too weak to establish defensible states of their own . . . It is only too apparent that cosmopolitanism is the privilege of those who can take a secure nation state for granted. (1994: 8–9)

Ignatieff links cosmopolitanism to an unexplicated notion of achievement, a notion of civilization as a historical achievement. The cosmopolitans are lucky because they inhabit societies which are rich, sophisticated and ordered. It is a historical achievement. It is an achievement secured against human nature. And it seems to me that the culture of high modernity, with its acknowledgement of the interdependent global system and the requirement of hermeneutic dialogue as a route to its always restricted comprehension, implies the advance of precisely that habit of cosmopolitan sceptical tolerance.

THE ACHIEVEMENT OF ADULTHOOD IN HIGH MODERNITY   It can be argued that if the fundamental character of the modernist project is the celebration of reason, then we would expect to find over time evidence of learning. It is clear in this context that learning is a critical notion as it allows both a modernist ethic of reason and responsibility to be advanced and critical commentary on the present to be deployed in public debate. It has been suggested that such learning can be looked for at the levels of both system and individual.

It is possible to speak of system learning as the economic substructure with its intimate linkages to the pursuit of natural science (Gellner, 1964) becomes ever more potent. It is also possible to speak of individual learning along with the development of the system. As the industrial-capitalist system extends its reach within the social world, one would expect the system's inhabitants to learn appropriate ideas/ skills. The response of agents to shifting structures will be pragmatic, the resultant learning will intermingle necessary and contingent changes to the learning selves. None the less, it is also possible to speak critically of divergences between productive level where there is material advance and the social/ethical level where there is less obvious advance. A lack of individual-level advance is a theme pursued by Habermas (1971, 1989). However, overall it is possible to affirm a modernist ideal which takes the pursuit of progress to be inscribed both in humankind and in the social system which we inhabit. In this case, once again, the shift to high modernity implies not less but more pressure to acknowledge the dynamic of learning.

It is possible also to look to the individuals who are taken to show, in principle, the results of reason deployed over time, that is, learning. The philosopher Gillian Rose looks at this business from the directly biographical direction; the business of learning over a lifetime is a matter of pursuing (and maybe achieving) adulthood, and she characterizes this as 'love's work'. The point is made in relation to the response of her family and friends to the diagnosis of her terminal illness. She comments:

> My friends and my family field the crisis of their own mortality brought on
> by my illness by serving hard and fast at me the literature and liquids of
> alternative healing . . . The injunction, which pervades the literature of

alternative healing, to become 'exceptional' . . . A crisis of illness, bereavement, separation, natural disaster, could be the opportunity to make contact with deeper levels of the terrors of the soul, to loose and to bind, to bind and to loose. A soul which is not bound is as mad as one with cemented boundaries. To grow in love-ability is to accept the boundaries of oneself and others, while remaining vulnerable, woundable, around the bonds . . . Existence is robbed of its weight, its gravity, when it is deprived of its agon . . . I reach for my favourite whisky bottle and instruct my valetudinarian well-wishers to imbibe the shark's oil and Aloe Vera themselves. If I am to stay alive, I am bound to continue to get love wrong, all the time, but not to cease wooing, for that is my life affair, love's work. (1995: 97–9).

The shift to high modernity implies a greater possibility of learning. The system becomes more subtle in its social articulation and its denizens (and constituents) become more adult.

THE ROUTINE SCEPTICISM IN HIGH MODERNITY   The first expressions of the modernist project in the eighteenth and early nineteenth centuries were optimistic, engaged and prospective. However, this type of work underwent a process of restriction and the outcome was the spread of positivistic social sciences, which took shape in the nineteenth century and found discipline-bound expression in the twentieth (Preston, 1996). The preference for a narrowly technical knowledge coincided with the rise to global pre-eminence of the West. It might be suggested that in the late nineteenth century it did make some sort of sense to claim that knowledge was all of a piece, and that the exemplar of knowledge was the late nineteenth-century natural science of the West as there were no other cultural competitors, with all other peoples absorbed within empire systems. A recent expression of this misplaced confidence was found in the post-Second World War settlement. However, the collapse of this settlement and the ongoing debates within the social sciences now allow the representation of the modernist project in sceptical guise, a scepticism we can also turn against our sense of ourselves.

In Bauman's terms, the matter is summarized as the shift from legislative to interpretive reason. Bauman (1988) argues that, in the confusions and dislocations of the shift to the modern world, it is the intellectuals who offer the newly constituted state the strategies and legitimations necessary to underpin its actions. It is on the basis of claims to knowledge of how the social system works that the legitimacy of the rulers comes to rest, and it is the intellectuals who provide this knowledge. Thereafter, the state and its intellectuals embark on the business of educating the people, of bringing order. The Enlightenment project was of establishing a rational state, and this is a political project. However, after the French Revolution a subtle shift begins to take place, and the intellectuals come to the view that their knowledge is not merely the guide to the state but the key to change. At this point a new project is forming which celebrates the role of the expert, and thus we have the role of the legislator.

Bauman takes the broad modernist project, the celebration of the role of the intellectuals in pursuit of a rational society, with all its conflicts and disputes, to have exhausted until recently all available intellectual space. In recent years a new position has been advanced, that of postmodernism. Bauman reports that it seems to postmodernist intellectuals that the role of legislator is no longer available. The system now runs on market seduction, and it needs only technicians, not intellectuals. Bauman rejects submission to the seductions of the marketplace (which, as Bauman points out, simultaneously requires the bureaucratic welfare policing of the lives of the 'failed consumers') and insists on the continuing validity and relevance of the modernist project. The reaffirmation of the ethic of the modernist project is coupled to an acknowledgement of the context dependency of the epistemology of the modernist project. The celebration of reason is particular to European received culture and may be taken to constitute its core. The universalist impulse of modernity has to be curbed and an acknowledgement of the resources of other cultures affirmed. At this point we can identify a new strategy of enquiry which grants the diversity of cultural traditions and attempts to foster a dialogic process of emancipation, the role of the interpreter. And overall, in the light of these arguments it is clear that the over-emphatic claims to knowledge typical of the modernisms of the nineteenth and twentieth centuries cannot be sustained in the period of high modernity, and a routine scepticism must be affirmed.

Political-cultural identity

I have argued that political-cultural identities are ways of reading enfolding structural circumstances. These subtle constructs are contested; they express a balance between private thoughts and public truths. The nature of political-cultural identity will be shaped by the exchange of powerful groups, established institutions and the informal resources of ordinary life. It seems clear that familiar patterns of political-cultural identity are likely to change in the future as the global structures which such constructs grasp become more complex in the way they are ordered. The changes in patterns of political-cultural identity will be many, for there will be a series of particular tales to tell. However, it seems to me that we can attempt to grasp these matters in general terms in order to secure a scattering of clues in respect of future developments. Overall, it seems to me that we can speculate that political-cultural identity will become more immediate (as people turn to their local situation), attenuated (as official ideologies decline and as political-cultural identity becomes correspondingly less prominent) and layered (as the spheres of possible commitment for individuals and groups become broader).

A political-cultural identity expresses our relationship to the community considered as an ordered body of persons, and may be elucidated in terms of the ideas of locale, network and memory. In terms of the notion of locale, the focus is on how an individual construes their relationship to the community they inhabit, and how thereafter the person considers that their community relates to the wider world. This involves the political understandings of individuals and the political understandings of local collectivities expressed in folk knowledge, common sense and folk ideology. The political-cultural understandings of an individual will record accidents of biography. In respect of given patterns of power/authority, understandings will be informal, practical, dense and unremarked. In respect of the formal sphere of politics, understandings will be episodic (what has been noticed or has impinged upon the individual). The political-cultural understandings of the local collectivity will be particular, episodic and informal. In terms of the related notion of network, we are looking at how individuals lodge themselves in dispersed groups and thereafter how the individual considers that the grouping of persons construes their relationship to other groups within the wider collectivity. It is the sphere of operation of ideologies, both delimited-formal, as the group propounds its position, and pervasive-informal, as the general cultural sphere is suffused with the articulated competing positions of many groups. And in terms of the notion of memory, we are looking at the ways in which individuals, groups and collectivities secure their understandings of the power aspects of patterns of social relationships in the material of folk traditions, institutional truths and the official histories of states.

I have also noted that it is possible to approach these matters from a structural direction and look at how the collectivity embraces the person. It is here that we can begin to speak of delimited-formal and pervasive-informal ideologies, great and little traditions, official ideologies, and the extent of the development of the public sphere (an institutionally ordered sphere within which rational debate might be undertaken). This is the more familiar realm of talk about political-cultural identity and we can recall the spread of material associated with ideas of nationalism and ethnicity, the programmes of social movements and the formal positions of parties, governments and states. All these represent the ways in which groups read and react to structural circumstances, and as these alter, so too do political-cultural identities.

I have argued that a political-cultural identity could take a series of broad forms: first, person-centred (how an individual construes their relationship to the community they inhabit); second, group-centred (how persons lodge themselves in groups and thereafter how a grouping of persons construe their relationship to other groups within the community); and third, nation-centred (how persons ordered as groups thereafter construe themselves in relation to other separate groups). At the present time it is clear that there is change along all these axes. The changes are subtle. In part they represent the inevitable lessons of structural reconfiguration. However, these changes are thrown into perhaps sharper relief, at least for Westerners, by the recent loss of the security of the post-Second World War settlement. It seems to me that we can essay a speculative foray into the likely dynamics of political-cultural identity in the developing period of high modernity in terms of the responses of agents to novel structural situations.

Immediacy, attenuation and layering

It can be argued that the early phases of the shift to the modern world had the effect of putting in place both the basics of the patterns of industrial-capitalist life with which the peoples of the developed world have long been familiar, and which are increasingly the routine form of life of those peoples within the developing world, and the familiar ways of reading these patterns at the level of the public sphere, the familiar ideas of state, nation and nation-state. As Gellner (1964) argues, it was in the early modern period that the rise of capitalism required a new political order which was realized in the guise of the state system, and in order to legitimate this institutional form nations were promptly invented. The upshot was that the political-cultural identity of an individual revolved around the particular groups within which the individual was lodged and the views current as to the relationship of those groups to the ordered collectivity of the nation. As the industrial-capitalist system becomes more evidently interdependent, global and tripolar, it is only to be expected that there will be a series of changes in the ways in which the system is understood and ordered. In part these changes will flow from a pragmatic practical recognition of new global circumstances, for as the world changes so too does our knowledge, but a related aspect of the process will be more reflective, a matter of the ways in which we construe the collectivity. In the shift to the modern world the invention of nations was actively promulgated and we have subsequently read our situations in these terms, but as the processes of systemic change advance it is likely that the grip upon our imaginations of these early modern constructs will diminish. In the matter of the dynamic of structural change and agent response, the ways in which agents construe their circumstances is of considerable importance and feeds directly into practical activity. Overall, I will sketch a way in which we can try to grasp the outline of these processes in so far as they impact upon the political-cultural identities of ordinary people in terms of the ideas of immediacy, attenuation and layering.

THE IMMEDIACY OF INVOLVEMENT IN POLITICAL LIFE   A recent argument in respect of the absorption of the United Kingdom into the European Union has spoken of the relocation of power and political meaning (the locus of attention of ideologies) at the supranational and sub-national level. The process is taken to parallel the restructuring of the whole European Union as an integrated regional group within the global system. The argument proposes that the familiar sphere of the nation-state and the legitimating ideologies of nationalism are contracting. It seems to me that we can argue by analogy to the system as a whole.

As the global system becomes more integrated and regulated/legitimated at regional level then political-cultural identity is likely to find a more local and immediate expression. In terms of the dynamics of structures and agents, this shift in the attention of agents is entailed by simple recognition of system change. The requirements for accessing the system in order to secure individual or group objectives change, and what could be accomplished in the past at the level of the nation-state via the familiar machineries of national and sub-national institutions must now be secured in other ways. If we are not to suppose that regionalization within the tripolar global system will entail an effective reduction in the power of existing groups and individuals, then we need to look to emergent modes of securing access to the system. The business of regionalization represents system learning as the logic of industrial capitalism extends and deepens its reach with the social world, and it is reasonable to suppose that the inhabitants of the system will learn in a similar way. In general, as the system becomes more all-embracing, groups and individuals will have to attend more closely to the local arenas within which these structural flows are expressed (and these can be the local offices of regional institutions and MNCs, the locally based parliamentary bodies and institutions of the public sphere, and the increasing spread of non-orthodox and/or non-governmental political organizations).

In the European Union, for example, one possible sign of this sort of process is the present enthusiasm for sub-national regional parliaments which are centres of power and political meaning made in contrast to the old national state-level ideas and institutions. One might also cite the growth in both the USA and Europe of new social movements, such as environmentalists and feminists, whose members typically seek to operate in non-traditional spheres.

As political power and political meaning move downwards towards the ever more sophisticated population, then people will pay more attention to their immediate sphere. As the industrial-capitalist system expands/deepens populations are drawn more tightly into the system. As they are absorbed they learn their new situation and as they learn they are less inclined to acquiesce in received ideas. In Pacific Asia, for example, recent years have seen a significant measure of political

liberalization. It has been argued that processes of economic development have generated sophisticated economies with newly created and
highly educated middle classes who look to participate in their polities.
In general, considering the process overall, it may be that it is a mixture
of reaction against the perceived loss of power to ever more remote
bodies, and new opportunity as power and meanings are drawn down
to a more local level as the system reorders itself, a pattern of quasi-
devolution intrinsic to the system.

THE ATTENUATION OF RECEIVED DELIMITED-FORMAL IDEOLOGY It is possible
to argue that the post-Second World War period has seen the public
national politics of all three emergent regions dominated by the
overriding demands of the emphatic rhetorics of the cold war. The
routine public politics of Americans, Europeans and those Pacific
Asians who were within the Western sphere have been grounded in
particular ideas of nation yet thereafter dominated by the ritual celebration of the fusion of the ideas of freedom, free markets and personal
free choice in the official ideological doctrine of the 'free West'. And we
might recall that it has been noted that it is characteristic of empire
nationalisms that they act to undermine local patterns of thought and
judgement, local expressions of belonging (Anderson, 1983). In this
context, the task of delimited-formal ideology is the demobilization of
a population, not its mobilization, and in the absence of structurally
available alternative patterns of action and thought, acquiescence is
rational. If we read the matter in this way then the familiar trappings of
nation-statehood, the flags, parades and anthems, in particular as they
have been submerged within a wider rhetoric of conflict, are wholly
apposite, for the business is a ritual. However, at the present time, clear
of the obfuscations of cold-war rhetoric, as processes of tripolar globalization continue it is clear that many new patterns of action and
thought are available. One might speculate that the habit of construing
the relationship of individual and ordered collectivity in terms of the
ideas of nation-statehood, so familiar to Europeans, and those other
territories which effected the shift to the modern world in the long
period from the eighteenth to the twentieth century, might well rapidly
fall away into relative disuse. As power and political meanings devolve
to the local level, a separate ritualized sense of the political may
decline, absorbed, so to say, in the practical sphere. We can speculate
that a process of attenuation of political-cultural identity might take
place as the familiar delimited-formal official ideologies of nationalism
decline in terms of their relevance to the lives of ordinary people.

In the classical European tradition of social theorizing the theme of
the supersession of politics is familiar within lines of argument which
suggest that social development can be taken to allow the substitution
of varieties of rational administration for extant conflicts. It is a deeply

ambiguous issue with liberals (such as Weber), democrats (such as Habermas) and conservatives (such as Hayek) warning against the spread of bureaucratic rationality through the social sphere. However, my speculations in respect of the attenuation of received delimited-formal ideology do not rest upon any putative emergence of new patterns of bureaucratic power within the tripolar global system; rather the reverse, for as the familiar nation-state retreats the power thereby relinquished is relocated in a number of institutional locations. The slow falling away of familiar received delimited-formal ideologies, the stuff of ritualized political life, does not flow from a reduction in the sphere of political life. We are not witnessing the death of politics, rather it flows from the new ways in which the possibilities inherent within patterns of system change can be grasped, a matter, in sum, not of the scientization of politics but rather its democratization (Habermas, 1971).

THE LAYERING OF POLITICAL-CULTURAL IDENTITY   If we suppose that system learning entails individual learning, then as the global industrial-capitalist system becomes more sophisticated in the articulation of its reach within the social sphere, individuals and groups will garner increasing knowledge of the system's operations. At the same time, as the system becomes more integrated, as present patterns of reconfiguration run their course, the opportunities for political involvement will become more diverse and individuals and groups will be able to work at a variety of levels (local, national and regional). It might be supposed that each level will develop its own typical forms of activity.

The local level might be expected to encompass a spread of activities whereby individuals and groups access in a non-orthodox fashion regional economic, social, cultural and political structures. It seems clear that non-governmental organizations (NGOs) and the proponents of new social movements such as environmentalism and feminism already operate in this way. We might speculate that such activity will increase.

At the present time the sphere of the nation-state is contracting. However, the range of administrative and formal political activities which revolve around the national state and its sub-national elements is large. It would not be true to say that the state is in process of withering away. Indeed, as the industrial-capitalist system becomes more subtly articulated within the social sphere, the range of activities pursued within the framework of the machineries of the state increases. The extent of the reach of the state should not be underestimated (Hay 1996). However, what is crucial in the process of regionalization within the global system is the end of the monopoly of power and authority which has been enjoyed by the national state over the modern period. The sphere of the national state no longer exhausts all political activity. And the sphere of that national state no longer exhausts all political legitimacy. The actions of individuals and groups which are oriented towards the state might now be construed quite differently, given that the formal machineries of the national state are but one sphere of action. The actions of individuals and groups might now be legitimately and effectively deployed in a series of spheres – local, national and regional. It seems to me that this subtle shift in the context of operation of the national state has the effect of empowering individuals and groups.

The new arena of possible political thought and action is provided by the emergent regional spheres within the tripolar global industrial-capitalist system. The existing national states have in recent years paid attention to the emergent regional system and this is evidenced in the recent plethora of multinational regional organizations – including APEC, NAFTA and the European Union. It might reasonably be said that it is the European Union which offers the most striking example of the institutional acknowledgement of regionalization within the global system. It is also the European Union which illustrates most clearly the ways in which regional patterns of economic, social and cultural life can find formal institutional expression which in turn can provide a vehicle for new political activity.

It seems clear that the present dynamics of change within the industrial-capitalist system are such that a series of relatively discrete spheres of action and thought can be identified, at regional, national and local levels. In terms of the routine experience of ordinary people, this implies that whereas in the past an individual would have had a master status as a political being in the form of membership of a nation ordered by a state, and thereafter a broad dispersed political-cultural identity carried in the routines of locale, network and memory, it would seem that today an individual might have no single master status as a political being and instead routinely affirm multiple political identities, and again thereafter a broad dispersed political-cultural identity carried in ordinary routines. In the context of the developing tripolar regional system, an individual can operate politically as a member of a local citizens' group, as a member of a national polity and as a member of regional or global organizations, and political-cultural identity becomes multiple and situational in character.

In other words, as the global system becomes both more integrated and tripolar the established state and nation lose their ability to restrict the person's activities and loyalties to their own circumscribed and ordered sphere. The ways in which individuals and groups can construe their relationship to the ordered collectivity becomes more open at local, national and regional levels as new strategies of thought and action are formulated.

The new tripolar global system

The substance of structural changes and agent responses can be reviewed in terms of recent patterns of events and commentary within the three regions of the integrated tripolar global system. As the processes of structural reconfiguration proceed new patterns of political thought and action will emerge and along with them new political-cultural identities will form. However, I will begin by noting the impact of the end of the certainties of the cold-war era because it was the abrupt collapse of the institutions and rhetorics of the post-Second World War system of blocs which precipitated contemporary concern for political-cultural identities.

The end of the cold war

In the post-Second World War period the general issue of political-cultural identity within the developed world had an overarching framework in the competition of the ideas of the 'free West' and 'socialism'. The period of the construction of these competing hegemonic ideologies lay in the years immediately after the war when American competition with the USSR precipitated the formation of two blocs. The key elements of the ideology of the free West affirmed the distinction between the realm of free-market-carried individual freedom and the realm of state-carried totalitarian unfreedom. The official ideologies of socialism promulgated in the spheres of the USSR and the People's Republic of China offered similar schemes to their populations. The delimited-formal ideologies of freedom and socialism offered political-cultural identities to the masses, and the political élite was offered roles and a sets of slogans to legitimate those roles. At the present time orthodox historians characterize the cold war as defensive on the part of the West while revisionist historians say the whole ideology was made in the West as a strategy of domestic political control, but that debate has rather been overtaken by events, in particular the ending of the cold war. In the broad perspective of the development of the global system, the received delimited-formal ideologies of inevitable conflict were destroyed over the period 1978–91. In the early period the reforms of the Chinese economy inaugurated in 1978 by Deng Xiaoping opened the way for an extensive marketization of the economies of the Asian socialist countries. The later period sees, first, Gorbachev unilaterally withdrawing from cold-war competition by initiating moves toward disarmament and *détente* (1985–9); and then second, the Eastern European bloc dissolving itself (1989–91).

Overall, the networks of ideological hostility and the central elements of the official ideologies of bloc-time have simply disappeared. The patterns of change have been most particularly acute in the context of the cold-war conflict of the USA, its European allies on the one hand

and the Eastern European bloc ordered by the USSR on the other, where the reunification of Germany, the Soviet withdrawal from Eastern Europe and the collapse of the USSR represented an epochal change. It would seem that there has been confusion among relevant political élites in the subsequent period as they confront the demands of the emergent tripolar global system.

THE EUROPEAN UNION   In the post-Second World War period the peoples, organizations and government machines of Europe understood themselves within the overall framework of bipolarity. In the Eastern European sphere matters were cast in terms of the achievement of a socialist polity. In the Western European sphere matters were understood in terms of the notion of the free world. The Western sphere was ordered at the macro-structural level in terms of the ideas, institutions and power relationships established/acknowledged by the Bretton Woods agreement. The USA was the core economy of an open trading region.

However, in the period of the last third of the short twentieth century this system came under great pressure and has slowly subsided. The following factors have contributed: first, the oil price shocks of the early 1970s; second, the financial implications for the USA of the war in Vietnam and the subsequent shift to debtor status in the Reagan years; third, the rise of the EEC and the Japanese sphere in East Asia; fourth, the (partial and uneven) globalization of the industrial-capitalist system; and finally the abrupt ending of the comfortably familiar bipolar bloc system. The upshot of all these changes over the period 1973–91 has been a movement into an unstable, insecure and novel tripolar global industrial-capitalist system.

Confronted with these slow patterns of structural change, the countries of Western Europe slowly moved towards a closer union. These ideas and institutional mechanisms were in place when the extent of structural change finally became unequivocally clear with the collapse of the USSR. The countries of Western Europe found an available reply in the guise of the European Community, itself a development of the European Economic Community, which had been founded back in the 1950s. The idea of the European Union was pushed to the fore. It has caused all sorts of enthusiasm and consternation across Europe.

By way of a speculative illustration of the notion of political-cultural identity we could pick out the key elements of European-ness: first, a political-economic form in which state and market interact, with the state having a directive role; second, a social-institutional structure which sees economy and polity acknowledging the important role of the community; third, a tradition of social-democratic or Christian-democratic politics; fourth, an idea of the importance of community (also for individuals); fifth, a tradition which acknowledges established institutions; and finally, a broad humanist social philosophy and social welfare practice.

THE USA   The Second World War saw the emergence of the USA as the premier political-economic, political, diplomatic and military power in the world. The power of the USA was used to establish and underpin the Bretton Woods system within the sphere of the West and the military/diplomatic confrontation with the Second World. The position of the USA was unchallenged until the middle 1970s, when the financial burdens of the war in Vietnam occasioned the first changes within the Bretton Woods system. The period of the late 1970s saw inflation and economic dislocation within the Western sphere and in the Third World. In the 1980s the military build-up inaugurated by Reagan led to the USA becoming a debtor nation. In addition, the USA was the major sponsor of the doctrines of economic liberalization which have further undermined the order of the global system.

The end of the short twentieth century has seen the USA continuing to press for an open global trading system, but these arguments are now made within the context of a nascent tripolar system and without the convenience of the Second World, which provided an excuse for US hegemony within the sphere of the West. However, it remains the case that the USA is the world's only 'superpower'.

By way of a speculative example of political culture we could pick out the key elements of American-ness: first, a public commitment to an open market economy; second, a public commitment to republican democracy; third, a strong preference for individualism; fourth, a tradition which celebrates the achievements of ordinary people; and finally, a cultural tradition of liberal individualism.

PACIFIC ASIA   The countries of Pacific Asia attained the outline of their present configuration over the period of the expansion of the Japanese empire, the chaos of the Pacific War and the collapse of the Western empires. The Pacific region over the post-Second World War period has been divided by cold-war institutions and rhetoric into a Western-focused group and a socialist bloc. The Western-focused group has been subject to the political-economic, political and cultural hegemony of the USA. However, the Western-focused group is undergoing considerable change and, in brief, this may be summarized as the beginnings of a political-economic and cultural emancipation from the hegemony of the USA. At the same time the countries of the socialist bloc, which had spent decades following autarchic development trajectories, are now opening up to the Western-focused group.

The key exchange in the post-Second World War period has been that of the Japanese and the Americans. Thereafter the countries of the inner periphery of East Asia have dealt with a long period of economic development in the political and military shadow of the USA and the economic shadow of Japan. The countries of the outer periphery of South-east Asia have more recently reoriented themselves towards the economic model of Japan. We can also note the related, more recent turn of the countries of Australasia towards the Pacific Asian economies, a turn that is routinely expressed in terms of a commitment to open regionalism, thereby arguably implicitly granting a continued political commitment to the West in general and the USA in particular. Finally we have the ongoing process of the reorientation of China and Indo-China.

We can offer a speculative illustration of the political culture of Pacific Asian-ness (centred on the experience of Japan): first, the economy is state-directed; second, state direction is top-down style and pervasive in its reach; third, society is familial and thereafter communitarian (thus society is non-individualistic); fourth, social order is secured by pervasive control machineries (sets of social rules and an extensive bureaucratization of everyday life) and a related hegemonic common culture (which enjoins submission to the demands of community and authority); fifth, political debate and power is typically reserved to an élite sphere (and political life centres on the pragmatic pursuit of overarching economic goals); sixth, political debate and action amongst the masses is diffuse and demobilized (thus there is no 'public sphere'); and finally, culture comprises a mix of officially sanctioned tradition and market-sanctioned consumption; and culture stresses consensus, acquiescence and harmony and eschews open conflict.

Changing political-cultural identities in the new tripolar global system

I have argued in the theoretical sections of the text that it seems to me that identity will continue to be a matter of locale (the place where people live), networks (the ways in which people interact) and memory (the understandings which are sustained and re-created over time). The route which I have taken in order to secure provisionally this conclusion involved setting to one side the familiar resources of the specialist disciplines of Western social science in order to reach back to the classical European tradition within which one can find, I have claimed, a deep-seated concern for the sphere of political action and thought, matters which might usefully be addressed, I suggested, in terms of an ethnographic/biographical strategy designed to access/recall the rich detail of the everyday lives of ordinary people.

Moving on from that base, I suggested that it would be reasonable to propose that political-cultural identity is secondary to identity but important in that it will express the way in which individuals construe their relationship to the ordered collectivity within which they live. A political-cultural identity would be a subtle multiple construct and would be established in part using the resources of locale, network and memory and in part using the resources available within the public sphere (that is, the sphere of politics and public). It seems to me that one can grant that the present configuration of the industrial-capitalist global system can be unpacked in terms of the dynamics of structures and agents, where the crucial agents have been states. It is the way in which state regimes have read and reacted to changing structural patterns which lies at the heart of the political projects they have pursued and which they have had to disseminate within the populations subject to their control. It is the mix of official ideologies and inherited local resources which provide the materials of the political-cultural identities of individuals and groups. It is clear that political-cultural identities are crucial ways of reading enfolding structural circumstances. It is also clear, therefore, that political-cultural identities are an intensely contested sphere.

I would argue that it is likely that as the global industrial-capitalist system continues to extend and deepen its reach within the social world, that identity will shift and exhibit less fixity and more fluidity, with new forms of cosmopolitanness, adulthood and scepticism. At the same time, it seems clear that patterns of political-cultural identity are likely to change in the future as the global structures which such constructs grasp themselves become more complexly ordered in the process of the creation of an integrated and interdependent tripolar system. It is likely that political-cultural identity will become more immediate as people turn to their local situation, attenuated as official ideologies decline and as political-cultural identity becomes correspondingly less prominent and layered as the spheres of possible commitment for individuals and groups become multiple. And these are matters which I have tried to illustrate in terms of recent patterns of events and commentary in the three regions of the integrated tripolar global system. It seems to me that these substantive concerns will influence political debate to a significant extent over the final years of the century.

Conclusion: new routes to new futures

Returning, finally, to my starting-point in the remarks of C. Wright Mills in regard to the exchange between private concerns and public issues which, he suggests, sparks the enquiries of social scientists, and reflecting on the experience of returning to a deeply silent UK after the excitements of Germany in process of reunification, it seems to me to be clear that the exchange between the slowly moving dynamics of structural change and the pattern of responses of agents is the main axis of our strategies of construing the relationship of self and ordered collectivity, of establishing political-cultural identities. The manner of establishment of such political-cultural identities is by no means straightforward as the sphere is intensely contested, with powerful groups, established institutions and the broad sphere of ordinary life all carrying a heavy stock of interpretive resources, ideas to be promulgated, embodied or merely taken for granted.

In the case of the United Kingdom, it is clear that the population is routinely invited to acquiesce in an official ideology – an evolutionary secure liberal-democratic state in which the British people quietly and pragmatically order their affairs – which, in truth, is a nonsense. It is also clear that the structural reconfiguration at present running through the United Kingdom, as it is running throughout the rest of Europe, will entail new patterns of political action and, in time, one would anticipate that these will issue in new patterns of political-cultural identity. In my opinion, the people of the United Kingdom should welcome these changes as they offer both an escape from the absurdities of the political-cultural project of 'Britain' and a clear route to the future within Europe. I have noted earlier that political-cultural identity is intensely contested. Yet the situation of the people of the United Kingdom has no paradigmatic status; it concerns me simply because this is the country in which I live. However, it is clear that one aspect of those structural changes running through the United Kingdom is their global extent. As other peoples in other places face their own patterns of structural change, they too will have to deal with the same awkward problems of reworking established political-cultural schemes in the process of formulating new routes to new futures.

Bibliography

Abegglen, J.C. 1994. *Sea Change*. New York, Free Press.

Abrams, P. 1968. *The Origins of British Sociology*. Chicago, Chicago University Press.

Aglietta, M. 1979. *A Theory of Capitalist Regulation*. London, Verso.

Anderson, B. 1983. *Imagined Communities*. London, Verso.

Anderson, P. 1992. *English Questions*. London, Verso.

Ariff, M. 1991. *The Malaysian Economy: Pacific Connections*. Oxford, Oxford University Press.

Aron, R. 1973. *The Imperial Republic*. London, Weidenfeld & Nicolson.

Barraclough, G. 1964. *An Introduction to Contemporary History*. Harmondsworth, Penguin.

Baudrillard, J. 1993. *Symbolic Exchange and Death*. London, Sage.

Bauman, Z. 1976. *Towards a Critical Sociology*. London, Routledge.

Bauman, Z. 1987. *Legislators and Interpreters*. Cambridge, Polity.

Bauman, Z. 1988. *Freedom*. Milton Keynes, Open University Press.

Bauman, Z. 1989. *Modernity and the Holocaust*. Cambridge, Polity.

Bauman, Z. 1991. *Modernity and Ambivalence*. Cambridge, Polity.

Beasley, W.G. 1990. *The Rise of Modern Japan*. Tokyo, Tuttle.

Benjamin, G. 1987. 'The unseen presence: reflections on the nation state and its mystifications', in mimeo. Singapore: National University of Singapore, Department of Sociology.

Bloor, D. 1983. *Wittgenstein: a Social Theory of Knowledge*. London, Macmillan.

Bourdieu, P. 1984. *Distinction: a Social Critique of the Judgement of Taste*. London, Routledge.

Brugmans, H. 1985. *Europe: a Leap in the Dark*. Stoke-on-Trent, Trentham.

Buckley, R. 1990. *Japan Today*. Cambridge, Cambridge University Press.

Buruma, I. 1994. *The Wages of Guilt*. London, Jonathan Cape.

Byrnes, M. 1994. *Australia and the Asia Game*. Sydney, Allen and Unwin.

Callinicos, A. 1989. *Against Postmodernism*. Cambridge, Polity.

Caute, D. 1978. *The Great Fear: the Anti-Communist Purges under Truman and Eisenhower*. London, Secker and Warburg.

Cecchini, P. 1988. *1992: the European Challenge*. London, Wildwood.

Chomsky, N. 1991. *Deterring Democracy*. London, Vintage.

Chua, B.H. 1995. *Communitarian Democracy and Ideology in Singapore*. London, Routledge.

Cohen, A.P. 1994. *Self Consciousness*. London, Routledge.

Cole, K., Cameron, J. and Edwards, C. 1991. *Why Economists Disagree*. London, Longman.

Colley, L. 1992. *Britons: Forging the Nation 1707–1837*. New Haven and London, Yale University Press.

Cronin, R.P. 1992. *Japan, the United States, and Prospects for the Asia Pacific Century: Three Scenarios for the Future*. Singapore, Institute of Southeast Asian Studies.

Crouch, C. and Marquand, D. 1992. *Towards a Greater Europe*. Oxford, Blackwell.

Culler, J. 1976. *Saussure*. London, Fontana.

Cutler, T. 1992. *The Struggle for Europe*. Oxford, Berg.

Dale, P. 1986. *The Myth of Japanese Uniqueness*. London, Croom Helm.

Darras, J. and Snowman, D. 1990. *Beyond the Tunnel of History.* London, Macmillan.

Dasgupta, A.K. 1985. *Epochs of Economic Theory.* Oxford, Blackwell.

Davidson, B. 1994. *The Search for Africa.* London, James Currey.

Deane, P. 1978. *The Evolution of Economic Ideas.* Cambridge, Cambridge University Press.

Delanty, G. 1995. *Inventing Europe.* London, Macmillan.

Delors, J. 1992. *Our Europe.* London, Verso.

Devan, J. (ed.) 1994. *Southeast Asia Challenges of the Twenty-First Century.* Singapore, Institute of Southeast Asian Studies.

Dobson, W. 1993. *Japan in East Asia: Trading and Investment Strategies.* Singapore, Institute of Southeast Asian Studies.

Dorfman, J. 1963. *Institutional Economics: Veblen, Commons and Mitchell Reconsidered.* Berkeley and Los Angeles, University of California Press.

Eagleton, T. 1991. *Ideology.* London, Verso.

Eccleston, B. 1989. *State and Society in Post War Japan.* Cambridge, Polity.

Eco, U. 1987. *Travels in Hyperreality.* London, Picador.

Evans, G. 1993. *Asia's Cultural Mosaic.* Singapore, Simon and Shuster.

Fay, B. 1975. *Social Theory and Political Practice.* London, Allen and Unwin.

Featherstone, M. 1991. *Consumer Culture and Postmodernism.* London, Sage.

Flemming, D.F. 1961. *The Cold War and Its Origins.* New York, Doubleday.

Frank, A.G. 1983. *The European Challenge.* Nottingham, Spokesman.

Franklin, M. 1990. *Britain's Future in Europe.* London, Pinter.

Fritch-Bournazel, R. 1992. *Europe and German Unification.* London, Berg.

Frobel, F. and Heinrichs, J. 1980. *The New International Division of Labour.* Cambridge, Cambridge University Press.

Fukuyama, F. 1992. *The End of History and the Last Man.* London, Hamish Hamilton.

Gadamer, H.G. 1960. *Truth and Method.* London, Sheed and Ward.

Galbraith, J.K. 1958. *The Affluent Society.* London, Hamish Hamilton.

Galbraith, J.K. 1989. *The Guardian,* 28 July.

Garton-Ash, T. 1990. *We the People.* Cambridge, Granta.

Gellner, E. 1964. *Thought and Change.* London, Weidenfeld & Nicolson.

Gellner, E. 1983. *Nations and Nationalism.* Oxford, Blackwell.

Gellner, E. 1988. *Plough, Sword and Book.* London, Paladin.

Gellner, E. 1991. *Plough, Sword and Book.* London, Paladin.

Giddens, A. 1972. *Politics and Sociology in the Thought of Max Weber.* London, Macmillan.

Giddens, A. 1976. *New Rules of Sociological Method.* London, Hutchinson.

Giddens, A. 1979. *Central Problems in Social Theory.* London, Macmillan.

Giddens, A. 1984. *The Constitution of Society.* Cambridge, Polity.

Giddens, A. 1987. *Social Theory and Modern Sociology.* Cambridge, Polity.

Giddens, A. 1991. *Modernity and Self Identity.* Cambridge, Polity.

Gipoloux, F. (ed.) 1994. *Regional Economic Strategies in East Asia: a Comparative Perspective.* Tokyo, Maison Franco-Japonaise.

Glenny, M. 1990. *The Rebirth of History.* Harmondsworth, Penguin.

Goodman, D. and Segal, G. 1994. *China Deconstructs: Politics, Trade and Regionalism.* London, Routledge.

Graham, O. 1976. *Toward a Planned Society.* New York, Oxford University Press.

Grimal, H. 1978. *Decolonization.* London, Routledge.

Habermas, J. 1971. *Towards a Rational Society.* London, Heinemann.

Habermas, J. 1989. *The Structural Transformation of the Public Sphere.* Cambridge, Polity.

Halliday, J. 1980. Capitalism and socialism in East Asia, *New Left Review,* vol. 124, pp. 3–23.

Hamilton, C. 1983. Capitalist industrialization in East Asia's four little tigers, *Journal of Contemporary Asia,* vol. 13, pp. 35–73.

Harrison, A. 1967. *The Framework of Economic Activity.* London, Macmillan.

Harvey, D. 1989. *The Condition of Postmodernity.* Oxford, Blackwell.

Harvie, C. 1992. *Cultural Weapons: Scotland in the New Europe.* Edinburgh, Polygon.

Hawthorn, G. 1976. *Enlightenment and Despair.* Cambridge, Cambridge University Press.

Hay, C. 1996. *Restating Social and Political Change.* Buckingham, Open University Press.

Held, D. 1987. *Models of Democracy.* Cambridge, Polity.

Heller, A. 1984. *Everyday Life.* London.

Higgot, R., Leaver, R. and Ravenhill, J. 1993. *Pacific Economic Relations in the 1990s.* St Leonards, Allen and Unwin.

Hobsbawm, E. 1994. *Age of Extremes: the Short Twentieth Century.* London, Michael Joseph.

Hobsbawm, E. and Ranger T. 1983. *The Invention of Tradition.* Cambridge, Canto.

Hodgson, G. 1988. *Economics and Institutions.* Cambridge, Cambridge University Press.

Hoggart, R. 1958. *The Uses of Literacy.* Harmondsworth, Penguin.

Hoggart, R. 1985. *A Local Habitation.* Oxford, Oxford University Press.

Hoggart, R. 1995. *The Way We Live Now.* London, Chatto.

Hollis, M. 1977. *Models of Man.* Cambridge, Cambridge University Press.

Holub, R.C. 1991. *Jürgen Habermas: Critic in the Public Sphere.* London, Routledge.

Honda, K. 1993. *The Impoverished Spirit of Contemporary Japan.* New York, Monthly Review Press.

Howell, J. 1993. *China Opens its Doors: the Politics of Economic Transition.* Hemel Hempstead, Harvester.

Hughes, R. 1993. *Culture of Complaint: the Fraying of America.* Oxford, Oxford University Press.

Huntington, S.P. 1993. The clash of civilizations, *Foreign Affairs*, vol. 72–3, pp. 22–49.

Ienaga, S. 1978. *The Pacific War: World War Two and the Japanese, 1931–45.* New York, Pantheon.

Ignatieff, M. 1994. *Blood and Belonging.* London, Vintage.

Inglis, F. 1993. *Cultural Studies.* Oxford, Blackwell.

Jaffe, I. 1995. Our own invisible hand: antipolitics as an American given, seminar paper. Glasgow, University of Strathclyde, Department of Government.

Jameson, F. 1991. *Postmodernism: or the Cultural Logic of Late Capitalism.* London, Verso.

Jeffrey, R. (ed.) 1981. *Asia: the Winning of Independence.* London, Macmillan.

Jenks, C. 1993. *Culture.* London, Routledge.

Jessop, B. (ed.) 1988. *Thatcherism: a Tale of Two Nations.* Cambridge, Polity.

Johnson, C. 1982. *MITI and the Japanese Miracle.* Stanford, CA, Stanford University Press.

Kahn, J.S. and Loh, F. (eds) 1992. *Fragmented Visions: Culture and Politics in Contemporary Malaysia.* Sydney, Allen and Unwin.

Katzenstein, P. 1985. *Small States in World Markets.* London, Cornell University Press.

Kaye, H. 1984. *The British Marxist Historians.* Cambridge, Polity.

Kearney, R. (ed.) 1988. *Across the Frontiers: Ireland in the 1990s.* Dublin, Wolfhound Press.

Kearney, R. (ed.) 1992. *Visions of Europe.* Dublin, Wolfhound Press.

Keegan, W. 1992. *The Spectre of Capitalism.* London, Radius.

Kennedy, P. 1988. *The Rise and Fall of the Great Powers.* London, Fontana.

Kenny, A. 1973. *Wittgenstein.* Harmondsworth, Pelican.

Kerkvliet, B. 1977. *The Huk Rebellion: a Study of Peasant Revolt in the Philippines.* Berkeley, University of California Press.

Keyes, C.F. et al. (eds) 1994. *Asian Visions of Authority: Religion and the Modern States of East and Southeast Asia.* Honolulu, University of Hawaii Press.

Khoo, K.J. 1992. The grand vision: Mahathir and modernization, in J.S. Kahn and K.W. Loh (eds), *Fragmented Visions: Culture and Politics in Contemporary Malaysia.* Sydney, Allen and Unwin.

Kolko, G. 1968. *The Politics of War.* New York, Vintage.

Koppel, B.M. and Orr, R.J. (eds) 1993. *Japan's Foreign Aid: Power and Policy in a New Era.* Boulder, CO, Westview.

Krieger, J. 1986. *Reagan, Thatcher and the Politics of Decline.* Cambridge, Polity.

Krugman, P. 1994. *Peddling Prosperity.* New York, Norton.

Lane, J.E. and Errson, S. 1987. *Politics and Society in Western Europe.* London, Sage.

Lash, S. and Urry, J. 1987. *The End of Organised Capitalism.* Cambridge, Polity.

Lodge, J. 1989. *The European Community and the Challenge of the Future.* London, Pinter.

Long, N. (ed.) 1992. *Battlefields of Knowledge.* London, Routledge.

Lyotard, F. 1984. *The Postmodern Condition.* University of Manchester Press.

MacIntyre, A. 1962. A mistake about causality in social science, in P. Laslett and W.G. Runciman (eds), *Politics, Philosophy and Society, Series 2.* Oxford, Blackwell.

MacIntyre, A. 1981. *After Virtue.* London, Duckworth.

MacIntyre, A. 1993. Indonesia, Thailand and the Northeast Asian Connection, in R. Higgot, R. Leaver and J. Ravenhill (eds), *Pacific Economic Relations in the 1990s.* St Leonards, Allen and Unwin.

MacIntyre, A. 1994. Nietzsche or Aristotle? in G. Borradori *The American Philosopher.* Chicago, University of Chicago Press.

McKay, D. 1994. *Politics and Power in the USA.* Harmondsworth, Penguin.

Macpherson, C.B. 1973. *Democratic Theory: Essays in Retrieval.* Oxford, Oxford University Press.

Marquand, D. 1988. *The Unprincipled Society.* London, Fontana.

Mayer, A. 1981. *The Persistence of the Old Regime.* New York, Croom Helm.

Meehan, E. 1993. *Citizenship and the European Community.* London, Sage.

Miliband, R. 1982. *Capitalist Democracy in Britain.* Oxford, Oxford University Press.

Mills, C.W. 1970. *The Sociological Imagination.* Harmondsworth, Pelican.

Moise, E.E. 1994. *Modern China: a History.* London, Longman.

Moore, B. 1966. *The Social Origins of Dictatorship and Democracy.* Boston, Beacon.

Nairn, T. 1977. *The Break-Up of Britain.* London, New Left Books.

Nairn, T. 1988. *The Enchanted Glass.* London, Radius.

Nester, W.R. 1990. *Japan's Growing Power over East Asia and the World Economy.* London, Macmillan.

Nisbet, R. 1966. *The Sociological Tradition.* New York, Basic Books.

Ormerod, P. 1994. *The Death of Economics.* London, Faber.

Orr, R.M. 1990. *The Emergence of Japan's Foreign Aid Power.* New York, Columbia University Press.

Overbeek, H. 1990. *Global Capitalism and National Decline.* London, Allen and Unwin.

Palmer, J. 1988. *Europe without America.* Oxford, Oxford University Press.

Pandy, B.N. 1980. *South and Southeast Asia 1945–1979.* London, Macmillan.

Panitch, L. 1980. Recent theorizations of corporatism, *British Journal of Sociology,* vol. 31, pp. 159–87.

Parkin, F. 1972. *Class Inequality and Political Order.* London, Paladin.

Phongpaichit, P. 1990. *The New Wave of Japanese Investment in ASEAN.* Singapore, Institute of Southeast Asian Studies.

Piore, M. and Sabel, C. 1984. *The Second Industrial Divide.* New York, Basic Books.

Plant, R. 1991. *Modern Political Thought.* Oxford, Blackwell.

Pollard, S. 1971. *The Idea of Progress.* Harmondsworth, Penguin.

Preston, P.W. 1982. *Theories of Development.* London, Routledge.

Preston, P.W. 1985. *New Trends in Development Theory.* London, Routledge.

Preston, P.W. 1994a. *Discourses of Development.* Aldershot, Avebury.

Preston, P.W. 1994b. *Europe, Democracy and the Dissolution of Britain.* Aldershot, Dartmouth.

Preston, P.W. 1996. *Development Theory: an Introduction.* Oxford, Blackwell.

Reading, B. 1992. *Japan: the Coming Collapse.* London, Orion.

Reynolds, H. 1981. *The Other Side of the Frontier.* Harmondsworth, Penguin.

Rieff, D. 1995. *Slaughterhouse: Bosnia and the Failure of the West.* London, Vintage.

Rix, A. 1993. *Japan's Foreign Aid*. London, Routledge.

Rodan, G. 1993. Reconstructing divisions of labour: Singapore's new regional emphasis, in R. Higgot, R. Leaver and J. Ravenhill (eds), *Pacific Economic Relations in the 1990s*. St Leonards, Allen and Unwin.

Rose, G. 1995. *Love's Work*. London, Chatto.

Sachs, W. 1992. *The Development Dictionary*. London, Zed Books.

Samuel, R. 1994. *Theatres of Memory*. London, Verso.

Scott, J.C. 1971. Protest and profanation: Revolt and the little tradition, *Theory and Society*, vol. 4.

Scott, J.C. 1976. *The Moral Economy of the Peasant*. New Haven and London, Yale University Press.

Scott, J.C. 1985. *Weapons of the Weak*. New Haven and London, Yale University Press.

Shamsul, A.B. 1996. Nations of intent in Malaysia, in S. Tonnesson and H. Antlov (eds), *Asian Forms of the Nation*. London, Curzon.

Sheridan, K. 1993. *Governing the Japanese Economy*. Cambridge, Polity.

Shibusawa, M., Ahmad, Z.H. and Bridges, B. 1992. *Pacific Asia in the 1990s*. London, Routledge.

Shirer, W.L. 1960. *The Rise and Fall of the Third Reich*. London, Secker.

Smith, A.D. 1986. *The Ethnic Origins of Nations*. Oxford, Blackwell.

Strange, S. 1988. *States and Markets*. London, Pinter.

Streeten, P. 1994. The role of direct foreign investment in developing countries, in *ADMP Series*. Tokyo, Sophia University.

Sturrock, J. 1986. *Structuralism*. London, Paladin.

Swedberg, R. 1987. Economic sociology past and present, *Current Sociology*, vol. 35, pp. 1–221.

Taylor, C. 1992. Nations and federations: Living amongst others, in R. Kearney (ed.), *Visions of Europe*. Dublin, Wolfhound Press.

The Economist, 9 July 1994.

Thorne, C. 1985. *The Far Eastern War*. London, Counterpoint.

Thurow, L. 1994. *Head to Head: the Coming Economic Battle among Japan, Europe and America*. New York, Morrow.

Tivey, L. (ed.) 1981. *The Nation State*. Oxford, Martin Robertson.

Toye, J. 1987. *Dilemmas of Development*. Oxford, Blackwell.

Tsurumi, S. 1987. *A Cultural History of Postwar Japan 1945–1980*. London, Kegan Paul International.

Turnbull, M. 1977. *A History of Singapore*. Oxford, Oxford University Press.

Turner, G. 1990. *British Cultural Studies*. London, Unwin.

Van der Pijl, K. 1984. *The Making of an Atlantic Ruling Cross*. London, Verso.

Van Wolferen, K. 1989. *The Enigma of Japanese Power*. Tokyo, Tuttle.

Vogel, E. 1980. *Japan as Number One*. Tokyo, Tuttle.

Walker, M. 1990. *The Guardian*, 7 February.

Walker, M. 1993. *The Cold War and the Making of the Modern World*. London.

Wallace, W. 1990. *The Transformation of Western Europe*. London, Pinter.

Wallerstein, I. 1974. *The Modern World System*. New York, Academic.

Walter, J. 1992. Defining Australia, in Whitlock, G. and Carter, D. (eds), *Images of Australia*. University of Queensland Press.

Watson-Andaya, B. and Andaya, L.Y. 1982. *A History of Malaysia*. London, Macmillan.

Watts, D. 1993. *The Times Guide to Japan: Understanding the World's Newest Superpower*. London, The Times.

White, R. 1992. Inventing Australia, in G. Whitlock and D. Carter (eds), *Images of Australia*. Brisbane, University of Queensland Press.

Whitlock, G. and Carter, D. (eds) 1992. *Images of Australia*. Brisbane, University of Queensland Press.

Wilkinson, E. 1990. *Japan Versus the West: Image and Reality*. Harmondsworth, Penguin.

Williams, G. 1989. *Marxism Today*, April.

Williams, R. 1958. *Culture and Society.* London, Chatto and Windus.

Winch, P. 1958. *The Idea of a Social Science and its Relation to Philosophy.* London, Routledge.

Wistrich, E. 1989. *After 1992: the United States of Europe.* London, Routledge.

Wittgenstein, L. 1953. *Philosophical Investigations.* Oxford, Blackwell.

Wolff, J. 1981. *The Social Production of Art.* London, Macmillan.

Woodiwiss, A. 1993. *Postmodernity USA.* London, Sage.

World Bank. 1992. *World Development Report 1992.* Oxford, Oxford University Press.

World Bank. 1993. *The East Asian Miracle.* Oxford, Oxford University Press.

Worsley, P. 1964. *The Third World.* London, Weidenfeld.

Worsley, P. 1984. *The Three Worlds.* London, Weidenfeld.

Wright, P. 1985. *On Living in an Old Country.* London, Verso.

Wright, P. 1992. *A Journey Through the Ruins.* London, Flamingo.

Yasutomo, D. 1986. *The Manner of Giving: Strategic Aid and Japanese Foreign Policy.* Lexington, KY, Heath.

Yoshino, K. 1992. *Cultural Nationalism in Contemporary Japan.* London, Routledge.

Zeitlin, I. 1968. *Ideology and the Development of Sociological Theory.* Englewood Cliffs, Prentice Hall.

Index